Remotely

REMOTELY

Travels in the Binge of TV

DAVID THOMSON

Yale
UNIVERSITY PRESS
New Haven and London

Published with assistance from the foundation established in memory of
James Wesley Cooper of the Class of 1865, Yale College.

Yale University Press books may be purchased in quantity for
educational, business, or promotional use. For information, please e-mail
sales.press@yale.edu (U.S. office) or sales@yaleup.co.uk (U.K. office).

Set in Adobe Garamond type by Integrated Publishing Solutions.
Printed in the United States of America.

Library of Congress Control Number: 2023933106
ISBN 978-0-300-26100-4 (hardcover : alk. paper)

A catalogue record for this book is available from the British Library.

This paper meets the requirements of ANSI/NISO Z39.48-1992
(Permanence of Paper).

10 9 8 7 6 5 4 3 2 1

for Lucy Gray

Contents

CONTENTS

Remotely

1

The Switches

It was a night like all the others. We looked out on the city streets in the moonlight and told ourselves that nothing was there. Not yet.

Soon after the onset of lockdown, a feeling crept up that something more extensive than the pandemic, yet vaguer, was happening. Life had receded, maybe, but we were left on the lookout. A worry was there, not to be dispelled, that perhaps our city and our home had been taken already. So the frontier was not guarding home security now. It was just a ragged street that had wandered into desert or mythology.

The hope in a lockdown was for safety, the envelope of home. But we could not escape the thought—hushed or unspoken—that we had opened ourselves up to a greater threat. People were hoarding toilet paper and the esteemed works of our civilization. Torn between shit and literature. Or some such prologue.

I can't put my finger on it, said Lucy. She talks in italic, or seems about to sing. *So many nights we came into this room, to be entertained. As if we deserved that. Yet the room felt occupied, long ago, not just by the television, but by this condition of remoteness.*

That was close to the heart of it. Our room had three mechanisms, or what we called "switches"; they were sesames of alteration. There was the electric light in the room. There was the way the television could be on or off.

And there was the remote. You could say it was a simple convenience, a way of not having to move the few feet to change the channel. But the "remote" made

me think of immense distances and unbridgeable separation. As if we were spin-
ning off into space like lost spectators. "Hello, I must be going" came into my
mind.

Or are you sitting comfortably, my dear?

Yes, I believe I am. Not that one can be sure. It's kind of you to ask, but also
weird.

I recall that fond question from radio. There was a program in Britain, *Listen with Mother,* where every story began like that.

Was it the Queen speaking in that nice empty voice she kept?

Is there something amiss?

Well, maybe just the feeling of a beast in the room.

Can you see it?

Not in the brightness of the screen.

There's the trick.

We were old enough to be wary of catching Covid, but there was also this indication—between a hum and a pressure—that something like a ma-laise had been going on since . . . who knew when?

Covid had been announced as a new threat to the world, but I don't think we were surprised. Hadn't we learned not to show shock?—I think of it as being deadpan.

So are we going to have to stay at home indefinitely, asked Lucy, *just an elderly married couple watching TV?*

Maybe that's the message, the whole point of Covid, that some time ago, without realizing it, we were taken over by this technology.

Oh, Lord, I see what this means—you're going to want to write about it.

This comic tendency is at the heart of our thing. I admit, I sometimes believe I live to have something to write about. Lucy writes too; she takes photographs; her head glows with daring ideas. But she is devoted to actual life. She always socialized more than I was inclined to do, and she reproaches me for hiding at my desk in the silence of composition.

We argue a lot, as a policy. And she forgives me for being wrong—or right sometimes. Call it gamesmanship. Long ago, we played tennis in that spirit. Being older and slower than she, and less of a player, I went in for slices, drop shots, spun services, and eccentric lobs, and she would curse at my cunning and not playing in the robust American way. But if she lost her temper, I had a chance of beating her. Then like a chump I told her that, explained the trick—and after that, she wiped me off the court.

I know, this sounds personal or domestic, but do not be disconcerted. This is a reverie on marriage and its conversation, but it will do its best to be a serious, searching book about TV and screens, likely to ask, "What are we going to do about this?"

Will you promise to be instructive?

I hope to get minds spinning. But the book may be read as a kind of novel, too, because she and I have always reckoned we were living in a story, talking to each other and to the TV. And one point of television was to give us all a way of talking to ourselves about what the world might be.

We have decided that argument is the liveliest part of ourselves. So as we settled into lockdown, we picked up the habit of following TV marriages—Edith and Archie Bunker from *All in the Family;* Walter and Skyler White in *Breaking Bad;* Larry David and Cheryl in those first seasons of *Curb Your Enthusiasm;* Marty and Wendy Byrde in *Ozark* (that was *the* Covid show, because those Byrdes were caged from the outset). Plus the gold standard, the wildest of all, silly yet essential, on fire with amour fou—the Ricardos in *I Love Lucy.*

That show is your everlasting drop shot.

Everyone loves *I Love Lucy.*

No one ever asked her if she loves it. Ricky seems to own her in the title, but isn't she kinda crazy, the way men are taught to regard women? When the wacko thing about women is why they like men.

I was about to resume, but she was not finished. *You've omitted an important show. I thought I should tell you. It's an answer to* I Love Lucy.

3

This was making me uneasy. You must not think we're some settled couple.

It's one of your favorites: I've seen you on the floor, barking mad with laughter at it. Isn't that why we called our dog Basil, and why you keep his old red collar on your desk?

Of course, the one and only—*Fawlty Towers.*

Just two seasons, 1975 and '79. Keep that gap in mind. And only six episodes a series. The modesty. The restraint. Where Basil and his wife Sybil run this small hotel at the seaside. And he's mad, just falling down the stairs absurd, a mantrap of chaos who thinks the world is out to ruin him with disorder. So he fights with the hotel guests, derides his staff, while Sybil beholds it all and never needs to say, "Why am I still with this wretched man?"

Maybe the most rueful comedy we've had. It's in an English tradition of marital misunderstanding. With a possibility of murder in the offing.

And don't forget that gap, '75 and '79. It was a show created and written by John Cleese and Connie Booth. They were married in life. He was Basil and she played Polly, the waitress and the chambermaid at the hotel.

The only sane person in the place.

But she and Cleese broke up. They were divorced before the second season.

They still wrote it together.

Does that remind you of us?

Everything reminds me of us. And Prunella Scales was Sybil the wife, grim, patient, and unyielding.

Craziest of the lot—because she knows what madness is but ignores it. Every day she realizes the catastrophe of Basil, but refrains from murdering him. Is that what you meant?

Years ahead, in Alan Bennett's *A Question of Attribution*, 1991, Scales would play the Queen. Like a suburban Lady Bracknell. She was the first person to do that.

Oh no, Her Majestic had been doing it for decades. With sourpuss grandeur, endless corgis, and protocol—don't speak to me until I've spoken to you. Absolute madness, without a raindrop of irony.

So we looked at those married series again like gossips in the neighborhood wondering which couples would stick together. We had our own perseverance; we argued and disputed, and then we made up. We had decided that couples benefited from a gap or friction in their lives. We learned this from favorite movies, the ones about couples that parted and then came back together again. The comedies of reengagement: like *The Awful Truth, The Lady Eve, The Philadelphia Story,* and *His Girl Friday.*

Must I always be married to Cary Grant?

That was the rage once. Stick around and you may see that any alert couple needs to get remarried once a week, or before dinner. It is a surreal sport, making these screen people into our friends.

And in lockdown the idea of talking together seemed not just occupational, but elemental.

One of the troubles about the lockdown is that you can't leave your other. You're locked together, as if you're in a series. Some days I wake up and long to take a flight, to get away.

Where would you go?

Tahiti. Tashkent. Hulu or Criterion. These imaginary places.

Who are we when we see ourselves there?

We're like the celebrity guests on The Larry Sanders Show. *Wondering if there's a script, or is it enough if we just start talking.*

That's it. Theoretical. I talked to Warren Beatty the other day—or fifteen years ago; he was on the *Sanders* show sometimes—and after a while, he asked me, "Am I my Warren Beatty, or yours?"

One smart fellow. I know how he feels.

2

A Theory of Entertainment

We try to think of ourselves existing in history, like people waiting in line. More or less patient, but with our fingers crossed, trusting that someone will be in charge.

That queue is scattered now; we are left in an unmapped zone where the facts are uncertain, and dreams struggle with numbness—isn't that the mood of modern advertising? It's not that it is selling any item now, so much as the theory of salesmanship hanging on like an old gospel.

We would prefer to hold on to reliability. You would rather not worry—and we say that TV is there to take our minds off all the bad stuff. But we gave up on our contract to stay real or rational some time ago—was that early in the new century, an uneasy calm in which we guessed that "turning points" and their inane sequence had been discontinued? So we're on hold, not quite going away.

You may not remember this as an event; it happened too long ago. The risk or incursion was not much examined at the time, because the new toy then seemed trivial and warm-hearted. Uplifting even: endless hours of fun. I'm talking about 1945–50, the dawn of TV. You see, *we let it in the house,* we welcomed it in.

This was only moments after a war in which, in Europe and the Far East, many homes were ripped apart beyond repair or belief. So much of our physical world had been demolished. Has it ever come back? We felt the horizon of extinction in our carefree evolution. It could seem a folly to rebuild.

There was a bombsite in south London where our gang played, a ruined house. This was a couple of years into the peace. In 1947, the house was still fenced off, with warning signs telling us it was unsound. And we could read by then, haltingly! So we went in like rats and rascals—no one prevented it—and there was a dining room, still laid for a meal. With the dust of old food on the plates. Nothing had been done to repair it. If we looked up, there was a hole in the roof with birds fluttering at its ragged edge.

How were you children able to do that?

We crawled beneath the fence and found a broken window.

And you had won the war?

That's what they said.

There was no doubting the danger to structure, not after Guernica, the London Blitz, Dresden, and the places in Japan we had never heard of until their great illumination. In a similar way, in those devastated countries there were homeless people on the road who might be refugees or marauders. They felt lost and despairing, yet they seemed dangerous to others. The old domestic order had been canceled. There was a legend of new bombs hovering over us, game changers before we understood how our lives had become as fleeting as a game.

Wasn't it playful or folly then that we let this beast in, treating it as comic or benign, and found a place for it in what we called our living room?

We were coming out of a dread of Gestapo knocking at the door. Knocking?—that's too gentle; those fellows tore doors off their hinges; they devoured whole villages. One thing about war is how it leaves you so vulnerable in what you had regarded as home.

Maybe our proper history with television is to sabotage the theory and comfort of home.

So we let it in. Without a thought. There was an episode of The Honey- *mooners* where Jackie Gleason brings a TV set home to please his wife. He tells her about the loans offered so working people can buy a set. It was an ad for the whole enterprise.

Every day, we still let it in the house and we have observed by now that its picture quality is brighter, more lifelike, more detailed in its texture, and simply more vivid than those larger archaic screens that still linger in our last movie theatres. It feels good to turn it on and have the light flood into our darkness.

Isn't that how we have gone beyond our nice flat screen? Whereas we had just one screen at first—the pale gray curve of plastic in a shell of mock walnut furniture, with an antenna to make us think of science fiction—we now give every person and child in the house their own screen. We call that a smartphone, which wants to believe we're being pretty clever, no matter that the phone screens are thresholds of remoteness. Instead, we say these small screens are a lot of fun. Aren't they entertaining? Isn't television a treasury, sitting patiently in what used to be our house? Like a hole in the roof.

It's light we have to have. From the photograph onwards, we have been so busy examining the styles and the genres of our imagery. But such time can seem academic if we do not admit that, like lions on the veldt seeking meat, *we have got to have light.*

That's why I turn the lights off in the room. So the screen's light will mean more.

I realize, we all have our favorites, the shows we delighted in for so many episodes, and felt transported by so that we forgot some of our worries. Isn't that what "they" and we mean by entertainment? And in the new millennium, there was this dawning of a fresh ambition in television series—as if it knew we might be ready to concentrate. Because television was growing up, or surpassing movies.

As if we believed we could save ourselves. Think of the excitement there was going from The Wire *to* Ozark.

Such dark stories for brave travelers. Yet sometimes there's a surge of triumph. Remember the commitment we made to *The Queen's Gambit* (2020, only two years ago as I write). Wasn't that a raw thrill? Adapted from a novel by Walter Tevis, scripted by Scott Frank and Alan Scott, and directed by

Frank, it's the story of a young woman, Beth, an orphan, who realizes she may be a chess genius, and how she emerges in the world as a champion and as herself. It's a story, but an advert, too, a spasm in the room that makes us feel more hopeful about ourselves. That's how we let it in.

This Tevis story wasn't overdone; it was just seven episodes, each about an hour long, and there it was on Netflix in October 2020 (that dark time in the pandemic). Never mind, the overcast of plague was lifted by the joy of discovery in the eyes of Beth (or Anya Taylor-Joy—a name made for casting) as she went from an orphanage in Kentucky to Moscow, where she takes on the world champions at the sixty-four-square game. We loved Beth escaping from confinement, so the show made the walls and ceilings of her world a display board for her chess thinking. I relished the 1950s setting and the shabbiness of Lexington, all lit up by diagrams of chess moves and this unschooled girl flowering into womanhood as a player. There were supporting people to treasure: Bill Camp as the janitor at the orphanage who teaches her to play and is quickly defeated by her, but who is drawn out of his gloom by her prowess; Marielle Heller as the indolent woman who adopts and then manages Beth; and Thomas Brodie-Sangster as the brash boy who is nearly as good a player as she is.

After seven episodes it ended: Beth was at the top by then. Her arc was complete.

I wanted her to go on and on. Why not turn her loose on backgammon or Middle East diplomacy? A show called The Diplomat?

We were afraid of empty nights, without her. Still, we need to know when to stop with a story: time and again in this book we'll be mulling over the energy of shows that last for years as business ventures defying the pressure in all story for an ending, *or a way of letting us know why we watched.*

With *The Queen's Gambit* it was easy to say we wanted Beth's end-game glory, whether or not we had a feminist agenda. Taylor-Joy's face, with burnished beaded eyes, made us yearn for her to smile. She and chess were sensations for a season. Yet by now, chess has subsided or gone back to being the obsession of fierce outcasts. (Didn't Bobby Fischer say, "I like the moment I break a man's ego"?)

The show won the Emmy for outstanding limited drama series: Scott Frank won for directing and writing; Anya Taylor-Joy was nominated (she lost to Kate Winslet in *Mare of Easttown,* and that was forgivable—*wasn't Winslet as good as TV can be?*). And Netflix, which reports its viewing figures rarely and then in the tightlipped way that empires admit to their ballistic missiles, declared that sixty-two million households had tuned in to it, or to part of it. A record! Something like everyone. That uplifting hope.

We could not wait for Beth's next episode, and that urgency may be the proof of entertainment. There's the word. In Act IV of *Henry V,* the Chorus asks, "Now entertain conjecture of a time / When creeping murmur and the poring dark / Fills the wide vessel of the universe." It could be an airline commercial? Entertain. Don't forget the idea of a screen being entered, a room beyond our room.

It's the inhalation of an atmosphere. But this is more complicated than our feeling lifted up in an adventure. The word "entertainment" seems to have originated in the sixteenth century to convey something amusing and diverting, but compelling. Even now, we suppose it takes our mind off sad things for an hour or two. But this usage surely derives from the richness of theatre in that age. For the tiny portion of the population that had theatres they could go to, the era of Shakespeare and the flourishing acting companies meant a marriage of poetry and the business of filling seats for the price of admission.

It was a business, and its operators, in 1600 or now, have been happy to treat it as a simple transaction: our fun, their money—granted how few people were involved in a culture that depended on live attendance. That system lasted until well into the nineteenth century, and it was only shifted or deepened by the creation of the photograph. That was an industry and a new discourse that mined the lifelike, and it reached from a keepsake of a wife or a child that soldiers kept in their tunic pocket, to be treasured if they found themselves dying, to images of unknown chorus girls that could be indulged for hours in the new voyeurism. Some soldiers kept both pictures—in separate pockets. But the photograph was our first mass medium because it seemed open for everyone. That very big concept revered the universality of those dead or alive, but forever lifelike in a print.

Those old photographs can be ravishing—they have enhanced the pathos of memory: look at the photographer Julia Margaret Cameron beholding the young actress Ellen Terry in 1863, or the wild-haired, wilder-eyed astronomer John Herschel, who named some moons of Saturn and Uranus. Those two were famous portrait subjects, but the camera was startlingly egalitarian: it was a new way of recognizing a pauper beauty in the slums, or a nobleman in the cotton fields. Photographs were useful and inescapable tokens of life—nearly everyone was using them by 1900 in a steady, automatic way. We still trust them to establish identity. But they are phenomenal in quietly acting out the plan offered in several Constitutions but seldom seen through to fruition—that we are all alike and equal, faces fit to be dreamed over.

I see twin possibilities: first that the entertainment in photographic discourse was easily monetized; and then that the precious slips of photo paper built an inventory of everyone, a culture of common virtue or vivacity that was entrancing. Some photographs may be better than others (like television shows), but they all share this mysterious allure: in giving us the lifelike they downplay life with an alternative. The photograph and its offspring let us think we had mastered life. But at the same time its surreal beast began to eat away at reality.

And we let this trick into the house, even if it has some qualities of an assassin. I do not use that last word lightly. If you want another example of what I am looking at—of why I am watching something I could not endure in life—notice that heavyset man over there, not quite brutish but morose or sorrowful.

He seems like a hulk with a hurt boy's expression. He is a local chieftain presiding over a family business that sometimes kills other men and degrades women. Those are not habits we admire, but you may like this guy if the actor and his writing prove warm enough—so you feel sympathy just because he seems gloomy in himself. Killer and chieftain, but he needs to see a shrink to try to sort his head out. We followed him over six years. Call him Tony Soprano. Some smart and lawful people say he and his show redeemed television.

Whereas pros in that business ask why their trick ever *needed* to be redeemed when it had the world by the eyes and was making so much money? How could redemption match up to that? Are we still harking back to 1961, when Newton Minnow, chairman of the Federal Communications Commission (founded in 1934), told a convention of broadcasters that television much of the time was "a vast wasteland"? Wasn't that like the president of Harvard (or Northwestern, Minnow's school) warning the world to be wary of its graduates? Or like a pilot on the tarmac passing on a last hint to us passengers that we might be advised to disembark?

What would the opposite of a wasteland look like, and could it be cultivated? Or was there even a chance—between 1945 and our unsteady future—that a wasteland might be the most appropriate education we could ask for? Minnow himself enjoyed live drama shows like *Playhouse 90;* he took pleasure in *The Twilight Zone* and Fred Astaire specials. He allowed that occasionally TV was very good, but no one was in doubt about his overall view of things. I suspect he never saw *The Gong Show.* So what does television need to be saved from? Or is the redemption schtick just another commercial for us suckers? What did Minnow think he meant by "wasteland"? Was it a huge bombsite, or just round any corner?

Perhaps Tony Soprano was more disturbed than he knew—more than the show's creator, David Chase, could have explained; more than James Gandolfini, who played the part, understood; and more than those who conspired in the dark glow of *The Sopranos* cared to think about. That includes us, the viewers who found inner fulfillment in the ways Tony and his people behaved so badly. There has always been this possibility in moving picture narratives that our feeling ignored, downtrodden, and unknown in life can be relieved by gaudy monsters who trash the self-important world. That is the song in *The Sopranos,* as it was in *The Godfather.* We let ourselves be entertained by this rueful portrait of a mobster who lacked confidence, and we chuckled at what a funny old life it was for us to be backing a gangster in our worldly way. Equally, Beth was a lesson that hapless orphans deserved great expectations. These stories are always urging us to be bigger than ourselves. And that can forget our smallness or vulgarity.

But is there emotional space in the world for so many needy swelling creatures—when many of them are not officially American? We know it can be a test to feed the 8 billion, and keep them in health or balance. (You remember balance?) But then consider the congestion of egos and desires that television is so nonchalant over. One man may kill another to get clean water and fresh bread. Or he may take up arms and vengeance just because his desire has been thwarted. What does the game of thrones permit? Desire is so hungry its targets hardly matter. We feel we have a right to be pleased or consoled. That's the insistence in advertising. Didn't America come up with the greatest of all jingles—the one about the pursuit of happiness?

That's how a theory of entertainment comes into being. That's why we have been reckless in letting this medium in the house when we had a buried understanding that the "forces" involved—show business, our government, and our feeble selves—reckoned that if the entertainment was novel enough then we would overlook warning strains in how unsettled we are. And 1945 was on an incline towards dismay and disintegration: the codes of progress and humanism had been dissolved, even if you felt the "right" side had won the war. So do not be overconfident about how we relax on our couch in the evening. It's as if on a bad night in Eden, Adam, Eve, and the Serpent had preferred to watch *Candid Camera* than hear the Lord read his solemn riot act. Everything on the box tended towards the facetious.

It was a smart retort from that Edenic trio to ask what the hell they could do about anything. It is our habit, or our escape, to say that there's nothing to be done about progress: the momentum leaves our helplessness untouched, and strips away our dignity—that pomp. So photography altered how we felt about ourselves, and whether we might expect to be understood—or liked. Movies had offered the liberty of fantasies that looked like life. But television knifed into our homes, less inspiring than useful; it seemed visible yet not quite visual. TV threw out the cinematic allure of voyeurism, and was so quick we hardly noticed the switch.

Not that the incline will stop here. "Progress" is headlong and accelerating, a force that adds to our insignificance every day. We slipped into the computer and the Internet, the smartphone, and the expansive scheme of data interpretation. What next? Especially if the pinch of physical survival gets a few degrees tighter. There could come a rationale and a crisis in which the persistence of individuals will have to be measured and controlled. This happens already, if you care to think about it. It is the way poverty closes down on many "unproductive" lives—as in shortening them.

Isn't it part of the theory of entertainment that everything in life is not quite all right? You see, the prompt for seeking entertainment is that there are things—we call them realities; we're sentimental that way—that we'd rather not think about or dwell on, or wake up screaming at. We need entertainment, a show, because our regular condition gets on our nerves.

That raises the question: are these awkward things natural and unalterable? Or are they something that we could attend to? Are we subject to an outside chance of improvement, or bound on a wheel of fire that has never given any hint of being under control?

Do you have a grant for this stuff?

Please, I am trying to concentrate.

It may seem tactless to raise the matter of poverty as a population control system. It is more appealing and viable to think of the system doing its best for us, encouraging us, cheering us up, and making a few sensible recommendations to go with the pizza. We have turned government into a dead-end game, and thus a good deal of television offers alternatives to the implacable grind of getting along.

Once upon a time (it was 1729, the year North Carolina became a royal colony), a desperate comedy writer suggested that the most efficient remedy for starvation in the impoverished classes was for the dead babies of the poor to be processed as palatable foods with market value. This was the insight of Jonathan Swift, and there were those who knew him who thought he was mentally disturbed. Desperate comedy writers easily acquire that reputation.

Like Garry Shandling or Larry David.

Despite the ingenuity of his plan and a few tempting recipe suggestions, Swift's Modest Proposal was not taken up formally. But the project was already being digested in diligent, matter-of-fact ways. So we live in this contract: that we allowed television into the house and gave it license to treat us as consumers. This could seem like the smart thing sometimes called a functioning society. It altered our citizenship, and took away our power to notice that trick.

Is that what "remotely" means? It does resemble prison. Don't you remember Sullivan's Travels, *where the film director (Joel McCrea) grows tired of making silly, fun pictures. So he takes to the road to find the real, hard America. But he ends up on a chain gang in the South. Life is brutal and unkind there. One Sunday the wretched prisoners are taken to a movie show for relief. They start to laugh. Then Sullivan sees the light: you have to settle for silly fun sometimes. What is that picture they watch? Is it Laurel and Hardy, or a Disney cartoon? What year was that?*

1941.

The year you were born.

3

What's On?

What are we going to watch tonight?
Perhaps it doesn't matter.
You mean, just turn it on and sit here?
Isn't that what we do? Soaking up the light?

For a week we had been going through old *I Love Lucy*s. It's easy enough to get into that collection—though it is still rerunning here and there on what I'll call the old, regular, and programmed TV. It's still there in hospitals and prisons and on the back roads left when the new highways came in. (I would guess the Bates Motel is always playing *Lucy*.) That Ricardo household gets crazier and more yesteryear, but I love her still. Though maybe decades later "madcap," the style, has yielded to madness, the inner meaning.

My wife is a Lucy, born in 1955, so her parents cannot have been unmindful of Lucy Ricardo. That "Lucy" on screen may have been the most loved woman in America in 1955—more than Marilyn Monroe, Eleanor Roosevelt, or Annette Funicello in *The Mickey Mouse Club*. The way in which we make companions of people on screen is remarkable and so much fun. But it has led us into many secret passages; we now find the labyrinth so natural we don't notice it.

People think they know *Donald Trump. That hideous intimacy he shits on us. Talk about body-snatched.*

Lucy and I keep lists of shows to see, things read about in reviews or recommended by friends. But then we mislay the lists and sometimes face the infinite possibilities, vexed and insecure at not having an obvious choice for tonight.

So we might start going over the archive of the medium. Isn't there too much to choose from these days? Do you remember *Red Riding* (2009) well enough to want to try it again? It was very dark, I think. I still have its atmosphere in my head, the anxiety and the dread of that north of England being out of control, but I'm not sure who did what in that story. Rebecca Hall came and went—was she murdered? I recall Peter Mullan seeming dangerous in it, but that is often his thing—he was like that in *Top of the Lake* and in *Ozark*. Would *Red Riding* seem like a fresh offering now, only teaching us how easily we forget? Could we regain the first zest of *Peaky Blinders* (2013)? Is it even time to go farther back, to the seeming reality of *Our Friends in the North* (1996)? Or would you be prepared to revisit the original *Forsyte Saga*?

You may have American citizenship, but you're still English.

Those Forsytes began in Britain in January 1967, just a few months before *Bonnie and Clyde* opened in cinemas, two ill-assorted period pieces in the same season, and both sensational. The *Saga* was adapted for television from novels by John Galsworthy (published in the period 1906–21), whereas *Bonnie and Clyde* sprang from noir snapshots of the Barrow gang in the early 1930s, and from Warren Beatty's urge to grab 1967. His movie was sex and violence in narcissist color, a rekindling of gangster picture attitudes cast in the antiauthoritarian elan of the late '60s. It was how to take your plunder to the bank on a career of robbing banks. It was a death wish meeting the sex drive. Even if you haven't seen the film, you know the panache of Beatty and Faye Dunaway in chic clothes and hard times.

In 1967, I was a movie man, a member of that church, inclined to regard television fiction as staid and formulaic. I sat down to watch *The Forsyte Saga* in a patronizing mood because this was mere television from some dusty novels, in black-and-white, and aimed at one's parents. Did the BBC expect us to sit still for twenty-six weekly episodes? Did they ever guess what habit they were onto with that project? From today's stance it looks more influential or significant than the BBC ever dreamed. *Bonnie and Clyde* was pretty kids getting their rocks off, but *The Forsyte Saga* was hinged on whether Soames Forsyte owned his wife like property or furniture, and maybe that question was braver in 1967 than getting Clyde to come. Tremors went through society as Soames raped his wife, Irene.

I remember, Vince Gilligan was born that year, 1967.

Was that the Gilligan with the island?

No, the creator of *Breaking Bad.* All those thoughts, like cushions on the sofa, tossed aside in a restless night.

In 1967, the scene where Soames raped Irene stirred up immense feelings in Britain. Eighteen million had watched the episode—like a third of the nation. It was shot with a sensuality rare on television. The actress, Nyree Dawn Porter, was modestly exposed. The actor, Eric Porter, not so. In response, the BBC did an item for its show *Late Night Line-Up* where a reporter went out on Oxford Street and asked passersby whether they felt more for Soames or for Irene. The majority, men and women, were on the husband's side, the man of property. Some said Irene deserved her rough treatment, and that Soames was only looking for love. You heard the old mantra about how a wife can't be raped by her husband. This is shocking now, but so commonplace you wonder what today's Oxford Street might say about *Euphoria* or *Sex Education.*

Then in the *Late Night* studio, the presenter Joan Bakewell asked four minor celebrities what they thought of it all. The item (you can find it on YouTube) suggests that the melodrama of many fictions could be usefully grounded by the voice of viewer response. The medium has always needed us as well as its set shows and business aplomb. *Late Night Line-Up* was a good idea, a commentary on how television was made, and Bakewell was deft at stirring us up in a cool way. The show was open-ended so the BBC Two channel carried on as long as it felt relevant. Just think of that ability to defy schedule, commercial breaks and guaranteed time. We would be better off if its model had persisted. The BBC was founded on the lofty idea of "nations speaking peace unto nations," but don't forget the possibility of unknown people talking back to the screen.

Don't we do that all the time? But are we heard, or attended to?

If we have given time and money to feeding "a culture" with "entertainment," shouldn't we wonder how that has eased away so many other ideas or energies from our heads and our possibility?

Lying on the couch, weak or weary, we may be excused from noting our invalid condition. But this book wants to be a history of attention as well as forgetting. We are so accustomed to the feeling of external control (that thing "they" do to us). It fills our time, diverts us, calms or becalms us, and leads us into sleep.

Is that why you sleep badly?

It helps us feel helpless, as if that is a last rite. We have succumbed to the idea that between indolence and insomnia we deserve to be occupied or pampered. Isn't it what we are here for; or the mechanism that stops other awkward questions? A couch can seem restful and appealing, something we have earned at the end of the day. It is home. Yet it is like being in a hospital under treatment—but being tactful about not mentioning it.

I don't look forward to visiting you in hospital.

I'll remember that.

You probably won't remember much by then.

You better wear a name tag.

I'll come each day with a fresh joke so you laugh until your stitches sting.

My *Girl Friday.* I'm not sure I look forward to your visits.

I realize this seems solemn. But our passing beyond the sway of religion and slavery, not to mention cast-iron class distinctions, into the new age of critical thinking, mathematics, and loneliness has been alarming enough to permit the refuge of lying on a couch, a sofa, a bed, or the floor for a bit of fun.

I wondered, why not write a book about long-form shows on television, on streaming and bingeing, and what that flow has done to us? What the plan may be. I love some of these shows and I will encourage you to see them. I can promise many great works, and the impassioned waiting on a surprising screen. Just don't expect me to include every show. Do you realize how many there are? There are now over 2,000 shows in just the Netflix catalogue. And new ones coming all the time, like rats hurrying after the Pied Piper.

Why pick some shows and not others? I'm not sure I have a satisfactory answer. I know I will leave out many worthy shows, ones that pleased me once upon a passing time. Don't we have to accept that we may never find *The Singing Detective, The Night Of, The Americans,* or the first *True Detective*? Not if we're keeping up with *The Staircase, Doctor Foster,* or *Alias Grace.* There are Nobel geniuses and people on Death Row who have never seen a moment of *Downton Abbey* or *The Donna Reed Show.* It gets to the point where you don't care what you've seen, or missed.

There are what many would agree were "important" shows in the history. But do they seem interesting or trustworthy now, or is "importance" beside the point of one damn thing after another? *Roots* was "important," wasn't it? We said it was a breakthrough, yet maybe its deepest achievement, in 1977, was to show America how racist and patronizing a place it was if it could be fobbed off with *Roots.* Then decades later a masterpiece, *The Underground Railroad,* was rather set aside by discerning viewers. Was it too painful to take? Or could we not erase the memory that *Roots* had been digested and then excreted?

I may expand on lesser shows because I happened to catch them, or be caught by them, while I was working on this book. It's tempting to live by a kind of pantheon, to declare that some shows are good, some bad, and some eternal. But that goes against the grain of the business that drives TV, the process by which "stuff" fills the air for a few hours for no better reason than letting us know the system is still "on."

Maybe *Candid Camera* is as important as *Roots* (or *Chernobyl*), or more rooted in our tricky being. Started in 1948, Allen Funt's good-natured practical joke show was unfailingly watchable because it had triggered the principle that anything on TV might be fake. It taught us to be wary of what we were seeing, and that was the start of what we now dismiss as "reality TV," without grasping how the medium started to dissolve our relationship with reality long ago.

Imagine an Allen Funt stunt where some heartland couple come to Las Vegas and go up to their plush hotel room. They open the door and enter, expecting to be so happy, but wow, it's the end of the world inside. Horrible and upsetting and going on all the time. Till that droll kidder Allen arrives with room service and tells the couple the "end" is just a theme show and a projection. So have a prawn cocktail with sweet potato French fries, an avocado surprise, and a spoonful of syrup.

Wouldn't you want that tonight? It's like waiting to see where *Babylon Berlin* was going—or *Crime Story*, or *Rubicon*. (There are many lost wonders.) Even so, this process could turn out uncomfortable, as if the couch might become a bed of nails, a slough of despond, or a flimsy raft tossed on the Pacific. (Do you ever wonder whether there could be a serpent within your couch, subtly stirring, less than fragrant, and as dangerous as that original tree of knowledge?)

So the covers need dry cleaning.

Why do we think we deserve to be entertained? What contract did the system slip into our method? What other levels of our nature or potential has this habit obscured? Can we tolerate a theory of being diverted, when the screen has the knack of suddenly confronting us with misery in Mariupol or Aleppo? Is it possible that we were meant to ruminate, instead of being "entertained"? Did we go down a wrong path in 1834 or 1895, a cutoff, like the one that misled the Donner party? Or is the question of our choice the deepest fallacy?

4

Chernobyl and *Chernobyl*

As I shared portions of this work in progress, Lucy advised caution over "Ukraine." Yes, of course, the situation there was so bad and undoubtedly *important,* she agreed. It was painful to watch the news reports every night, as the broken communiqués mimicked the ruined state of many buildings. Everyone was anxious over Ukraine; we had all heard of Mariupol by then. I shudder to think where that country will be by the time this book is yours.

By then Ukraine may seem if not quite dated, then of the past. We are weak in our memory. These intense actions slip away: some go to series, but others are not renewed. I'm not sure I really recall Aleppo.

Can Ukraine or its onlookers be so lucky? Is the street empty today, or is that a suspicious gathering on the next block? There was a time when our history talked of wars that went on for thirty years, or a hundred. It is customary among historians to regard the disturbance of the twentieth century as stretching from 1914 to 1945, as if 1945 ended all it needed to conclude. Does history really come in these primed chapters?

I felt the gloom of Ukraine was here to stay for a while, if only because it has been with us so long. No need to trouble you with how the unresolved status of Ukraine reached back to the sixteenth century, or the ninth. That ninth was interesting. But the record was filled with alternatives to any notion that Ukraine simply belonged to Russia or served its wishes. More to the point of this book, there was *Chernobyl* and how we viewed that hot spot again as fresh war set in.

This was a television miniseries, made by HBO and Sky and released in

2019. As such, it seemed to prove the medium's assumption that any catastrophe could work as a show.

That's my worry: that our crises can be tidied up so quickly and turned into series. I have a feeling—I know it's stupid—that some worldwide chronicle of catastrophe needs to stop dead in its smooth tracks. So "previously on . . ." becomes "we interrupt this . . ." And armed men appear suddenly at Downton Abbey.

Chernobyl was created and written by Craig Mazin (he had written *Scary Movies* and *Hangovers* beforehand—careers now can zigzag), and all five episodes (of just over an hour each) were directed by Johan Renck.

It attempted to describe the mishap at the Chernobyl nuclear power station, in Ukraine, that occurred on April 26, 1986. For a time, "everyone" knew about that incident, and many reading this book will have seen some of the series. Even if you missed it, or turned it off because it was too harrowing, you have no wish to brush it away, let alone bury it under thick concrete (the eventual "solution" to parts of the contaminated site of Pripyat, the city that had been created to serve Chernobyl).

Like an eager critic, I want to say it is a great series, among the best in this book. But that is not sufficient. More than itself, *Chernobyl* asserts a stricken marriage of drama and documentary. God save us, the show says, this thing happening is so awesome and scary, how can we not face it? But can we do so without employing a framework like fiction? The show won the Emmy for outstanding limited series, but it's demeaning to offer the word "limited." It ought to be within the reach of television to startle us with scenes from the awkward marriage of actuality and narrative. The medium should explode its "limits" every night. If it doesn't dare to be so revolutionary, it starts circling on a treadmill. Think of this as our last chance if you need a scary jolt.

So this is not a show to address the benefits or the dangers in nuclear power. It is an exposé of how bureaucracy, official self-protection, and common human fear—the urge not to look at the real thing—amount to a campaign of untruth that intensifies the damage being done. So the show was also prescient on the later conflict between Ukraine and Russia, the one we think of as ours now. It hinges on Soviet authority denying what had happened at Chernobyl and how it had to be cleaned up. It is a story about dishonesty and corruption, such as Dickens might have inhaled. It teaches us there are disasters in our system tugging against every care and nervous decision. Pripyat will be available again in twenty thousand years.

You see, we make mistakes. Perhaps that is all we make, all the time, but television in its valiant mindset is so often intent on telling us how great and secure we are. What grand idiots.

Should you say that? Won't people be upset? Won't that stop the engine turning over?

For dramatic clarity, *Chernobyl* picks on a few individuals to say that story can surpass entropy and persistence. Anatoly Dyatlov (Paul Ritter), deputy chief engineer at Chernobyl, tries to cover up what has occurred. Vassily Ignatenko (Adam Nagaitis) is a first-responder firefighter at Pripyat who tries to deal with the fire. Lyudmilla (Jessie Buckley) is his wife, who must behold Vassily's ruin. Valery Legasov (Jared Harris) is a scientist ordered to solve the larger problem. Boris Shcherbina (Stellan Skarsgård) is the Soviet official who is his tormented superior. Ulana Khomyuk (Emily Watson) is a composite of several scientists who understood the issues at Chernobyl and labored to have the truth made clear. And Barry Keoghan as Pavel.

These people are brave and agonized. But the show does not want us to identify with them or rescue them as endearing figures in the way Jane Fonda's character Kimberly Wells attracts emotional support in *The China Syndrome* (1979). That is not to attack Fonda—her urgency got that movie made, opening twelve days before the accident at Three Mile Island, a vision to shatter disbelief. But she is a natural seeker of our love and approval; that is in the nature of an American movie star. There are degrees of honor and courage in the characters in *Chernobyl*, but they are plain figures caught in a harsh situation and in failure. Under Soviet conditions that truth will not come out. That can be as dangerous as the half-life of strontium-90, or whatever. Discourse and critical thinking in Soviet Russia (as in all other states) were under an overcast of propaganda and deliberate self-deception that are the core of advertising.

And don't forget how, at the outset, we see Legasov killing himself. Two years after the incident and the inquiry. He hangs himself. He was sick, they said, from radiation, but he was in despair, too. He was like our narrator checking out before the story started.

And it all runs together, so have you noticed that Legasov is also George VI from *The Crown*? Jared Harris. He spits up blood there, too.

The show was banned in Russia, but technology made that hard to enforce. In the area of the former Soviet Union, many people were able to stream the show—in just the way our kids hack into stuff we are watching (and paying for) on our screen.

You can think of *Chernobyl* as an analysis of the willful blindness of the Soviet Union. So several years after it was made, the show seems to draw attention to the plight of liberty and truthfulness in "our" Ukraine. But it is not anti-Soviet or anti-Russian. It is a plain statement on the impediments to truth and understanding anywhere. Don't forget that as *The China Syndrome* opened much of the American nuclear power industry assailed it as an irresponsible fiction. You could say that the American film was also some explanation of why, even in the greatest nation on earth, only limited or formal efforts have been put forward to understand racism, the threat of global warming, the way poverty makes us die early . . . or why must there be advertisements on TV?

Perhaps that last point seems contrived. Not so. Few things are as close to our damage. We have to be smarter and more honest; it is within our nature; candor is a proper subject for television. No medium intent on information and critical thinking should endure advertising. Or the smug homily that there is nothing to be done without it.

There are so many frightening things in *Chernobyl:* the physical degradation of contaminated people; the anguish of those losing their loved ones; the fatigue in opposing stupidity and corruption. These things are bravely handled in the ways of fine acting, good writing, and the evolution of decisive scenes. This is excellent or accomplished television. As if that helps.

What left me most uneasy was the view of Pripyat after it had been shut down against the world, and left to wait until "it" was safe. It was called an area of exclusion or a zone of alienation. The film had used locations in Vilnius in Lithuania for this, but its model was the look of communities in Ukraine and the Soviet Union—or elsewhere. Maybe Vilnius or Ukraine are less photogenic than the suburbs of Dallas or Las Vegas. Still, *Chernobyl* ends on piles of empty buildings, Lego cities, the places where once upon a time we decided that people should live, or wait. In emptiness, these sites have an air of regret, and that was there before the catastrophe. There are zones of alienation where we live in San Francisco, places the regulars try not to see. Where the homeless long for home. We are becoming veterans at looking away and there is indecision in whether television opposes that or permits it.

Chernobyl *makes me feel torn. I am impressed that it was done so well. But horrified that it was there to be done, and that I am watching it in safety. It is such a test, to look at reality and turn it into a story. Even now in Ukraine, there is combat in the vicinity of other power stations. Television is so like us: it aspires to the texture of reality and then turns its back. Is that what we require? And one day, maybe, some regime will say Chernobyl didn't really happen. It was always in italic. But I recall the sequence where men go out to kill all the animals—that's the first time I noticed Barry Keoghan.*

5

Going Vegas

Is it unkind to cut from the forlorn streets of Pripyat to a view of today's Las Vegas, where traffic and the neon are shimmering with life? But maybe the commotion of that downtown is misleading. After all, this is a kingdom where moral decision has been turned into a test of chance. That is why so many people there are tense and dangerous from waiting—for a card to be turned, for that silver ball to settle in a notch, for fruits to line up on a slot machine, or for daylight to return.

Las Vegas was our first "anywhere" place, a gaudy set put down in the desert, an escape, an idea. A piece of art direction. It was the theory of TV made manifest in stucco, neon, and scary hope. At first, it could be explained away as a naughty diversion, a lurid aside. But it was the American future, irrational yet lush, rich and empty, a complete on/off call.

It was the introduction of "nowhere" as a getaway idea in America. A place you wanted to be, a slick anonymous hotel at the end of the Ellis Island line. With Candid Camera *in every hotel room.*

At five o'clock in the morning once, all-night gamblers went up on casino roofs to see the glow of bomb tests sixty-five miles to the north. They got the light show and then the slam breakfast—sunny side up or scrambled. The urban gathering seems in awe of how the desert is watching and waiting. Ochre, ruffled and breathless in the morning. Desert has deeper history than cities; it knows its day will come again. Las Vegas had offered a trip into the West, a racy vacation, but it was a virtual trip before we had acquired that concept. A theoretical venturing into a nullity and a place that could not last. Is that establishment over there an occult chapel, a fortune teller's cave, Area 51, or the Liberace museum?

I thought that had closed.

The idea persists.

Alas poor Liberace, we knew him well.

Many modern habits (the pre-apocalypse protocol) were pioneered in Las Vegas, that deadpan intersection of desert and edifice, of heat, hope, and chance, expectation and patience. It was a destination where transformation or catastrophe were part of the roulette.

You have to wonder about a civilization that finds entrancing desert, and puts Las Vegas there. It's like being on an aircraft, flying over the gorgeous West, where every row of seats has shuttered out the spread and the light to study ridiculous movies eight inches by six.

Once upon a time, we liked to think Vegas had been placed in its nothingness as a getaway from respectable society. Timid law-abiding miscreants pictured that desert destination as a way of being liberated or escaped.

Or call it the American channel.

That old frontier wildness. The deadliness of the place was advertised as exotic. Its greed was reappraised as our long shot in the dark. Nevada had been founded on principles of divorce and gambling at odds with how we were supposed to be. Had the republic ever set up institutions so opposed to its ideal, or so flagrant for desire? It was an ad for getting out of line.

So weary pilgrims would get a flight and a reservation in a hotel, and the chance to discover a million dollars or ruin at the tables. Without any trace of blame or responsibility: no one really thought the game was rigged—it didn't need to be; anyone could see that most of us were cast as loyal losers. We entertained the notion of being with a showgirl or a sisterly hooker. We glimpsed big shots, sheikhs, and Armani hoodlums in sultry private rooms. And we existed on the novocaine thrill that what happened in Vegas stayed there. So we were safe to return to Des Moines, Concord, Bedford Falls, or wherever, just a little tanned by danger and bad things.

This was a mythology, but one that appealed to anyone crushed by disappointed habit, doing the right things and feeling like a chump. If we dreamed of orgy and murder, or of the bells chiming as money cascaded in our laps, Vegas was our deadpan church, and there was a biblical reassurance in desert seeming so close with heat pumped up from hell. Of course, that heat had to be finessed. In Vegas, the piled cash, the hooker's glance, and the ice cream depend on air conditioning, and that surge of cool is not just physical and comforting but a moral cancellation. Another irresponsibility. For the first decades of Las Vegas visitors could think the a.c. had nothing to do with weather and water. So the city and the culture of the place were a drive-in screen of dysfunction.

But then in time, in what we thought of as the postwar magic of Americana, we saw that there was less point in going to Las Vegas, for it had come to us. In terms of design, the motel-hotel structure began to seep into fresh residences. The unlikely hope of the place infected more and more of the stalwart nation. The subversive imperative that we would have to gamble to get by in America gained ground. Professionals in the stock market agreed that their whole show was a poker-faced casino. For more than a hundred years the economy had assumed it relied on industry, hard work, conservatism, and capital. Ingenuity and whatever—you know the litany of what makes us tick. But a truth was coming in, that it was all chance while the only thing to be relied on was our greed and the way it and money had overgrown economic purpose, moral righteousness, and those tidy schemes for possessions and property.

You are describing Ozark!

Property was turning to assertion and self-advertising. Have you noticed that lying may be excused if it can call itself promotion? With ironic honor, mocking but mischievous.

There was this, too: that as the issues in our temporary placement grew more pressing—

Like the water at Hoover Dam going lower. Or the day you turned on your shower and a diamondback slid out of the pipes.

It was a Vegas game. We had to decide between thinking ourselves out of that drought, treating the problem with facts, critique, and sacrificial ingenuity, or taking the gambler's exit by saying, Oh, I bet it will work out, meanwhile let's catch the latest Cirque du Soleil, and the new filet mignon at Smith & Wollensky. Let's have fun while we can. That idea of saying stuff stays in Vegas was brushing all awkwardness aside, and it took wings on the assertion of television advertising that we were all going to have a terrific time. We like to tell ourselves that we have gritted our teeth and put up with advertising, but it has put a hand inside our glove puppet from the ass to our mouth that prompts our rictus smile.

We were at the Mirage, and I took a photograph of an upstairs floor in the hotel and what seemed like a hundred yards of corridor and rooms, locked in windowless light and air conditioning. And the corridors mirrored one another and fanned out like the pockets on a roulette wheel. It looked like a scene from a luxury prison.

And that deserted corridor, with all its cells, had luster and poise as if some supreme commercial was playing. The sound was turned off. You couldn't see a picture. But you felt that mocking constancy that you could be all right if you pressed ACCEPT. I say mocking because of that innate nudge and its smothered grin, as if to ask, "Aren't we idiots to be doing this?"

And in every one of those cells, along every corridor, on every floor, there would be a television screen, ready to console and calm anyone who had lost his life at the tables but didn't have to provide plastic until tomorrow morning. At some time in the last decades of the twentieth century it became apparent that stretches of America looked like this.

With a desert outside. And inside.

The habit I am thinking of is that Nevadan absentmindedness, slipping us free from caring what time it is, or will be. There is an unspecific temporal availability in Vegas casinos, the crystallization of all our anticipation in the turn of a card. The streaming in being at the tables—laying out the cards, the chips and the theories of counting, or contemplating your steak dinner with baked potato, sour cream, and chives, with a side of crested spinach. Plus the generous cocktail. That setup was so pressing, so poised for ridiculous magic and salvation, we lost touch with night and day or what time it might be, of having anything else to compete with being at a table. It was an early warning that we would not get out, and the rows and floors of identical rooms were a model taken from institutions. If Vegas is there in another fifty years, I wonder whether some new casino will take over from the Venetian, the Wynn, or the Bellagio, and be known as Rikers.

I always guessed prison reform was your thing. And room service could be the warders.

Just don't trust any commentator on America who hasn't been stranded in Vegas.

The steak dinner looked exquisite. It was there every night until the hotel sent guys in workout clothes and Old Spice up to your room to escort you to the street, where even in the nocturnal heat and the stupor of neon you understood that 77 percent of the people on the street were losers too. The first person who got Vegas was Nathanael West, and he saw it so early that he still thought of it as Los Angeles in *The Day of the Locust* (1939), seven years before the Flamingo opened. But West felt the derangement in hope, and the vengefulness in its disappointment.

In Las Vegas you feel your metabolism adjusting to timelessness, and if you walk out on the Forum at Caesars, that enclave of boutique shopping, where the artificial lighting slides from dawn to dusk, or the other way round, you can feel free, or lost. The passage of time was automatic shuffling.

Something like this happened last night, or whenever: I think it was night, here in San Francisco. I had fallen asleep on the couch as if it were somewhere between a launchpad and my tomb—you know that premature burial game.

Lucy and I had watched season four of *Ozark,* in three nights: seven episodes broken down as two, three, and two. We loved it, and we saw how close it was to the pattern of gambling with characters who are driven by the mischance of money.

Now that the show was over, we wondered what we could do in its absence. You know that hollow feeling when a binge runs out of light. So we agreed, why not watch the season once again, as if it was another couch into which we needed to settle more deeply. (We had not yet appreciated that season four would have a second half, and Netflix wasn't saying yet when those episodes would arrive. They came in 2022, but I'll come to that.)

So we started off on four again with the opening sequence where Marty and Wendy Byrde are in the car with their kids, coasting along on a sunny day in a kind of dream, with a song on the car radio, until a semi comes towards them on the wrong side of the country road. Thus Marty swerves (he is a lifelong swerver) and the SUV goes into a gorgeous cartwheel, turning over several times. Magnificent to behold, yet not good for you if you were inside.

What happens to that car? It must pay off later. Or are those Byrdes dead already?

Lucy, you got some 'splaining to do—I said this in a shameless Latin voice, but her idea that the Byrdes had always been ghosts or other than alive was piercing.

We agreed that the car crash was the lovelier for not being settled. Its unwinding went on forever. So we were wondering were those strange Byrdes dead or alive, which raised the question, had they been living dead from the start? The "Living Dead" is one of the great American dreams. The Byrdes said they were laundering money and raising a family. Just getting along in the picturesque Midwest to erase their debt to the Cartel. But *Ozark* was providing death as a by-product of cleaned cash. We were always waiting for spectacular fatality. Like the kicker at the end of season three when the awesome Helen, as tall as Janet McTeer and as commanding, got offed in an instant so that her blood and membrane fell on the Byrdes like rain or confetti. I hope that's not a spoiler.

This question spread in my mind as I started to sleep, like one of those spilled drinks in a commercial for the most absorbent tissue a great civilization ever made. Or the threat of syrup getting into your phone. Sort of thing.

When I woke up Lucy had gone away, but I was there on the couch still, in a poised sprawl before slipping towards the floor. Yet again Marty was ducking out of a crisis to take a phone call, while Wendy and Ruth glared at each other in their pent-up dismay. Wendy's hair was lank and dyed, while Ruth vibrated beneath her hive of curls. It was always *Ozark*. I didn't know where I was, but I understood what I was doing there, and if it hadn't been going on forever then I was available for a while longer yet.

There was a message on my phone, a flash, breaking news for a fractured culture: "Never underestimate how much Americans are willing to spend during a crisis," it said. At last the dogged engine of our progressiveness was revealed.

You do see, this book is a pained rhapsody over America. Not that the country is or need be the greatest nation in the world. But it has a chance of being the last one.

Hi, I'm in the bath, she called down the corridor.

6

Inattention Must Be Paid

You know, when I'm in the kitchen, making eggs or whatever, I put the radio on. Or Spotify. But I don't quite listen. It's liking sound or company. Not wanting to feel alone. And you do the same thing with the TV. Do you realize that? You leave the room sometimes, with the set still playing. For an hour or more. Like leaving a light on. You go away. Anywhere.

I want to feel sure it will be there when I come back.

Like breathing in the night. Hearing a companion asleep.

I had felt it would be rewarding to study *Ozark*. The show seemed an unnerving commentary on regular America, not just the middle of the map but the dark fields of the republic. As it played in the era of Donald Trump it was hard to ignore how *Ozark* meekly observed a nation and its business as lacking any imperative except success or staying afloat. While the Byrdes scrambled to survive, there was no way the show believed in ideas worth surviving for. That's why laundering money was the deadpan nerve center of the show—not even raw cash, but taming control of it.

Decades after the cheeriness of early TV, here was a show—as good as any of its time, I felt—that had no shame or irony over the emptiness it proposed. How had the medium advanced? How had we watched and not noticed alteration? *Ozark* was more honest, inventive, and grown-up than *I Love Lucy*, or *The Fugitive*, or *M*A*S*H*, but there was no escaping the burden of the new show, or the consequences that left for the society huddling to watch it. How were Lucy and I to ask ourselves whether we could take it?

Was it proper or productive to keep paying such attention to the smothered regret in the faces of Marty and Wendy? Or were we giving up their ghost?

By January 2022, in three and a half seasons, *Ozark* had had thirty-seven episodes, at a running time of around an hour each. Call it 59 minutes a pop, and that's 2,183 minutes, or more than thirty-six hours. That duration is immense by movie standards, where three hours is still a stretch—and these days it can feel stretched very thin. Movies are listless now, as if the medium knows it has lost the audience. Yet *Ozark* episodes are as crisp and pert as something made in 1941. They hold on to pace, economy, and exactness, those blessed virtues, as if they were a serial telling us—*don't go away, come back next week.*

But thirty-six hours seems impossible or ancient, as if a story lasting that long is faintly ridiculous. It's implicit in such a show that, for all the plot, it isn't going anywhere. So you don't have to follow the dotted lines of narrative because the situation is always the same. You could come in on any episode and be what is called comfortable with it. In all of *Ozark* how many shots of Laura Linney looking anguished have there been? Two hundred, five hundred? That may be as potent as the Byrdes turning from sparrows to vultures.

Don't knock it, buster. Aren't we having a good time, instead of just watching ourselves come apart?

But in our own ongoing story, otherwise known as our life, a hundred hours is only a long weekend. A moment you will have forgotten six months later. We enjoy stories, but our lives also work in repetitive series that erase narrative. The other day, I estimated that Lucy and I had eaten scrambled eggs on toast . . . 4,210 times in forty years. Give or take. Some better than others, but as consistent as the eggs, fluffy yet solid, and good stuff. Not that I remember one from another.

You have nothing better to do?

That's a kind of happiness.

We are not literature. We're boring: selfishness is the forlorn attempt to deny that. As if we might be actors playing ourselves, it's a way of reaching out for significance, like saying "Rosebud" as you die.

Let's say that streaming can't exist without time—or without the bleak sensibility that guesses attention is not as important as school wanted to teach us. You get the idea that in passing time we intend to ignore the possibility that time is passing us by, as if we're not there or as if it is ridiculous to suppose we matter.

No episode of any show is really important beside the calm patience of episodicness. It's the way, in streaming, that no piece or drop of water in our swim is crucial. You can't pick up a handful of water, but the feeling of the current tugging at your hand is so inspiring. The stream works only because every drop or molecule is the same as all the others. You may be reminded in this of Werner Heisenberg's uncertainty principle and the elegant puzzle he detected in being unsure whether matter was best regarded as particles or as flow. Stories or streaming. This principle was first described in 1927, the year in which we also had to determine whether a movie was made of pictures or sound—or were they scrambled together?

More and more, I feel the strange appeal of doing nothing.

I've noticed that, too, like not doing the washing up, not making the bed, not taking out the garbage, not—

I know this is not regular mainstream television criticism, but it seeks the essence of how the medium functions. We have been raised in the tradition of Film Studies or Narrative Humanism 101 to follow the precept by which geniuses work (or like to think they do). They are always making deliberate and crucial decisions: this word or that, rosebud or rhubarb, let the close-up hold or cut away to a long shot of dark smoke in the sky. This is trying to pin down meaning and consequence, and celebrate the function of particularity. But as the great film from 1941 admits, "Rosebud" doesn't really matter; it was a pretext, a McGuffin, a trick of dollar-book Freud. Because it was more important that time was passing: Charlie Kane went from on to off; the film stopped; we walked home thunderstruck—and started to see *Citizen Kane* over and over again, adjusting to its room and its couch.

Orson Welles admitted he couldn't look at his great film again. It was as if his DNA could no longer spiral in the streaming of the movie. There was nothing playful left. He could claim that few directors had spent as much time and indecision as he had going through the frames of a film over and over again. If you doubt that intensity, get yourself into the editing studio on a film, and marvel at the neurotic repetition of shots and sequences—refining them and then blowing them apart—to get the movie what they call "right." It is a process in which the actions, the things said, the particles, become arbitrary or artificial, no more or less than notes in a piece of music or the scoops of light on running water as the river passes by. A movie can't be "right," only final.

You will know that in film studies, in reading about movies, you can't do a paragraph without tripping up over words like "important" or "riveting." That culture longs to believe particular movies and instants are loaded with grandeur and significance. It's like the inhalation that precedes "Rosebud." But be ready for this letdown: most movies are just like other movies, so it may not matter which one you are seeing and claiming as a masterpiece. And most viewings of *Kane* are endless scrambled egg.

Or hardly hearing in the kitchen.

Consider how many things there are in life that we cherish but do not think to call a masterpiece: one fresh-baked wholemeal loaf is indistinguishable from another; one stick of asparagus is like the regiment; you can say the same about a sunny June morning in London, a view of the ocean in a storm, or—not so far removed—a convincing act of sexual congress. I know, the people involved in the latter like to say that really was *the one,* the best, where the earth moved or a bell rang. But that is our generosity talking when we might not be able to tell one coitus from the other, or from a good loaf of bread. While enjoying most of them.

You're so open-minded.

So you can't indulge the mysterious personality of the couch without knowing it saps or surpasses attention. And as if we hadn't yet formulated attention deficit disorder, it's plain that we are taught to believe that attention is . . . well, us at our best. When I say "taught" I'm invoking the enterprise we call education, and I remember Mrs. Mower or Mr. Treadgold (the scolds of my childhood) saying, "Now pay attention, children," as if nothing was ever going to work without that given. But I'm suspicious of attention. So many useful things—like breathing, or sleeping, or . . . I leave this list up to you—carry on without it.

We are at an awareness that guides this book, and our understanding of television and the couch. This may be the wasteland Newton Minnow noticed, but it is an exuberant garden, too. We are facing a realm of inattention, not just as a domestic practice, the way "entertainment" is absorbed, like oatmeal or carbon. I doubt the human being is really capable of inattention; it's more that his and her mind wander until they see fraternity in a sewing machine and an umbrella. That can be a prelude to useful questions about where our civilization is going, and whether it might be better described as a mere condition or inertia, without all that pompous stuff about intention, progress, and how grand we are.

As we undertake to follow narratives, we put ourselves at the author's desk: we foresee concluding arcs for the characters; we imagine incidents about to happen; we take for granted a degree of moral resolution. So Shakespeare might have foreseen all along: *I am going to have to kill Cordelia*—the old man must appear at last carrying her dead body. But if I am to kill her, I must take care that there is purpose. I had fragmented visions of Marty Byrde bearing the corpse of Charlotte, or of Wendy herself putting Marty out of her misery. Can you see that revelation? Don't go away—these matters may yet be attended to.

I guessed that *Ozark* might not be so drastic. After all, without Charlotte or Marty there could not be another season. And no matter the farewell speeches, and Jason Bateman being otherwise tied up doing Hyundai commercials, you never know when money will start streaming again. In 1960, *Psycho* seemed put away for good—but then, two decades later, Anthony Perkins had to come back, three times. And we know money never knows—it takes no responsibility. So we understand that finality has given way to one damn thing after another.

I'm making eggs.

Please be sure you put the scrambled *on* the toast.

No way, that turns the bread soggy.

I like it like that.

Sunny side up, sweetheart! That's how Heisenberg took his eggs! Preserving the particle and the flow.

7

A Machine for Making Light

At the end of the nineteenth century and into the twentieth, the fraction of us who had read novels or seen plays was revolutionized by the movies. It was a moment when to be alive might make you faint or cry out in the dark. That's not too sweeping or portentous an idea. Movie was the revolution that meant more than Mao, or Disney.

Reality was bypassed. Still there, but like any old movie.

Because the fragment of ourselves that had attended to the lines of type on a page, or the unwinding of a drama on stage, felt the tempest of a new kind of storytelling that became—in a few years—material for everyone.

Suppose you could not read; suppose you could not afford a ticket for a play, or lived in places where there were no theatres, so the craze for flickers swept you away on a rush of rapid eye movement. Just pay attention, children, and muster the dime you need for a seat in the dark. We were lost, sweetheart, all of us, and those who said they were found were crazy.

The melodrama of the novelty cannot be underestimated—we make a grievous error by not admitting and exploiting the revolution. It had been exciting enough to have photographs. Lifelike images that permitted a kind of emotional and intellectual ownership that had not been possible before. But once those pictures moved, the degree of latent desire was electrified. The element of story could be conveyed with a suddenness and an immediacy that was impossible before. The intensity of attention or concentration, and the way that mechanism exalted aspiration and longing, I think that was an onslaught on human nature from which we will never recover. It goes on and on, you see, and in the spirit of wanting to be entertained we barely keep up with the radical changes in our understanding.

Consider the parts of this onslaught (but know the parts are as interactive as the ingredients of weather):

- The medium is a violent juxtaposition of light and dark, of our huddled intimacy and the world's brightness: in its inescapable format it dramatizes "enlightenment" and the threat of darkness—it is like a spiritual tension but the only deity in evidence is the machinery itself. The stories the medium tells may do all they can to cleave to nobility and virtue, but the mechanics are primitive, dictatorial, and cold-blooded. Manichaean, and at odds with every advertised businesslike plan for pursuing happiness.

- And this wonder is implacable, impelled by some invisible force. The machinery is its own being, and we are of no concern. You may cry out in the middle of a movie, "Save the child!" or "Save me!" You may be having a heart attack or a thorough spiritual crisis, and the mechanics do not hear or notice you. They are not deflected or touched. So it is curious that the stories the machine unfolds seem to want us to be touched. What we were undergoing was the first metaphor for our not mattering. The process (they call it entertainment) was simply a machine that devoured and shat out those lovely things, the light and beauty and fun. But it was so powerful as to let us know we had given up any hope of control, or even participation. And this happened at the very moment when our "they" said: you must all be educated and reasonable; you—all of you—can then vote; why not have a little social security and health insurance; drive on the right-hand side of the road; don't you see what a fine life it can be? And this monster treated us as if we were not there and had no existence, beyond our ticket. The advertised show, the entertainment thing, was a model of subservience such as had never existed before. And these movies were seen "all over the world." More people knew Charlie than acknowledged any leader: that was the spur to Chaplin's *The Great Dictator*. This was a tyranny that coincided with worldly attempts at command, like Communism, Fascism, and Democracy. And above all Capital Consumerism. Those were the genres on offer in the twentieth century. But they were all subservient to the power, and to the realization that every individual going after happiness would be better off dead. This scenario had an odd resemblance to the aloof silence of God, and that reminded us how God's deepest purpose was to determine, at the moment of our demise, whether we were on or off, hit or stand. We were not exactly our unique vivid selves (though those ads were appealing). We were the mass. And a mass has to have a medium, or else it goes crazy.

- The reach of this authority is countered by the medium's constant insinuation that its famous and lovely reality is not there. For example, you may be seeing the deserts of Arabia but you are not there; you may be seeing someone as delectable as Mary Pickford or Charlie Chaplin, but you can't touch; you may watch the murder of a man, done in increasing detail, but you can't intervene or save him. You are not responsible. What you see is the expression of your helplessness. The huge stress on realism is also fake. Sooner or later this will undermine our faith in reality and in ourselves.

- And all of this, every instant in every movie, is hinged on the possibility that in a fraction of a second the image on the screen can be convulsed by change: you may be looking at Mary Pickford, and thinking how sweet she is, and then quicker than you can close your eyes, the image is of a tidal wave breaking on a shore and bringing devastation. It's not just that this transition is scary and startling. It leaves us with the imponderable: what does this wall of water mean to Mary? Because we cannot experience a "cut" without trying to explain or heal the arbitrary shift. Every cut is a suture.

8

Paying for the Room

Cinema was not just a novel entertainment. It was a new plan for our time and being, a departure from domesticity and the clearest hint of an exciting world beyond—so we were taken out of our homes to meet it. And from the start we felt its thrilling overlap of real and surreal, or a threat to order. We would see things that were out of sight.

In a frenzy of designer dreams, the picture business decided to build theatres. These were very large by our standards today, and they were an empire of decoration that would seem comical and touching in our Bauhaus cubes at the multiplex. The walls of many theatres or cinemas from the 1920s were extra screens. Their suggestions of Spain under the Moors, of pashas and their odalisques, of the Arabian nights, of an Orient freshly discovered, or of an Olde England fit for knights and their ladies, were trailers for coming attractions.

But it was a close-run thing. When Thomas Edison and William Dickson invented the kinetoscope, its eyepiece was meant for single individuals looking on their own, in privacy, *or secrecy.* At the outset of cinema, by 1900, many urban homes were already electrified: the one-viewer show could have been pumped in, like the light, or television. But we weren't sufficiently brilliant to grasp that.

It was the advance of electrification that let cinema slip in ahead of television. Thus the masses were beckoned into large, ornate rooms that seemed lacquered in the adrenaline of dream. And electrified. For most people, these palaces were awesome or intimidating. The theatres might hold a thousand, or two thousand, and invariably they were packed. Having waited in line to get in, you felt privileged being there. Your spirits were raised before anything began in the way of house lights dimming and the foundation light (the force behind you) coming on. There was one other act of public participation that came close to this intensity, and that was going to church. No wonder every screened cut had the potential of a miracle.

Going to the movie theatre meant being part of a crowd of strangers, a congregation. There had never been so steady or sweeping an enactment of community. You could smell each other; there were honest fears about infection. So it was no wonder that many of the first practitioners—from D. W. Griffith to Chaplin or Sergei Eisenstein—believed the medium would galvanize and unite the world. Equally, there were others confident that the medium revealed the doom that awaited civilization: you can feel that in Erich von Stroheim, Fritz Lang, and the adoration of what we call menace or horror. Its gravest preacher would be Alfred Hitchcock.

But as in a church, the crowd knew it was there for several purposes: to have fun (to be taken out of oneself and into some spirit or romance); to pay for the show; but to be present at a vivid demonstration of human nature. Whether through exuberance or fear, the audience understood that they were part of a narrative experiment: could the characters survive and feel happy? Or would dread come in like a tsunami, or a knife in the shower? This was not so different from church programs in which we were offered the chance of being saved or not.

These movies were fashioned for those who might have a hard time reading novels, or who could hardly negotiate the intricacies of Shakespeare on stage. For all of us. The chief reason for feelings of community and togetherness was that the illiterate, the uneducated, the poor, might be lifted up to a state of pilgrimage. This was a political window to see through as our outer society was tearing itself apart. For cinema coincided with the Great War (a conflict such as had never existed before, fought with new lethal weapon systems), with the Depression, and then a Second World War and the two bitter mottoes in its fortune cookies at the victory party: the Holocaust and the Atom Bomb.

It was a terrifying era in which nothing matched the boldness of the hopes inspired by movies that we might all of us be all right. Sitting in the dark, holding on to our seats and our companions, desperate not to miss a single cut and in love with these people we would never meet. It was as brave and wild, but as fearful as a slave state.

Think of the Second World War as the turning point in the passion for cinema that had lasted forty years. The war marked the fullest identification of the audience with the international project, not just in the fighting drive of war movies but in the use of newsreels at movie theatres to report the war's progress, albeit with rapturously dishonest assurance. In the U.S. as in most countries, the audience at the movies was bigger than it had ever been, or would ever be. In the years just after the war, the American audience hovered near 100 million tickets a week when the population of the country was around 130 million!

Going to the movies was not just something Americans elected to do—it was what they did habitually. They went without caring what the film was! They understood the medium so much more quickly than great critics or greater auteurs.

It was an era of wholesale fantasy: few of the war movies knew how to present war in its reality, or had any intention of doing so, and if they had tried, the devastation would have been outlawed by censorship. So the life-like medium was drifting farther from the truths it might be able to grasp. Yet the medium was reaching a peak. You can say that a "great" film (or a piece of slick shit) like *Casablanca* was specious wishful thinking enough to pump that wistful mood into our souls.

But the era of the war had so many landmarks in cinema history: I'm thinking of *Bringing Up Baby, Citizen Kane, The Shop Around the Corner, His Girl Friday, Sullivan's Travels, The Lady Eve, Shadow of a Doubt, Meet Me in St. Louis, The Best Years of Our Lives, They Live by Night, Letter from an Un-*

known Woman. The thought hardly occurred to the 130 million, but for a few enthusiasts it was possible to believe the cinema was tending to greatness and distinction. Was it like an art? As if some movies were as worthy as novels, symphonies, or paintings. And the pattern was broader than America. The same period produced *Grand Illusion, The Rules of the Game, Children of Paradise, Bicycle Thieves, Odd Man Out, The Red Shoes,* and *Brief Encounter.* Not to mention *The Story of the Last Chrysanthemums* (1939), a Japanese film you have likely not heard of but which is a model of reflective humanism, actually produced in a country that was—according to our folklore— contemplating enormous acts of cruelty and duplicity.

Not all of those pictures have stood the test of time, but the medium did not bother with that test. And now there might be masterpieces, films to study and write about and to introduce in places of higher learning. Or was that just a sign that the medium was nearing death?

I admitted the snob I was in coming to *The Forsyte Saga,* and that is part of the disdain a movie person felt for television. Even now, while knowing that the *Saga* was a turning point, I can't persuade you or myself that it was very good. But television had escaped the crushing cultural need to be good, let alone great. More fundamentally, television *was.* It persisted, on a screen, before the screen had become part of the wall, but then it was turned on in the way the lights were turned on. No one would have said this even if it had been intuited, but television was so humdrum it didn't matter. That was a new way of understanding our place. And if you are dismayed by this place, just get along with it and do your best.

The cinema's aim and grandeur were over. The halls and corridors of the Granada Tooting (my cherished cinema in childhood) were an attempt to resemble some historical and mythic atmosphere. I looked it up, and I find that the theatre opened in 1931, with Cecil Masey as its architect and the Italian Gothic interiors designed by Theodore Komisarjevsky. It had three thousand seats, but sometimes I felt inclined to explore its galleries and corridors; they were as compelling as anything on the screen. I saw *Samson and Delilah* there and believed that epic could have been filmed in the Granada itself. That theatre (like so many others) was from a gilded album of the Romantic Past, call it Once upon a Time. But the cute thing about television was that it had come down (like a Tardis, or the monolith in *2001*) out of nowhere and taken over our drab domesticity.

There was a first urge in which the audience reckoned to dress up a little for television, especially if they had neighbors over—and for a while some people had a television set while others did not. This was a matter of caution, as well as poverty, as if a few of us did sense the threat that the medium presented: it was rumored that looking at TV was bad for your eyes, that cathode rays might be sinister, and that was a metaphor for some more profound, unidentifiable damage that was occurring. I watched the start of the *Forsyte Saga* with neighbors in west London who were not just better off, but secure in that privilege. So my arrogance was fueled by reckoning that these people had too much Forsyte in them, just as the furnishing of their sitting room aspired to the pompous décor in the show. So I wore a tie and a jacket to watch the show. This was like early BBC newsreaders wearing evening dress on radio.

And whereas for the Forsytes we sat upright in good chairs—to signal attention—the medium has long since yielded to the lush slackness of the couch and the sofa. Viewership is more horizontal now, more slovenly, more inclined to dozing, and given over to coming and going, to taking inattention as a right, and working one's phone. This contempt is awesome, and so deeply instructive as to be terrifying.

Your editor might be reading your book, observing TV, and working his phone—all at once.

The horror.

Look on the bright side—you have an editor.

For a while at least, the television set itself down in regular living spaces with implacable self-importance. It demanded nothing less than centrality and a place where no windowlight marred its screen. Sometimes real light had to be excluded—in the way later on the vistas of desert and mountains would be eliminated on airplanes so that dehydrated movies could be perceived in the air-conditioned gloom. In many situations the set had a neurotic antennae (the most sensitive thing in the house?) that had to be adjusted all the time. People were cursed for walking across the room and sending the lines into nightmare. A strange sense of science fiction hung over the living room.

And still it didn't work. "Remotely" then had basic meanings. "Reception" was as elusive a concept as life after death (and sometimes it looked like the blurred imprint of spiritualism). Still, families persisted with the scattered snowstorm and sudden flapdoodle in the picture. How did this flawed technology carry the day against all its disadvantages? Why were we doing this, instead of listening to the radio, reading, doing embroidery, sticking new stamps in our albums, playing the piano, sitting at a table for canasta, or just engaging in a little ruminative conversation?

So many intrusions or losses gave us reason for hating the television; its vulgar containing box was one of the first proofs of our being humiliated by progress. Yet all too soon the parasite became as essential as the other household services—and as entertaining. We could tell ourselves that TV was just like the movies. But that was a lie, or a feint, the new magic. The medium was better compared to weather, to a state of thought—like being in love with someone (yet at odds with them—as in family), or being prisoner to a vast, indifferent continuum. Like a soul on earth contemplating the theoretical abyss of space, or what TV in its addiction to advertising would call "the final frontier." Like Icarus surveying the sky.

At first the offerings seemed to be particular shows, or programs—like the News, the coronation of the young Elizabeth II, a Cup Final, *Dragnet* or Milton Berle, or some sensation or disaster, as in "We interrupt this program . . ." There was the clue: that a tumult lay behind the schedule of what to see; that numb enormity was the lurking destiny of TV. So who was in charge of that and managing it? And wasn't the medium and its business poised for interruption, like sprinters in the angular hesitation of "Set"?

In the immediate sense, the "they" in charge was the dealer who sold your TV set, around $450 in 1950, or more than $5,000 in today's money. And might drop in to adjust it, or to despair. Beyond those vexed but profiting guys there was the indistinct authority that ran television, and here the choice was very different. In the United States, the new medium came to be organized around competing networks. They would soon line up as CBS, NBC, and ABC, and for several decades they owned this new horizon just as Spain and Portugal had once administered and shared the wealth beyond mere Europe. And these networks sought their working income, and their profitability, from the sponsors or the advertisers who attached themselves to shows.

As if the country could voice no sense of the national impact of a new form of discourse. This was one of the most disastrous decisions (or lack of decision) in the history of our culture, and the ruin goes on, no matter that viewers often think of their TV as being free from ads. There was an alternative. Great Britain recognized that television was so important it deserved state regulation. Thus the BBC (founded originally in 1922) was entrusted with television, and subscribers were asked to pay an annual license fee: in 1946, it was raised to 2 pounds for a household receiving radio and television. (It is 159 pounds now, about $200.) That revenue is expected to pay for the administration of the BBC and the production of programs. In American eyes, this plan can seem paternalistic or vulnerable to undue state intervention. The BBC has not always avoided those dangers. But America should ask whether its own television system could have produced *Monty Python's Flying Circus, Fawlty Towers,* Kenneth Clark's *Civilization, The Forsyte Saga, Our Friends in the North, The Singing Detective,* or even Alastair Cooke's *America.* The idea of a Python sliding across the stately nudes that Clark admired brings us to the brink of surrealism, the madness always latent in TV.

There is no quick answer to that question about intellectual daring in the U.S., but it will run through this book, and until we get there, it is worth asking whether a society needs a BBC to achieve *The Crown*—or is the question better posed the other way round?

But what could the head of the BBC or the leadership at an American network do? We know, more or less, what they did, so it is not hard to assign credit or blame. But go back to fundamentals and think of the opportunity facing you in a switch—on or off—that you can bring to life.

If you command a television outlet—whether it is a small local station in New Hampshire or Netflix—once you've turned the switch on you have to do something, and keep doing it. You can't turn the switch off without letting the viewers think you have ceased to exist. We want electric light—we are in a fury if it cuts—and do not ask what the light illumines. So "content" in TV can be secondary to persistence.

That problem still functions at the highest level, in Manhattan or Los Angeles. And here we begin to get into the nature of content in a serious way (or as *Python* would say, mocking my gravity and the predicament of the BBC—"And now for something completely different"—that vain hope).

Television had staples from the start, like the News: that alters every day, like the weather forecast; but in another way it is the same old items shuffled around with the same tense reporting faces. All you have to do is maintain the coverage and overlook this flagrant handicap: that TV news is held hostage by the need for some gestural footage that can accompany banal spoken paragraphs on what is happening. It turns on the assumption that news happens and cannot be explained—so it will be shown and summed up. Don't forget how far that condition has affected the way we all "understand" our world.

The News was a format that television appreciated: it needed a standing set, the apparatus for running extracts, a few appealing host figures (though stopping short of glamour or charisma), and a loose network of correspondents and stringers. It would take in filmed extracts from the hot spots and tragedies. But the show was a thirty-minute slot, sure and steady, so long as the hot spot kept itself within bounds. The News was a series and quite quickly the audience became team players: they liked Huntley and Brinkley, or Walter Cronkite, or why not a woman of color? Why not? You know why. The News seemed to be a mirror to the wide world, but it was channeled into a settled American scheme of national eminence and virtue. Some nights the news was grim, or some years, but the format was reassuring. One late afternoon in November 1963, Walter Cronkite at his desk turned to the camera to say the president was dead. Many felt he was close to a tear (and that was charisma: it is treasured by those who saw it). And Walter was said to be the most trusted man in the nation, far more so than JFK.

The network newscasts were much alike, and they prospered for decades, with huge audiences tuning in at the cocktail hour. They are still there, with diminished following, while they and the cable networks have understood that the standing set and the abiding attitudes were ready to shade into the haranguing of disputing talking heads. In addition, the flowering of opinion—and the way the regular flowers turned into wild and sometimes toxic blooms—became the new news. It was a way of admitting that no one truly knew what had happened and so the News was a sea of discord and partisanship. It was no more reliable than official intel verdicts on the state of things here or there. In time, the tenor and behavior of politics followed suit until the series called America arrived at a logjam of seething dispute and automatic lies. And so the News—still on the same kind of studio set, with seated talking heads—became a show in which the old scheme of identifiable reality had been abandoned.

The other staple series was the commercials, and here was the first television offering that carried the clear suggestion, "Well, you don't need to watch this." It was a clever trick, to drop the implicit hint that the engine of the medium was best ignored. All that it required for accomplishment was idiots on the couch, and we accepted that casting.

At first, the commercials felt archaic, or defiantly unmovielike. Against every precept of marketing (which was virile and cheeky in so many American marts by then), the commercials were so boring as if to say, "Well, of course, you're doing something else in these interludes." Like combing the cat or caressing your sweetie. But the stilted sales pitches contained a new play upon that old movie trope, desire. For fifty years, motion pictures had put some vivid imagery on screen that asked, "Wouldn't you like to be gunning these hoods down the way Jimmy Cagney does it?" or "Just gaze upon Monument Valley, or the kitchen of Joan Crawford—can't you see yourself in those locations, as states of bliss?" Or take a look at Marilyn Monroe and imagine she is yours—and she seems more than willing. "Are you looking at me, honey? Well, you must be because I'm the only one here."

Those longings and so many more were impossible for the multitudes of us, though one had to admit that some vacant guys had almost incidentally started killing people because they had nothing else to do, and the trigger hand did recall all those gangster spasms. Even in *Bonnie and Clyde,* Warren Beatty slides his six-gun in front of Faye Dunaway's face—if she had been as short-sighted as he was she might have thought it was something else. Plus innocent stooges do drive to Monument Valley; real housewives can renovate their kitchen so it takes on iconic grandeur. And Arthur Miller did marry Marilyn Monroe. For a time.

Still, cinematic desire was intrinsically out of bounds. We only wanted it so much because we couldn't have it. That's what made the movies such a grand romantic medium, and so misleading.

But commercials were the real Black Friday jamboree for desire. You couldn't have James Dean or Natalie Wood, but you could see a new Ford or a smoldering Philip Morris cigarette and say I'll have that. And all you had to do was go out and make the purchase. All of a sudden the screen gave up being romantic and turned transactional. Now you can get the goodies online.

Commercials were on their way to being thirty-second movies, shot with the material sensuality that was going out of fashion in movies, but constructed in the noir detachment that was ready to ask, "If you're watching this shit and calling it oatmeal, just pay attention to the surreal wit, the tacit pornography, and the cynicism we're into." If this was our mass medium then the world was a joke. A foot of film in a commercial cost more and was more artfully labored over than a foot of film in the grandest feature film. And as the '60s slid by, so the audience for television surpassed not just the declining cinema audience but every memory of the three thousand–seat dreamscapes. And the commercials filled up to ten minutes in every hour of our screen time. This was a kindness to programmers because they had less need to think up something—anything—to justify being on, on the air.

What are we going to switch on tonight? We're going to watch the set being on. I know that sounds demeaning, and a disgrace to the notion that we have minds and critical faculties. But think about last night and what you saw, and recollect the times when just to be awake, you picked up the remote, started pressing its button, and became your own editing device. The potential for lassitude and giving up the ghost is beyond counting. It's called *the remote* to indicate convenience, but don't overlook the metaphor that has for you.

9

There Has to Be a Next

Sometimes we sit there in the dark, without faces to see. We let the tremors of one show pass away and wonder whether we are empty enough to try another. Perhaps you do the same at the end of the day.

You know, I like to feel it is very fine to have some urgent story to follow. Something that never occurred before. As if life itself is happening, so fresh and rare. But then after a while I wonder if the freshness is just an affect, the way of doing story.

How could it not be?

A fear sinks in, a depression, as if every lovely moment was thought of and shaped, shot and reshot, so the freshness is just dry twigs of celluloid.

Naturally.

Yet it's not quite natural, is it? Not as daring as it wants to be. There is someone screaming on the street.

If television was prepared to go on forever, how could it handle fiction, the narrative form that was expected to propose a situation and then settle it? So "once upon a time" was heading for "the end." In those two words, we faced a cultural reckoning. It might be tragic or triumphant, moralistic or absurd. Conclusion repaid the commitment in reading, and it reflected an author's fatigued exultation in getting the whole thing over with.

The ways of reaching this terminus cover an enormous range. At the close of Scott Fitzgerald's *Tender Is the Night,* the narrative voice notes ruefully that Dick Diver, the man who might have been so much, has disappeared into the Finger Lakes region of upstate New York—"in any case he is almost certainly in that section of the country, in one town or another." Yet the wistful voice also leaves room for the chance that Dick may be dead, caught up in some personal scandal, or waiting for his last page, doing whatever he can to overlook the doldrums of his life. I put that book down with more regret than I ever mustered for Jay Gatsby.

Or in the case of Tolstoy's *War and Peace,* at page 1,215 in my edition, the author is mulling over issues of human freedom and the comparison of Earth in space with the individual's aspiration to be free, and he comes to rest with,

"In the first case, the need was to renounce the consciousness of a nonexistent immobility in space and recognize a movement we do not feel; in the present case, it is just as necessary to renounce a nonexistent freedom and recognize a dependence we do not feel."

Taken out of context, that may not seem helpful, but coming at the end of maybe two months reading the novel, it had a grandeur and a mystery— didn't it? I mention it now only because "a nonexistent immobility in space" does remind me of television and our haunted couch life with its nagging wonderment.

From the outset, television felt the headlong compulsion of a situation that never ended. Could life go on forever? Think of it on terms with the News without ending or apocalypse, a show that can be slotted in eternally. Almost without rationalizing the process, the medium needed certain elements of story—characters, a situation, suspense—but without the threat of resolution. Like *The Fugitive,* the pilgrim must go forever. You didn't want to risk development because then the show would be over, along with its franchise and its revenue. Put it this way: there was every inner potential in terms of dramatic logic that Lucy or Ricky Ricardo might strangle each other, but Lucille Ball and Desi Arnaz were riding a rocking horse of momentum— if only for the commercial future of the medium.

I Love Lucy had negotiated the fact of Lucille's pregnancy so that Lucy's state of "expecting" was made part of the show. That was sweet, and an obvious ideal. But if the real couple had determined on divorce, which was often under fraught discussion in the same years, so many pressures would have stilled that urge more reliably than any kind of marriage counseling. Though creatively, the show could have done worse than getting the two of them into therapy sessions. That would have been intriguing and comic—not so far ahead it would be a prompt for *The Sopranos*. But in the '50s not enough Americans were impressed by psychotherapy, and no one at CBS or Philip Morris could have countenanced that degree of frailty in this far-fetched yet idealized couple. It was fine for the Ricardos to act crazy once a week, and it indulged what was called Ball's madcap energy, but it was as beyond the bounds for Mr. and Mrs. Arnaz to seem insane as it was to watch them reading the close of *War and Peace* together.

Don't think I don't love *I Love Lucy*. The show is still often very funny; it pushed Lucille Ball into her best creative character, an earnest woman under so many pressures she was losing her mind. In addition, it was a show that did so much to shape early television, not least the principle of collaboration. In fact, *Lucy* grew out of a radio show, *My Favorite Husband,* which was a measure of how far Ball's downhill status seemed settled. She was close to forty and she had been making movies for more than a decade without establishing herself as a star. So she thought to try television, and in that she was assisted by Desi, who was a shrewd businessman and alert to his wife's screwball potential, no matter that he could not stop having affairs with other women. They took the idea of a married couple comedy to CBS and they were encouraged by producer Jess Oppenheimer, and by the writers he drew into the plan, Madelyn Pugh Davis and Bob Carroll Jr.

But CBS did not think Lucy and Desi would seem married on the air—there was racism in this unease—and it was the couple's decision to do a pilot and pay for it themselves that carried the day.

The show made its debut in October 1951 (a week after Stalin said the Soviet Union had the atom bomb). Philip Morris had agreed to be its sponsor and at the outset there was a comic skit where animated figures of Lucy and Desi climbed down a packet of cigarettes as if that were their house.

It was shot live for the most part at CBS in Los Angeles, and a weekly episode ran for about twenty-three minutes. It had directors: William Asher handled 101 of the 180 episodes; veteran cameraman Karl Freund (he had photographed F. W. Murnau's *The Last Laugh* and Fritz Lang's *Metropolis*—shadowy masterworks) shot 149 episodes in advertising's bright light, using a three-camera system that Desi had suggested and which became a standard in studio television.

Can we reconcile the versatility of Freund, photographing the interaction of the good girl, Maria, and the malevolent robot woman in *Metropolis* (both played by Brigitte Helm), with the singularity of Lucy trying to hold down the obligations of an American housewife amid the derangement of her schemes and crises? Week after week, we waited for Lucy to have a breakdown. Ball was businesslike and far more reliable than Desi. But she regularly cracked up in the show and lived under the umbrella of that curious title in which long-suffering Ricky loved his mad woman anyway.

Some talented student should cut together scenes from *Metropolis* with segments of *I Love Lucy*. It could illuminate the sitcom and leave us trembling. A frenzy was there already in the way Lucille Ball played the part and soldiered on after Desi had fallen by the wayside. Long before we had the technology, the surreal interaction of images from decades apart was in the air. Perhaps there was no surer destination for the happy-go-lucky sitcom than the intimations of horror in *Metropolis* with the sweetheart turning into a witch. How many of our women today know that arc and feel themselves flying on wings of desperation—like Icarus's sister?

Do you think of me that way?

You do scream at machinery.

Better that than attack you. I am a Lucy, there's no helping that.

If you think this is a stretch, or out of bounds, just ask how far the strain and madness in Laura Linney's Wendy Byrde fits with those long-suffering, good women the actress has played. Television now can give us everything: I could cut from Linney in *Ozark* to Linney in *The Truman Show* or *John Adams* or even *Mystic River*. Not always so nice, but steadfast, loyal to being what a woman should be.

I am exploring instability, but those significant co-contributors on *I Love Lucy* were simply serving the radiant pathology of the two stars, and their supporting players, Vivian Vance and William Frawley. This happened at 9 p.m. on Monday. That it was shot on 35mm film (at Desi's instigation) ensured the show's long life in syndication, and thereby ordained the infant stage in the life of television shows. Here was another iteration of Hollywood's wish to be a factory, turning out the same product week after week. This seemed fixed and consistent, but so much TV was rooted in the ferment of going crazy. It was just that Laura Linney had to wait for *Ozark* for that clarification.

I Love Lucy was a situation comedy locked in place. The husband was a successful bandleader, exuberant and volatile, but deeply in love with the wife who was always getting into scrapes and schemes trying to find her way into show business. That could drive him crazy, but he usually tidied things up. This permanent crisis was graced by very tight scripts, the absorption of guest stars, a sure way of working on the studio set, with a live audience, and with the liberated mayhem in Lucille Ball. It was not that she was "like" many American housewives, but her endless predicaments reminded enough women of their own helter-skelter existence while the structure of the stories reassured men that they knew best and could sort it all out. Real women were going mad and Lucy told them it was understandable.

It's not just that the show deserved to be a hit (playing in sixteen million homes in the '50s). To this day it can be watched without tedium or superiority. Somehow a woman who had largely missed the point in color on screen became a household favorite in black-and-white on the small screen. Lucy didn't try to seem beautiful, and television has been scared of that loftiness.

By the fall of 1951, *I Love Lucy* rated number three in television viewing; it was as reliable as Stan Musial. Thereafter it was number one or two up until 1957. It won every award available; it made a fortune for CBS and presumably for Philip Morris. It also made the Arnazes rich: at the outset they had formed Desilu as their production company and then they bought the old movie premises of RKO as a site for producing big situation shows for the next couple of decades. Ball bought Desi out of Desilu, and then in 1968 she sold her holding to Gulf & Western for $17 million (about $140 million in today's money).

The famous couple were always breaking up, and they would be divorced by 1960. But their business fortune and its influence were secure. Ball went on with successful shows that were less original and which could not hide her age. Of course, you know this work, even if you are the age of one of Lucille's grandchildren. That is because the show is always playing and earning somewhere. More than that, you feel its imprint in so many other shows from the golden age of television and in the canned laughter that echoes down the decades. *I Love Lucy* represents the age in which the business and talented and likable people found the narrative setup of this medium that was based on a situation that would never end. This was an arrangement of intense energy—true heights in the history of physical comedy—rooted in an exaggerated but recognizable take on married life in which the woman went wild and the man stayed reasonable. Why could that not go on forever? It was the rhythm and the destiny that television always aspired to— hectic, yet stable. It depended on the drive and timing of Lucille Ball to prevent you from realizing with every episode that you had seen all this before, for years.

Thirty years after its glory, every top TV show leaves something for us to be ashamed over. The screaming has stopped. You have to wonder what happened.

It reminds me of *Succession*. That segue may seem perverse; the tones of *I Love Lucy* and *Succession* seem so far apart that it is reckless to put them in the same sentence or value system. But in the culture of the remote the two shows—and a million others—are side by side, available. So our scheme of segue has been altered by the endless motility of the remote button and the torrent of material that is available every night. It is in the nature of the stream that the notion of rational segues, or making sense, has been washed away. We are all citizens of the cut now. You know that an erroneous buttoning can carry you from the interminable recipes for insurance to predictions of how the mud, tank oil, and ice of Ukraine will soon be given the sauce of blood and lies. Television is the first medium that has had no option in its technology but to admit our chaos. And very likely it will be the last. It's easy to argue that *Succession* is more "sophisticated" than *I Love Lucy,* but only if you are ready to recognize sophistication as a shroud.

So think of *Succession* as some kind of sit—a show, that is, determined by a situation. If it helps, let me push that label a little further. It can't be exactly a sitcom (though for me the chief appeal of *Succession* is in its dark humor). Could it be a sit-gruesome? No, that's awkward. Sitnoir? Dangerously obscure or academic. Sitshit? Blunt but to the point. Let's keep working on the possibilities. But meanwhile let's stress the elements of the sit.

Succession had had three seasons then (a fourth was promised). That made twenty-nine episodes, each one coming in at an hour. So it is a saga, if you like—The Roy Saga—in which the surface seethes with activity, yet nothing really alters. At the beginning, in 2018 on HBO, the entourage of family and associates was poised to see what would happen to the aging billionaire Logan Roy, a master of so many enterprises. Would he pass on his shares and tyranny to others? Would he die or provoke assassination by some of his offspring? Or would his misanthropy turn on all those would-be heirs, and slaughter them? Would the story of *Succession* end in his funeral, or in his ascension to some hellish heaven as an ultimate power? Had he been not just Dad but God all along?

The Scottish tycoon was the age of his actor (Brian Cox, then seventy-two), but despite attacks and health alarms, he had the virulent energy of

Cox the actor—it cannot have deserted Cox's busy mind that he had been the first screened Hannibal Lecter (in *Manhunter,* 1986), vexed to see that monster falling into other hands five years later. That says nothing against Anthony Hopkins—the two actors may be friends—but what keeps Roy alive and odious are his need for vengeance and his certainty that no one else in his group is worthy of his position. In the sit of *I Love Lucy,* the suspicion was how close Lucy was to being crazy, but in *Succession* we accept that Logan Roy is the epitome of demented, sardonic hostility. His heirs are not in his pathological class. He is such a master that his madness does not matter. It is his show, so all the others scramble around him, like the insects his Lear has stirred up. How strange it was to hear Cox say that Roy loved his kids.

Except that Lear does advance in his play: one daughter resists the story her tyrant father wants to tell; others succeed in dethroning him; he is cast out onto the heath and to madness; and ultimate tragedy awaits him. No such destiny is possible in *Succession;* the warped sanity of its sit must go on forever. No doubt, the creators of the show—notably Jesse Armstrong—have contemplated such things as a near-fatal stroke for Logan Roy, some kind of dementia, or even termination. At the close of season 4 this may be the way the series exits: "How to Murder Logan" could be a season. But not until then. And even then? . . . I nurse the thought that on some exotic Cayman heath the show can close on Logan in an ultimate explosion of egomania. Only power can end power. Thus he obliterates himself and all of us, knowing that he can never be succeeded, and giving an impious Scottish finger to us, the audience that worshiped *Succession* so slavishly.

The proof of this is in the texture of the show's unfolding week after week. We follow shifting groupings of the would-be successors—Kendall, Shiv, Connor, Roman, Tom, and Greg—in colloquies of conspiracy and betrayal. Sly while eager, lying but ingratiating, devoid of shame, the aspirants are ruined morally because their souls are toxic from breathing power and desire. And in all these maneuvers, they are held together by their phones, the earpieces by which they are attached to the story and the tidal rhythm of betrayal. HBO doesn't do commercials, but like other shows *Succession* is a constant annunciation for the iPhone. What the people say matters less than the vulnerable intimacy of being in touch. You can turn off the sound and simply watch these unreliable molecules in their patterns of intercourse. (There is no need for actual sex in the show—as in so much TV that has been surpassed or eclipsed by sheer power urges.) After a season, you could even karaoke what they are saying, because we have become collaborators in their corruption.

I am not disparaging the actors running their routines—Jeremy Strong, Sarah Snook, Alan Ruck, Kieran Culkin, Matthew Macfadyen, Nicholas Braun. It is a very professional show, but most actors will admit that it is easier having to be wicked and treacherous than it is attempting a banal and inept level of decency. So these actors can stay within their attitudinizing. Cox's creative soul is by now as curled as his disdainful lips or his suspicious gaze. He was a fine actor, but after Roy I doubt he could play Lear because the audience would insist he was doing Logan. He is his own commercial now— his simpering voice-over became part of a series of ads for McDonald's during the third season of *Succession,* enough to make common burgers seem fit for gourmets or cannibals. The *Succession* storyline may go in and out. The insults vary a little over the years. But the vicious game does not alter. Its wounds are the same, cruel and humiliating, but the damage is theoretical, for these characters have no blood or life to lose.

This is the overheated yet undercooked monotony of *Succession.* If I were talking about Lear, that condition would mean ruin. If Lear were perpetually on the heath, with eyes being gouged, insanity rising, and catastrophes following on like summer after spring, then the play *King Lear* would be dead in our history. It survives, and moves us, because Shakespeare had determined on a narrative arc to satisfy the energies the story has aroused. There are so many characters in the play that we care about and want to see through to the end. But in *Succession* we know the stooges are hollow pawns—or actors—in Roy's board game.

Why are we watching? Because we envy while hating the lifestyle of the rich and famous? The show lets us fantasize over luxury life, the décor of mansions and astonishing hotels, the Murdoch of wealth. Yet it encourages us to despise the state of irresponsible wealth and the way it destroys character. *Succession* is about high power but it says next to nothing about what power can do to society. The Roys do not grow because they are fixed on money. So their petty greed is isolated from the state of greed at large. We have our cake while eating it—that is a mainstay of television. And it repeats the shocking but lulling contrast between the world and the playground in the commercials and the humble nature of our living room.

Don't simply conclude that that split response is a mark of our dishonesty. In watching Lear, we dream we might be kings no matter that we may end up homeless and deranged. Fiction as a whole says, imagine yourself here or there. There's no cause to feel that voyaging is reckless. It is in the nature of story. Still, the becalming danger in this neurotic helplessness is to say, quietly, that money and power are our irreversible gods. There is no one in *Succession* to like, because the monster himself has poisoned affection. Yet there was a cockeyed nobility in *I Love Lucy* and its four central characters being foolish but likable. Just as that sitcom urged us to embrace the mistake-riddled Ricardos, so it offered a view of marriage and friendship that was worthy or becoming, if at the level of, as Shakespeare put it in Puck's mouth, "Lord, what fools these mortals be!" The Logans are crazed about being smart, while the Ricardos treasure their foolish ways. But that ordinariness went out of fashion.

Whereas, if the finale of *Succession* becomes a riot of murder, in which Logan, with bare hands and naked malice, disposes of his children, their spouses, and all the assistants, we would walk tall in amusement and awe. That cynicism is our new air. In the seven decades between the two shows, our hope has gone from silly summer to macabre winter. In the heyday of *I Love Lucy,* it would have been unthinkable that any audience could have been hooked on such gloating iniquity. It's in being so well done that *Succession* is such a killer of time, or a way of saying time has collapsed on us.

It did end?

I'm sure it did.

You saw it? Are you sure of that?

Didn't he die, the old man? Didn't the show go off in all directions?

Some series turn deranged as they end. Like feeling death coming on.

So they try out every story angle they never got around to. Wasn't there an election in the last Succession*? I seem to remember that.*

I think they meant to have it roll over into our ordinary chaos.

They? You mean the Roys, or their ghosts in reality?

There was no longer any telling one from the other.

There you are: out of office, out of funds or defense, that monster had taken over our storytelling. Wasn't that when he did that terrible town hall in New Hampshire?

CNN let him in.

It's always us letting the demon in.

10

Patriot

Step aside from a celebrated hit show. I am going to write about *Patriot* because I seldom find anyone who has heard of it, let alone seen it. But it's interesting, and we agree that among thousands of shows we are bound to miss many that are worthwhile. In the same way, you are not going to say "Hi" to everyone on the street, or hear their confession.

Having streets is quite crucial, don't you think?

It's a way of reminding ourselves that in a big scene with Gatsby, Daisy, and Tom (that desolate trio) there could be a couple of others off in a corner talking quietly. They do not seem impressive or impressed. They do not push themselves forward with "What About Us?" Indeed, they are less onlookers than mere bystanders or extras in a documentary, people off the street. They have no idea that there is a cloud hovering nearby, *The Great Gatsby*.

If you go looking for *Patriot* you will find it—on Amazon Prime. Doesn't that sound likely? You may be engaged in an odd way. But you may also wonder if I've made it up, or tossed the project aside long before a pilot, because it just didn't seem to work. Still, beyond story and the stories we love there is so much unresolved stuff in life. The current we work with.

Most of *Succession* is lip-smackingly to the point. It's like a spell cast by a dangerous Merlin. That is a mark of Brian Cox's timing, but it's the stamp of the medium, too, a kind of television that has been planned and aimed to the last frame. The slamming shot that puts the eight ball in the top pocket.

The mechanics of the plotline are like clicking intrigue in Logan Roy's chess-playing head.

There could be a Beth he has to play against, and she humbles him.

They should hire us as writers.

We don't see into Roy's business operations in searching ways—he does power as his product—but the articulation of the plots is a testament to a kind of show that never loses its grip—because then we might turn off. We have to keep watching since Roy has his merciless eye on us. He can't die because television is reluctant to stop.

Even in television shows that aren't going anywhere more definite than *I Love Lucy* or *Succession,* the overhang of control can be very pleasing. We love the Ricardos in a pretty shambles; we wait to see the devious Roy relatives whipped and shamed. That expectation keeps us watching. But tight control can become claustrophobic. So there's all the more interest in anything prepared to experiment with being out of control. Yet how can the scheme of television exist in that wayward place?

The medium bristles with executed planning. The show may seem spontaneous and lifelike, but it is a grind, a mechanical iteration that does not vary. *Succession* is the same in London and Los Angeles, and all the customer needs to understand is how to summon it on his remote system. Like water in our pipes, the show is there waiting to be turned on. It is like all movies: it was done long before we thought to sit down and watch. Now and forever, it will always be its designed self. We trust this consistency, but we are slaves to it and its indifference over how commercial power functions.

Beyond that mechanical persistence, television is an extensive business. We may have had to subscribe and then agree to $4.99 for a running of the show. In our living room, we understand by now that this commerce has overwhelmed the business of movies in theatres. And somewhere someone is making a lot of money from what we choose to see. The vagaries of *Patriot* are part of the immense business plan of Amazon, a corporation even mightier than Waystar RoyCo, a global media enterprise.

We also appreciate that smart creative minds have conspired to make *Succession,* for whatever it is. Do not take that process for granted—or forget how much we contribute to it. While we came to believe that films were made or auteured by directors (a claim that begs many questions), we have picked up the model of a TV series having a showrunner, the origin of the idea, and then the all-encompassing manager who hires writers, directors, producers, crew people, and actors to execute the plan.

But never leave out the business structuring in the creative attempt. I mean the organizing of commercial resources, and the researched estimate of what we want, or will accept. These shows cannot function without a consideration of our desires. You don't have to examine the process for long without appreciating that this is like the analysis, or the diagnosis, of ourselves that goes into the advertising, or the selling of itself to us. It's not necessarily the case that this analysis is accurate or wise. But "they" are trying to manipulate us in the dark for their profit. That is what titans like Logan Roy have managed, and that is why it is bizarre yet understandable that Roy's profound business strategies are omitted from the gloating of his chess mastery.

One can assess this assembly of a series as creativity, but it is management logistics, too, timing a show to the second and ensuring that the action goes forward without lulls, small talk, or the risk of inattention. The point is forever being pressed into our consciousness. There is never going to be a moment in *Succession* in which Roy's business pauses and the camera moves aside to show us that nothing much is happening in the garden beyond the human figures—except for the fertile persistence of the plant life. If the tracking camera moved in close we might see the tireless life of bees and hummingbirds. It might begin to feel like being in a garden. But *Succession* knows not to go there. There is no there there, even if it might be possible to think that Roman Roy, say, is captivated by the scent of roses. To such an extent that he sometimes wonders about escaping the Roy menagerie to be a gardener.

As if Jay Gatsby is really a gardener.

Which leads to the offhand marvel of *Patriot,* a show that steadily asks us to wonder why we are still watching, and how this ever got on television. Does it quite exist? Have we all made it up? I have seldom watched it without dropping off. All of which raises the question of how television and sleep are related.

Patriot ran for two seasons, and eighteen episodes in 2015–18. It was conceived by Steven Conrad, who wrote and directed the majority of the show. Inasmuch as he seems to be "the artist" on view, I could say that he is fifty-five now, born in Fort Lauderdale, with a number of movie credits: he wrote *Wrestling Ernest Hemingway;* he has directed *Lawrence Melm* and *The Promotion;* and he came on board after several other writers to script *The Secret Life of Walter Mitty* (starring and directed by Ben Stiller) and *Unfinished Business.* This is not a career that has taken hold, or picked up evident character, and with the best will in the world I see little connection between Conrad's prior credits and *Patriot.*

Yet how can I describe *Patriot* without lapsing into the mindset that it is purposeful, and even successful? John Tavner is an agent of American Intelligence, part of an absentminded project to stop Iran from getting nuclear weapons. In much of that he operates under the casual guidance of his father, who seems high up in Intelligence, without being in possession of that faculty itself. John has a license to kill in his work, and he bears himself with a sleepy implacability. For reasons beyond understanding, his cover is working for a piping company in Milwaukee. He has a wife and a mother, too. As in no other film I could think of, the action goes often to Luxembourg— though the film annoyed that grand duchy by shooting in Prague. It's not that Luxembourg is used or relevant. Rather it is a kind of vacancy, a place where one can wait for Godot.

Then in the same span of time, as if in retaliation, the series *Capitani* (2019) was both set in Luxembourg and filmed there. I felt the storyline of *Capitani* was labored, and much of the acting lugubrious. But I was pleased by the rural charm of what was Luxembourg: its woodlands were more interesting than the murder that occurred there. It felt like stuff *Patriot* might have shot, but forgot.

The way I have described *Patriot* suggests an offbeat espionage and adventure story, but it shows little interest in that, just as it feels no worry over Iran getting its Bomb. From the outset it was signaled as black comedy, but it is more usefully presented as a surreal travesty of plot outlines. Of course, the tradition of surreal travesty in TV series we can binge on is limited. Even as I try to write about it in a way that might persuade you to enlist, I find it hard to believe the official report that *Patriot* was generally well reviewed or that it found a substantial audience. I point these things out because the virtue and charm of *Patriot* lie in feeling lost or inadvertent. It is not like a TV show.

There is no tension in the James Bondish outline of the story. There is nothing adventurous about John Tavner. Discussing an actor's appearance is a delicate matter, but I think Michael Dorman had been cast as John or directed to be more dogged than decisive. He has a downcast air. So often he gazes into the camera, glum and detached, like a man contemplating a meal he has no urge to eat. He is on screen a lot of the time without ever achieving old-fashioned movie presence. It is not that he believes in the Iran business, or seems to care much for his wife, or his parents. We like to think of our 007s brimming with purpose and skill, but Tavner is remote even in big close-up; he seems assigned to his role, without consent or enthusiasm. Much of the time he grunts or sighs "Cool" to what is happening, but he doesn't seem affected by the world around him, and he is painfully uncool.

You might decide this show is comical or satirical, but that is not a satisfactory explanation. There are passages where the humor sinks in, and blooms, but not much more quickly than a bud coming into flower, and without any display of being the prime purpose of the show. In the same way, the title seems beside the point: Tavner plods around in his job, but nothing justifies (or mocks) the high concept of him as a patriot. Sometimes he feels like a vagrant who has blundered into a show that has been discontinued, yet somehow its pulse flickers on.

The texture of the show is patiently unimpressive. As well as faces gazing head-on into the camera, but without much expression in delivery, there are moments in which inert action holds and lingers on screen, often at an unusual distance, and without an attempt to shape or focus its mise-en-scène. There is a handsome police inspector (Aliette Opheim), but she maintains as impassive an image as possible. Kurtwood Smith delivers the most clear-cut "supporting" performance, the funniest in *Patriot,* as one of Tavner's bosses, but he feels out of place just because of his genre precision. Late on in the series, we meet Tavner's mother, and it is pleasant to recognize Debra Winger in the part, an actress we have liked but who has not worked enough. She looks very good when she appears (aged sixty-two), but she has so little to do, despite being allegedly the U.S. Secretary of Transportation. She doesn't get to be Debra Wingerish. Equally, John's father (played by Terry O'Quinn) is a bogus authority figure, forthright but unreliable. He often stares lengthily into the camera, as if pondering something significant to say, before giving up the effort. There's no attempt to use these parents to mount a psychological portrait of Tavner. He is not the lead character in a compelling drama; he is not sympathetic or possessed by ideas. His patriotism is never stressed. Instead, he feels like an actor who arrived late for the audition and missed his own backstory.

The plot never thinks to be followed or believed, yet some set pieces take a lot of time. The imagery is sometimes carefully composed, with unusual stress on full figures. I don't think it is well directed, but it is shot through with an unsettling surrealism, so absorbed in calm absurdity without obvious opportunities for laughter that the idea of a large audience is hard to swallow.

One favored vein of critical writing about screen work could try to say that Steven Carver must be a neglected auteur, an errant genius even. But I'm not sure *Patriot* has such ambitions in mind. I can't exclude the possibility that it is intended as a desultory mess, something that has somehow happened. It could be a show done by Melville's Bartleby, someone who would prefer not to do it. The show becomes intriguing in its indifference and its accidental quality. These things are oddly aligned with our stale couch and its drab room.

At the end of the second season, John Tavner is in the middle of the English Channel, swimming his best, while dragging a large bag full of money. This is like a Beckett tableau, a metaphor for futility. It is shown at some length—or more than seems appropriate—yet without giving his swim any air of heroism. It may be that Carver was unsure whether this was the proper, dramatic end of *Patriot,* or was there a chance of one more season getting the green light? We should keep such indecision in mind with these shows, and wonder whether there could be (or could have been) lots more story to come. But that would be easier to accept in *Patriot* if there had been more narrative beforehand. This pondering may not sound tempting, but a provocative goal has been reached—I think—which is to leave us uncertain why we are watching.

That is hardly businesslike in a mass medium. But don't rule out the prospect of a medium that will ask that question, while providing just enough to get into half-hearted temptation. Whenever you're on hold on the phone, the music to listen to is antimusic. You wonder if you are there. So I came to believe that in sometimes falling asleep as it drifted by I was getting with the spirit of *Patriot* and beginning to ask myself questions about lying on the couch, wondering whether I was ill. Or gone.

11

A Winged Couch

When our participation in television is so domestic it's worth asking how far the shows offer a taste of "home." I am writing after an evening in which on MSNBC we had the first glimpses of homes in Kyiv being fired upon and burning, with Ukrainians taking to the street. This was fragmentary stuff but it was riveting and frightening, and it made the security on our sofa seem more tender or threatened. We live in what realtors describe as a nice or desirable part of San Francisco (though not the most precious heights). But for a year we have seen from our windows a red tent where someone lives on the corner. I am just trying to underline how far "home" is a motif in the television experience fit for infinite variety. Home can be the standing set where Archie Bunker had his chair in *All in the Family* or it can be that rented lakeside house in *Ozark* where Marty Byrde will one day stuff the walls with unlaundered cash. That gets you thinking about money as insulation.

This reminds me how in *Patriot* the characters do not seem to have a home. My impression of John Tavner is of a vagrant, going to strange places but having no base. That is how he wears the same nondescript clothes and seems unattached to any domestic order. This bears on what we feel about his uncertainty, somewhere between numbness and being lost. Domesticity seems alien to Tavner, and so the sense of a mysterious quest is central to his being—so long as we can live without the promise of the quest ever arriving at any destiny or comfort. Intermittently, specific décor comes and goes, but it provides no emotional substance or handholds for the characters. No stress is put on this, but the sense of being lost draws Tavner and the others closer to a condition that overlaps with the threshold aura of a séance or a supernaturalism.

In a similar way, in *Succession,* the Roys exist in many luxury mansions and hotels without needing access to closet space or reassuring holes where they keep their "things." They are so mindlessly affluent, in a kind of penthouse Vegas, that they pick up new clothes, fine tableware, and electronic toys for every episode. Owning the world, they do not bother with favored possessions. Let alone bump around together on the kind of durable standing sets that are familiar from *I Love Lucy* and so many other shows. The love in *I Love Lucy* has a lot to do with the familiarity of certain spaces and pieces of furniture. You can say the same of the coffee shop in *Friends* or Walter White's home in *Breaking Bad.* We come to know these rooms nearly as well as we inhabit our own, moving in the dark, knowing where the door handle will be.

In British television, there has been a tradition of superior or enviable décor—above the regular standards of furniture stores, but within reach as antiques or prized pieces—that runs from *The Forsyte Saga* to *Downton Abbey.* Some of the people in those series may have behaved badly, but they respected the décor and the BBC's warehouse of props. Pleasing interior design has been a testament to conservative values and a way of behaving that is still esteemed in Britain. After all, if you can dress correctly and with elegance, and if you know which fork to use in cannibal courses, then you may be on small-talk terms with your spouses or your children. Or you are allowed to lacerate people if you speak with the tart propriety of Maggie Smith's Dowager Countess of Grantham.

For that strand of British society nostalgic over the past, there is a habit of going to quality stores for old furniture (I remember Phelps in Twickenham in west London—it closed in 2004 after 133 years in business) to purchase a good nineteenth-century chair, a painting that is somewhere between old master and upstart pretender, and a set of Spode dinner plates. Such television shows cherished that past and quietly advertised its purchasability.

Antiques Road Show (1979) was the crown of that attitude. To watch the shows was to partake in a reverence for domestic order (and political reaction) that has to be guarded against the nearness of a kind of wasteland, evident in Beckett, or in *Patriot,* or in the scattering and confusion of home and home-land that is pressing in on us every night on TV.

For instance, last night, as well as watching scenes from Kyiv, Lucy and I saw Stanley Nelson's documentary *Attica* on Showtime. To appreciate the macabre place of home in that grim prison was shocking. Then we witnessed how the authorities preserved such stupid order that the prison system re-created a landscape of slavery. To behold authentic footage of naked Black men beaten and humiliated in the vengeful white dread of anarchy was to understand the stricken meaning of home in the code of white property.

This is how I have always seen this book organized: around the idea of the couch and the room for which it and the television set are the nuclei. Yes, the couch is winged in that it is a means of infinite imagined transpor-tation. But it is also as fixed and limited as a prison cell or that table at the doctor's office where you are asked to hop up and place yourself on the white paper roll so that Doc can make a first estimate of your condition.

I keep stressing the power (or the stealthy loss of power) in being supine with the television. I can believe that many of you, some of the time, elect to watch TV from an upright chair—repeating your stance at a theatre, in a classroom, or at a political meeting, where the rows of chairs are a diagram of community. But the significance of the sofa and the couch is in the way a chair becomes a bed, permitting more sprawl and abandon, and a degree of unguarded commitment to the séance. You may have had a checkup lately on that doctor's bed; you may be close to one hundred percent. But as you watch Ukraine, *Attica,* or *Ozark,* your sinking state appropriates a passivity or invalidism that alters you. If I were to propose that the mind functions differently when the human figure is vertical or horizontal, I would have little evidence to support the theory. But try dismissing it from your mind and recollect the wondrous muddled states you know from waking up, and asking yourself whether you are all right. It is critical folklore—it has been for decades—to say that watching movies resembles dreaming. In which case, keep room in your mind for the possibility that getting close to sleep is a portal to the surrealism that television quietly activates.

Being at home with our set amounts to a kind of sit, and it can feel as easygoing as radio—or the electric light itself—mass media that did not require us to leave home. So we seem to be in our element, or at ease. But examine that notion carefully. The intellectual transportation in television can be compromising. In just one night, Lucy and I watched an hour or so of footage (some of it live) from Ukraine as well as watching Stanley Nelson's careful assemblage of old footage from the Attica incident.

Looking at Ukraine made us angry and scared, to think that a self-serving tyrant should use this moment not just to kill Ukrainians, and to deflect Russia's own attention from its parlous state, but to add further dismay to a world already crouched against a pandemic, the ravages of racism, the extent of poverty, and the unlimited threats embodied in global warming.

We are exhausted by the ordeal of the past few lockdown years. We wonder whether isolation has made us crazy. Talk about a horizontal audience, or one ready for what used to be called a little entertainment. That can still work. Only a few nights ago, when Ukraine was the warning word, Lucy and I escaped into a movie, *The Kindness of Strangers,* a finite story, written and directed by Lone Scherfig, with Zoe Kazan, Andrea Riseborough, and Bill Nighy, and we thought it was a delight. We felt at home with its humane attitudes, its Dickensian view of a world of wealth and its opposite, and the uncanny playing of those three actors and the film's larger cast. Moreover, it is a movie about a mother (Kazan) and her two small children who are at a point of being homeless.

In San Francisco, we say there are more than twenty thousand people who are homeless, and many of them are camped on the streets, to the distress of the city and its government. That includes the person in the red tent at the corner of our street. We have helped that person (a little, a very little) and we sometimes grow indignant over something needing to be done about it. But our mayor is trying and it's not as if San Francisco is less than conscious of being liberal or progressive, as well as having plenty of powerful residents who would not let such campsites stay on their streets. And who have enough discreet access to the police force to ensure timely removal while they are gazing at their TVs and deploring the onset of homelessness in the cities of Ukraine.

What has this got to do with the winged couch and the kingdom of television? Well, it gets at context, that weather system scarcely controllable in a medium of so many channels and platforms. In a city where the benefits of home (its intimacy) cannot be kept apart from the condition of homelessness and our high-minded indifference. The red tent does not have a television. I doubt its occupant has an iPhone or a power source for keeping it supplied. In short, the being out of contact in our city and its society is not out of sight or beyond belief. Call it dread, as we watch the ragged caterpillar of refugees lining up in Ukraine.

Some of these thoughts came into focus in thinking about Attica. Lucy and I were in horror at what had happened in that New York prison in the fetid summer of 1971. Long ago? We had never seen the ghastly footage, or understood that the deaths incurred in the relief of the Attica strike were all brought about by National Guard officers deployed to solve the vexed situation. Initially, the official storyline had said that some prisoners cut the throats of the hostages to draw attention to the wretched conditions in the prison. Not so. All the deaths came from ill-considered shooting by the National Guard.

This had started as a protest strike at Attica that involved the taking of some hostages—and an interruption in the institution's regular service, or call it the iniquity that we were comfortable not noticing. But these hostages (prisoners within the prison) were not mistreated. And the speeches by the insurrectionists asked for reasonable improvements in the conditions at the prison. For a few days these talks (often live on TV) had seemed promising. Some visitors—like lawyer William Kunstler and State Senator John Dunne—had been making a case for reform. But then the powers that be felt insurrection was threatening their dignity. Governor Nelson Rockefeller lost patience. He had based his identity on being brisk and competent. There are times when authority is desperate for action now. The "anarchy" had to end. The damned live coverage of these eloquent prisoners had to cease. The National Guard was sent in, though neither Rockefeller nor Nixon had even visited the prison, let alone spent a night in a cell.

The mutiny was shut down. Prisoners were compelled to crawl through the mud. They had to run a gauntlet of beating. They were made to stand naked. They were fundamentally abused, as if the affronted system needed to say, "Look, we can do this! Don't forget." It seems like a chapter in an old history, like the ships landing in Virginia with their cargo of slaves.

It is evident in *Attica* that a majority of the inmates were Black, and the record indicates that more than a thousand of the two thousand inmates were involved in the "fight" or the strike or the protest. The attempt or the outrage was that prison life be put on television. At the time, that population was twice the number Attica had been designed for and prisoners might spend up to sixteen hours a day in their cells, with inadequate medical facilities and restricted rights of visitation. Attica is near Lake Ontario and Lake Erie, between Buffalo and Rochester, 267 miles from New York City or nearly eight hours by bus. But it had been *here,* now, on television.

More than fifty years later, the footage seems historic, or a crisis in our progress. But there is still a prison in Attica, the same one as before. It can hold up to two thousand inmates and they are said to include some of the most dangerous criminals. These days, that danger is reckoned to be so pressing that there is no longer daily TV transmission from Attica, just as there is no live stream of homeless campsites in all the rooms in our city's grand yet insecure hotels. But we could still study Stanley Nelson's *Attica,* while going back and forth to take in the hazardous coverage from Kyiv and other cities in Ukraine. (When I say hazardous I am referring not just to the intrepid citizens and camera crews, but to the undermining of our safe calm at home.)

And while seemingly alert we are so unable to do anything about it that might be useful that we cannot dismiss the possibility that we are dead already on the couch, no matter that it comes with brave wings and a scheme for flight. It is tempting to think that being watchful is a measure of responsibility. But experience indicates that some of us will watch anything in the nightly indolence of "What can we do?" Television breathes helplessness, like an infection that slips past any mask.

12

At Random

I am trying to contain the profusion of television. It is a system in which all weathers are happening at the same time—and maybe one day soon turbulent weather will be like this, with fire becoming icicles, and floodwater rising as steam.

I was raised as a movie critic or historian. In that work, somebody said, Very well, here is the film for you—it might be *All Is Lost* or *Céline and Julie Go Boating.* Sit yourself down, the system said, watch the picture, and then write 1,500 words on why a stranger should or should not see it.

What? You want to see the film twice because there are things in it that need time to settle in? Well, that does not fit the tradition of press screenings. Never mind, we'll manage it, but that leaves you less time to write about it.

What? Now you want 2,000 words because both films are about being on the water, and that's too significant to omit?

I sit down with the movie in a lifelike model of concentration. For two or three hours it's me and the picture. I may take notes; I may begin to sketch out an opening paragraph. But I am attending, very hard, in a demanding and focused process. *I can't miss a thing.*

I liked that way of working, and took pride in making up my mind fast and doing the set words inside the deadline. That is only professional expertise, but it does ignore the chance that proper criticism or "understanding" needs much more time and thought. Or so much time, forget about it?

In that respect, watching television—even in the semblance of a kind of criticism—is much more complicated. Perhaps I felt early on in *Ozark* that the show was for me, or for my urge to use television to write about America. But that wishing spilled over so many nights and weeks, and in the bingeing I realized that I could pause, go back and watch an episode or just a few minutes again, and again. It was there for me, which seemed very satisfying. As if I was close to making it myself. And the domesticity of TV watching brought other things. Between episodes. Lucy and I might get into a conversation on something entirely different or "unconnected"—only to find that the very next episode of *Ozark* seemed uncannily aware of what we had been talking about. It didn't have to fit, tongue and groove, but the coincidence made mischief out of concentration. This could be funnier than the show, maybe, yet it was also a path in the woods that could lead into a larger sense of life.

Lucy and I had been to the movies together for decades. We sat there in rapt silence and attention, as if looking at an infant starting to walk, the precious thing. But there was one night at a theatre in New Hampshire, at *Alien,* when the feisty creature burst out of John Hurt's chest and Lucy told me she was going home now—yet I stayed out of some legend of professional commitment.

I remember thinking of leaving you that night. You seemed so calm about it. As if that creature might have started eating the cast and you would just watch the camera angles.

We are overawed by the solemn elevation of a film. There it is on its screen, implacable and immaculate, as if its makers might be dead by now, or like gods. We did not chat because that could disturb other people. So we did not get into such issues as what were sane people doing, making and watching a scene where an infernal organism erupted from a character's chest?

Of course, the silence was proper; one could be ejected from a theatre for breaking its rule. And in that grave respect, the cult developed that movies were as grand as art, the window or the mirror for us all. Isn't it pretty to think so?

But you will have observed how different life can be when you're watching TV with a beloved. Lucy is in this book not just because I love her et cetera, or because "Lucy" is a marker in television history, but because the passage of co-spectatorship (or mutuality) is so extraordinary, because it is less interested in how the film has been done and more concerned with what is being done and what it does to us.

Is that what Lucy is doing? One of the things about being married to you comes at breakfast, going over what we saw the night before. The conversation.

To extend the *Alien* example: as years passed, Lucy and I had a son, Nicholas, who noticed me working on the four *Alien* films (another book). He asked to see *Alien* but Lucy and I agreed that it was not "suitable"—I think he was eight. Then he beseeched and implored and I was inclined then to open up every movie to everyone.

You're so open-minded, sometimes you're not there.

So we made a plan. I would watch *Alien* with Nicholas. At the first sign of his distress, or fear, the screen would be killed. I was so stupid. Thus we watched, and I watched him, my finger on the remote's OFF button. He observed the scene, without going mad or descending into hell—or not that I noticed. He sighed when it was over; a sigh at eight can be professorial; he seemed to feel something was expected of him. "Cool," he said. "How did they do that?" It was a reasonable question but I'm not sure that outweighed the recklessness or whatever of offering such a prospect as entertainment.

So what I am getting at is the untidy benevolence and psychological utility of watching television in a spirit that takes conversation, dispute, mockery, and interruption for granted. Is it possible that the culture made by movies would have been more decent or constructive if we had always watched in the readiness to speak up and wonder how deranged we needed to be to accept so many movies in silence and respect?

Companionship is demanding: it says, look, that show you're looking at is so small a thing. While we were waiting the seventeen seconds before getting a new *Ozark* episode, Lucy might interject—*Do you think we could watch a* Call My Agent *instead?* Or I remembered Chelsea would be playing Manchester City in fifteen minutes. I think I had to go over to that.

No! Call My Agent*!*

You can add on every alternative; it's hard to come up with anything you can't see on your screen. But alternativism is inherent in modern television and a mockery of the concentration we like to hold dear. Can you not see that your flat screen is oceanic deep, so patient, so calm, containing multitudes, so engrossing and distracting that choice may fall into disrepute. This is close to incoherence, but the impact is tranquil. Some evenings we almost wish for an extra button on our remote, one that gives us RANDOM, from anything in the history of the medium (aka eternity). Do you see a habit looming, an urge that dispenses with programming and heads off into immeasurable randomness?

You may recognize this as madness or a folly that you would prefer not to see in an author. But maybe reason has had its day. So I will confess that I still find great pleasure and input in sitting on the couch with the remote and going through the seven or eight hundred possibilities with just five seconds on each hit. I have to do this alone. Lucy is not partial to the steady self-interruption.

I watch the whole show and second guess after the fact. Our timing differs.

But if interruption goes on long enough it becomes a new steadiness, an ordering. Then lo and behold, it won't be long before you see storylines and delightful cuts appearing before your eyes. Furthermore, after a night of this—are you still there?—you may be astonished to find the helpless portrait of everything that has accumulated. There is a politics in this process as it shivers from the new treatment for erectile dysfunction to explosions outside Kharkhiv.

Of course, that cut is very pointed, and perilously didactic. The more tender or illuminating cuts have no such heavy-handed purpose. They may be as insinuating as a Busby Berkeley chorus line from *Footlight Parade* meshing with some listless pornographic interlude where . . . Yet again, I am close to stumbling against a point, some wry conclusion about what has happened to screened sexuality in ninety years. Try again—suddenly I find the soccer ball making the net billow in some unexplained game and long-distance views of clouds gathering over Monument Valley. We are at a point to prove the surreal principle: ask two strangers to pick an object and put it on a table. No link exists between the two. But then show that table and its two things to someone else and he and she will recognize the connections between the two:

- An orange and a penknife?—the one opens the other
- A shoe and a stepladder?—climbing has been defined
- A gun and a dollar bill—you can do that one yourself if you're American
- A sewing machine and an umbrella?—that was the surreal test first conceived in the 1860s

Objects and scenes are alike—we can't help this, resist it, or take credit for it—but in that helpless resemblance we are sinking into the affinities, the narrative or the inspired muddle of existence as no other medium has allowed before.

So you must try to be patient if this book forgets where it is going or achieves the magnificent surprise of coming upon something that was lost.

The composition is disturbed. Like that figure on the couch somewhere between fever and departure, sleep or hallucination, I do not feel in charge of what is happening or why. I can understand that this may be disconcerting for a reader. But you must be able to escape from the strict entrapment and specious comfort of things making sense. The shape of this book—its Contents, if that is the code you aspire to—is a riot of succumbing to whatever is available. When Lucy and I had our chance viewing of *The Kindness of Strangers,* we just responded to the echo in an unknown title when we found it on the Netflix platform, and also because the show had Bill Nighy, an actor most himself when he hardly knows what is happening in his show, and is not certain whether that quandary is fit for farce or tragedy.

Wouldn't you go for a series that was just Bill Nighy and Bill Camp? Think of that pair in The Wind in the Willows *as Ratty and Mole, or doing Sherlock Holmes.*

So, like anyone at a loss over where to find sense, I am going to make the next chapter a commentary (that sounds useful) on two shows I love. The one is *Our Friends in the North,* made for the BBC in 1996. The other is *Ozark,* the series that began on Netflix in 2017. Don't go away.

13

Great Shows

Ozark was created by Bill Dubuque and Mark Williams. Dubuque is from Missouri (the home of Ozark country) and in friendship with Williams, he had written a few movies—*The Judge, A Family Man,* and *The Accountant.* Williams was a producer and he directed *A Family Man,* as well as two Liam Neeson adventure films, *Honest Thief* and *Blacklight.* I'm going to admit that the Williams films strike me as accomplished, routine, but anonymous works. Once upon a time, that accounting would have seemed limiting and pejorative. But I am trying to shrug off the automatic shade of auteurship because the medium sometimes wakes people up or coaxes them out of couched sleep.

Let's say there was a friendship and a professional partnership between Dubuque and Williams that may have found fire in meeting the actor Jason Bateman. Bateman was born in Rye, New York, in 1969, and then moved to Salt Lake City and California. Working hard as a teenage actor, he did not graduate high school. His workload was intense, with many movie roles and a few television shows before he established himself as Michael Bluth in the hit series *Arrested Development* (2003 onwards), where his character is the center of a disturbed family, striving to hold things together, but nearly submerged himself.

That is significant: while Bateman may be placed now as one of the most familiar lead actors in America, it is not as if he is known, or loved, by the public. What distinguishes him is a deft neutrality, a willingness that lacks self-assertion, much less neurosis or ego. This can be traced to that era in screen acting where authentic stars were universally recognized but undefined or withdrawn. One can observe this in such universal figures as Gary Cooper, Cary Grant, William Holden, and . . . well, it's up to you, but we are discussing an acting in which these stars feel the need to do less and less in being there. I don't want to turn mystical or hero-worshipping with this tendency towards simple presence. But it is vital to the nature of the camera and the screen. It compares with the persistence over decades of some newscasters and talk-show hosts. This is a condition that gave us Johnny Carson, Walter Cronkite, and Bob Newhart. So I think Jason Bateman's functional reticence is at the heart of *Ozark*. But is it appealing or chilling?

He gives me the creeps sometimes. Then I like him. He's like you, sweetheart.

This is not to marginalize Laura Linney, who plays Marty Byrde's wife, Wendy. Linney is a brilliant actor, though she is more inclined to express herself in her work. But it is harder for actresses to put on the kind of passivity I am ascribing to Bateman. We live in a medium where women have not yet escaped the need to be attractive. Female underplaying is dicing with death. Linney is not an overtly sexual actress, but she has always had energy in a way Bateman seems to have ignored. Count on this as one more unfairness to women and wonder whether it is inherent in human, social nature, or something that might still be put to rest in a more positive future. Still, in much of *Ozark* we feel a latency in Wendy that could prove vicious and dangerous. It lies in wait. Timing on television can take years.

The Byrdes live in Chicago, with their two children, Charlotte and Jonah. Marty is a financial adviser; Wendy is a public relations officer in politics. Don't their names sound like old sitcom names—small, sweet, and happy? That's a foreshadowing of the show's deadpan irony.

These Byrdes could be comfortable or dull, but Marty is involved in a money-laundering operation attached to a Mexican drug cartel. He is in trouble because his partner has been defrauding the cartel, something Marty knows nothing about. So the cartel strikes: it kills the partner, and Marty is

saved only by the frantic ingenuity with which he proposes a new laundering operation based in the region of the Ozark lakes in rural Missouri.

The cartel agrees to this, but to underline its earnestness it kills the man
with whom Wendy has been having an affair. They drop him off a skyscraper.
This shows us that the Byrdes, while together and fond, are not locked in
romance. Wendy has an emotionalism that needs outside release. By contrast,
Marty has little expressive dynamic: it's just that he is quick, good-looking,
efficient, and the wings of the new Byrde enterprise. But he is withdrawn,
like a watcher. Marty has made survival into a religion, without having to
take oaths of faith. He is entirely transactional. And so the Byrdes break out
and go to the Ozarks, where few TV series had ventured before.

The sit is set for a crime series, with sinister music and a strange runic
logo, but lit up with aerial views of large lakes and wooded shores. Part of
the sit is that the show could be read as an advertisement for vacations in
Ozark country, unless you are deterred by the grimness that transpires there.
For this sit leads to endless murder, the burden of absurd amounts of cash,
and the ongoing process in which the Byrdes' life—poised on being a happy
family—is corrupted by the monetization of all anyone can see. It is not that
Marty and Wendy will survive—and any show needs characters who will
last—but how they are degraded in that process.

The narrative is so well organized that Bateman's Marty might be its
showrunner, dodging the peril of every situation, and apparently united with
Wendy in trying to raise the kids decently. This is not stressed in the show
(there is no ostensible satire), but it's hard to digest *Ozark* without seeing
how the models for a regular American life are being ridiculed or reversed.
Imagine the show filled out with a banal supply of commercials: for life insurance, electronics, leisure activities, and all the potions and medicines to
maintain well-being. And some urging to come to Ozark for a vacation.

That's why Bateman's need for order and efficiency is so telling, for he is
embarked on sheer evil, and carries himself in the assurance that if he doesn't

notice the damage then it will not be there. Is this contrived, or the keystone to American process that simply omits a moral point of reference? How long before we identify the overall allusion to being safe on the sofa, onlookers instead of participants? How are we meant to assimilate this narrative with our own efforts to ride out the tempest called money? That's where Marty's deadpan tone is so shocking. Not that Bateman seems ruffled, not even when he's beaten up and threatened within an inch of his being. It's in his distraught calm that Bateman is so amazing as an actor.

He makes Marty a technician: he could be an astronaut in some Apollo crisis, or a field commander withdrawing from Kabul. He could be a president trying to speak well of the state of the union. But he handles himself less with courage or skill than with an indifference. It is in underplaying his dilemma that Marty begins to be an automaton. And daftly superhuman: for Bateman also directed nine of the episodes (he specialized in the opening episodes of a season, to get the process settled in). Not that his style is more evident than that of other directors on *Ozark:* Andrew Bernstein (seven episodes) and Alik Sakharov (eight) and Robin Wright (two). There are several other directors employed, but I can't tell one from the other, even if Sakharov (born in Tashkent) may have a tougher edge—he did direct the four episodes that conclude season three, and they reach a magnificent murderousness fit for the Corleones.

Too much individual expressiveness might overbalance the show's dispassionate flow. That's where Bateman's impersonality (as coproducer as well as lead actor and sometime director) is so influential. For *Ozark* builds to a point where what happens in the storyline is not a matter of individual choice. It is in the nature of money's streaming, a factor that is no more explained or defended than the word of God in a religious story. It's at that point that one may grasp the shocking abdication of *Ozark,* or a dull but inescapable ache over how we are watching it.

Of course, the Byrde family grouping is assisted by several local characters. I'm thinking of Harris Yulin as the dying man who has a basement room in the Byrdes' house and who becomes a confidant to their son. There are Peter Mullan and Lisa Emery as the Snells, opium farmers in the area. They are Gothic throwbacks to a rural past and they have the most intense love relationship in the show. There will be Janet McTeer as Helen, the cartel lawyer who watches over the Byrdes. And there is Ruth Langmore, played by Julia Garner, who won three supporting actress Emmys on the show.

Ruth was a phenomenon from the start: rural, impoverished, uneducated, but harsh with yearning to be someone. Garner made her ragged and unkempt, seething beneath her demented hair, small-minded and foul-mouthed, but possessed of animal spite and cunning. She feels the chance that Marty could teach her and lead her forward in life. We half anticipate a love affair between them. I think this could have been there, ruinous for her and a speed bump for him. But the whole show flinches from sexual life, as if that might diminish the unsurpassed passion of money.

From early on, we guessed the ultimate decision in the show could affect the two children. There are many TV series with children, but few where they grow up. At the outset, hustled away from their Chicago, these kids are innocent or bewildered. But they learn so much in adjusting to their new life and being on the brink. This is not resolved after four seasons, and a test is coming: will Charlotte and Jonah stick to the family line, will they break down and get into the madness their parents resist? Can they be better than their parents, or just more efficient if improvement no longer signifies?

That narrative pressure means something has to happen. I can imagine Dubuque, Williams, and Bateman arguing over future plotlines and the imponderable question: how long can the sit stay in place before it has to explode? As yet, Charlotte has been less developed than her younger brother. But the actress playing her is twenty-two and the character deserves more agency. Jonah, who seems eighteen by now, has some of his father's mathematical coldness—could it be enough one day to usurp Marty's position? Could the audience stand up to a resolution in which Jonah became an associate of the cartel, in which he even finesses his father? Is that too much like *Succession*? Or could it be part of the ways Wendy has been going mad throughout the story, and might be the spearhead of a coup? Haven't we always felt an Electra or a Mrs. Macbeth behind the tortured smiles of Laura Linney?

I have no answers, but I hope you can see how far *Ozark* and *Succession* share the energy through which family may be exposed as a silly dream that real Americans are ready to dishonor. The thinking on storylines amounts to a fever.

But whereas *Succession* has been ready to stay a board game, *Ozark* always had the threat of blood sport. Just think of the way Helen was removed.

Yes, these endings could be frightful. They might frighten away the large audience that has sustained the show and made such money. But an outrage is not out of keeping with what has always lurked in *Ozark*. This is a novel-like structure in which the ideals of our society are close to being terminated. I can propose it as great television, but it could lead us to a point of admitting that the whole medium is our nihilist disgrace.

Our Friends in the North? I don't know where that title comes from. Does it carry a note of disbelief that these provincial people might really be our friends? Or anyone we care to know? Can we hear the loftiness of Margaret Thatcher talking, as if to say those people in the North (Labour voters) will never see things her educated way, so she feels bound to talk down to them as "friends," as if one day they might be saved. Or discounted. The poor bastards.

There seems to be a note of disdain or mockery, a way of saying those northerners will never face the way meritocracy has replaced society. Do you recall how Mrs. Thatcher outflanked not just socialism, but the thorough observation of people in their downcast reality, by claiming that the vague noun "society" did not actually exist? It's like Marty Byrde declining to notice or abide by responsibility—or as if evolution intended to have nothing to do with morality. How else can it advance without the necessary fascism in biology?

If *Ozark* depends upon Chicago outlawry escaping to the country and colonizing it, so *Our Friends in the North* assesses how people in Newcastle upon Tyne, 250 miles north of London, can adjust to the shifts from a Victorian, industrial economy to the slick ways of the South as Britain slides towards the millennium. *Ozark* is utterly modern in seeing how the transactions of commerce have smothered earlier notions of belonging to a place. Indeed, the Byrdes adjust to rural Missouri in only a few episodes, whereas that farming couple, the Snells, are hopelessly stranded in a past that will be manipulated by change. *Ozark* is a brisk, utilitarian hell. There's no reason for the Byrdes to pay the area any heed because they are committed to the America of heartless modernity. Missouri had its habits and its history, but Marty can turn those features into playing cards.

Peter Flannery wrote *Our Friends in the North* on an old model of creation. He had been born in Jarrow in County Durham in 1951, hearing stories of the Jarrow march, a dramatic demonstration in October 1936 against unemployment and lack of privilege during the British Depression. About two hundred "crusaders" made that march. They were assisted along the way by trade unions and the public, but their plea was largely overlooked by the government.

Flannery wanted to write plays based in the life he had known. In his late twenties he became a resident playwright with the Royal Shakespeare Company. As he watched a production of the two parts of *Henry IV,* he conceived the idea for the broad canvas of *Our Friends,* a chronicle based on four friends from Newcastle.

That play was produced by the RSC in 1982 with Jim Broadbent in a lead role. The BBC was so impressed they urged Flannery to make an adaptation for television. This took years to accomplish, with support from Michael Wearing, Alan Yentob (the head of BBC Two), and the producer Charles

Pattinson. There were disagreements and most of the usual fluctuations and betrayals in setting up any show. This is moviemaking, but with more scope for creative vanity than the old factory system ever allowed.

At last, Yentob's successor Michael Jackson determined to give the project a budget of 8 million pounds (half of his production allowance for the year). Thus it became a TV series in the winter of 1996, nine episodes of about seventy minutes each. It was meant to cover the years from 1964 to 1995, from the Harold Wilson government to beyond the imperium of Mrs. Thatcher.

That span tests a naturalistic show, so the characters age tactfully over the nine episodes. But faults in that respect do not mar the attempt by television to talk about what was happening in its Britain. The series is done as drama, but the documentary sensibility never goes away. We feel it in the views of narrow tenement streets and the gimcrack display of modern times that begins to eclipse the old England. This is a television that expects the audience to be aware of what happened in the North, in the South, and in the minds of its people.

By contrast, *Ozark* gives no hint of what was happening in the America and the Missouri of the years of Donald Trump's power. How could we watch the show without having to ask what that leader implied about us and what dire weather system he was making manifest? Or would that bluntness alienate consumer views and entertainment in Ozark country and in other parts of the nation? It seems to me—and I am English, recall—that American television fiction has given up the challenge of addressing the country in its stories, and in being a mass medium with a target beyond complacent exploitation. That is decadence and hopelessness. And it is further explanation of why the viewer needs to be depicted as an invalid.

Our Friends in the North presents four friends in Newcastle in 1964. Nicky is a university student who has been in America volunteering for civil rights. He is drawn to be a journalist and reunited with a girlfriend, Mary, who has little ambition beyond being happy. They are lovers briefly but then drift apart. She falls for Tosker, a lazy opportunist. They will marry without much thought about it. There is a fourth friend, Geordie, who seems to promise his own decline. The show will track these four, and many friends and associates, over thirty years.

This was done for 1996, when the casting took advantage of several young players. Nicky is Christopher Eccleston, Mary is Gina McKee (herself from Sunderland, eleven miles from Newcastle), Tosker is Mark Strong. And Geordie? Well, here is the twenty-eight-year-old Daniel Craig, wearing some bad wigs but in the best work he has ever done as a man who becomes homeless and derelict. To look at that show again now is to marvel at the wealth of acting in Britain, and to see how far its debt to social and political realities never touches the spick-and-span Marty Byrde.

Our Friends in the North is not a perfect series. It knows such a pinnacle is out of reach. Done in haste, under conditions of budgetary restrictions, television has a right to be untidy. That roughness contrasts favorably with the pious refinement of so many movies.

There are problems. The aspect of *Our Friends* that takes Geordie to Soho and the new pornographic trade, running up against a gangster (played by Malcolm McDowell), is a little uneasy and opportunistically gaudy, or sexy. That involves an extensive yet superficial exploration of corruption in the Metropolitan Police. The great weather storm of 1987 feels unduly convenient and theatrical. There is also the treatment of political abuses in Newcastle extending to Westminster that now needs footnotes to tell us how the character Austin Donohue is in part T. Dan Smith, a Labour Party leader who ended up in prison. Even so, I admire Alun Armstrong as Donohue, an honest man who has made too many compromises on housing projects for the less affluent: Mary and Tosker live in a flat that has damp everywhere— this is the proper treatment of décor. I am also tickled by the early presence of Julian Fellowes playing a suave and odious politician, Claud Seabrook, immaculate in his cynicism. This is the Fellowes who would become the creator (and effective proprietor) of *Downton Abbey*, the ultimate degradation of the BBC's weakness for older homes, sprightly aristocrats, and their plummy décor. *The Crown* seems to lament the court system behind the feeble family, but there are millions in Britain who revel in the display of privilege, good furniture, and "manners."

Nicky's parents may be too predictable a portrait of stranded northern grit in whom underplaying has been sentimentalized. But as I watch Peter Vaughan and Freda Dowie in the roles I succumb again to a faith in actuality. The lives of these characters wither in ways we all know or fear, forgetting and falling, no matter the suckers we are for television commercials for longevity. This is not just hair turning gray or extra weight in the hips and the midriff—the adroit way Gina McKee holds such things at bay is an endearing wonder. It is a step towards enlightenment when her wife and mum think to enter politics. But McKee is as interesting a player as Daniel Craig was in 1996, before his own specter of Marty Byrde took him over.

I always like that Gina McKee. There's something offbeat about her, a wryness that gets in the way of being romantic. I heard they redid The Forsyte Saga *in England (2002), and McKee played Irene, with Damian Lewis as Soames. Did you ever see that?*

I never did. Put it on the list.

If we ever get there. With our list we could be sinking.

In the hands of several directors—Simon Cellan Jones, Stuart Urban, and Pedr James—the context behind the lead figures in *Our Friends* is furnished with love and severity. The show is hailed as a classic now, and in 2022 there was an update done for radio. Seeking out the original will reward you, no matter that you do not quite know Newcastle or Mrs. Thatcher. Such forces start to disappear in history, especially if our grasp on English actuality hinges on *The Crown*. Julian Fellowes (by now Baron Fellowes of West Stafford) is a famous success from *Downton Abbey* because of our adoration of that show's skill and humor, its players and its dream of wealth—but fleetingly in 1996 in *Our Friends* he was impeccably hateful as a smug shit Home Secretary.

The age was there by then when politicians were like people who had their series. Not a platform. Blair and Clinton . . .

We keep coming back to home and the necessity in watching television of asking yourself where you are and what you think you're doing. Is this the collective unconscious we are inhabiting, or have we graduated to mere unawareness? Have we decided that it is all easier if we agree not to matter? So while watching Peter Flannery's series decades later you can realize that "our friends" must be ourselves, while "the North"—the land of grim failure and being old-fashioned—begins six feet from the couch.

14

Next Night

The next night Lucy and I wandered into reruns of *Seinfeld*. We hadn't meant to go there; we tried a couple of other series and decided after fifteen minutes or so that they were unworthy of us—the ability to kill a show is something novel in screen entertainment; how few of us actually walked out on movies in the great, placid kingdom of that medium?

But there was *Seinfeld* on the platform's table of contents, the one-word title, bold red letters on a yellow oval, the kid face of Jerry so ingratiating. He really was a nice-looking guy.

"Why don't we try that again?" one of us said, and it felt like our rabbit hole even if we are both rather more Larry David people. We'll come to that. The culture of those two, Jerry and Larry, is as endless and mysterious as Laurel and Hardy. We are talking top of the line.

And something so casual, so apparently undesigned, that it's a wonder it was ever there on our screens. I can imagine people at the outset—watching *Seinfeld,* or even working on the show—saying, "Oh, this will never go. They'll have to cancel this."

Do you want another episode? Lucy asked, after we had watched two in a row. We swallowed five before we went to bed, Lucy reading her book on Magritte while I fussed over adjusting my CPAP machine. We might as well get down to basics.

There was so much reason to think the show was a loser in the making. So in 1989, the production company had decided to call it *The Seinfeld Chronicles.* Though the show was plainly all New York, they would film it in Los

Angeles (a pilot was done at Desilu). It had attributes hardly noted at the time: it was very white; it was very male; and nothing happened beyond the bickering and maneuvering of four uneasy people. One could write about this show as if it was a play by Beckett or Harold Pinter. That occurred as a stray thought, but I don't know now if I can avoid it.

Talking of stray thoughts, you realize Garry Shandling was there before Seinfeld?

You see, there is Jerry, a very cool, pretty guy, working hard to be relaxed about being amiable and ordinary (as opposed to being on TV), but as you come to realize, fraught with unease, if only because he is the central figure on a show. He is a stand-up comedian who often goes on the road. We see him there, doing his routine, and he seems pretty good, with glimpses of a packed audience rocking back and forth in appreciation.

Every now and then Jerry returns from a gig in Minneapolis or wherever, to live in the shabby square footage of his apartment—it is one of the essential set-sits of television. But it is so down market, nowhere a successful comic would live. It's as if there is something holding this Jerry back, an unidentified force that prevents him from being Jerry Seinfeld (in red on yellow).

He lives alone, but his routine is organized to counter that. He flees from solitude. So he is visited all the time by Elaine (Julia Louis-Dreyfus). They were a couple once, but they broke up for reasons of unsuitability that neither of them can understand or live with. Because they remain a couple, no matter that Elaine carries a needle, ready to jab at Jerry for failing her or just for being Jerry. For his part he is interested in other girls—very interested—but he can't talk about them with Elaine without turning shy or guilty. And she doesn't seem to have another romantic life, though anyone can see without dispute that she is as cute as Jerry and nearly as lovely as Julia Louis-Dreyfus. I mean, it's plain that once upon a time these two had sex, but not now.

They are in mourning for each other.

Which makes the role of George Costanza (Jason Alexander) so strange. He and Jerry were friends at school, and they talk as if they have been talking most of their lives. They are buddies yet totally unsuited. I still can't believe that a Jerry would give George ten minutes. Just as Jerry is thoroughly viewer-friendly, George is an insecure creep, avowedly unattractive, interfering—in short, let's face it, an asshole. But the two of them are smart and articulate enough to be aware how inappropriate they are as friends.

Are they trapped? A lot of TV bonds are like that. People on a chain gang.

Now, you can say it is stupidity to believe friends have to be suited. And you are as right as you are in rejoicing over the company Stan and Ollie kept so long. Or in the way Magritte and a CPAP machine can be side by side. But you get to wonder at their affinity or persistence—Harold Pinter would have you wondering, and he would have seen that Jerry and George are a version of the unlikely bond of Jerry and Larry. I mean Larry David, co-creator and co-writer on *Seinfeld,* and apparently a constant nagging perfectionist on set, a kind of director. The two men had been New York comics and writers in the same milieu, but they came together just months before *Seinfeld* began.

Then there is Kramer (Michael Richards), a goofball, and a neighbor to Jerry. He has no evident job or income; he is like an aroma lingering in the building; and he is half-dressed, unshaved most of the time. You can believe he has body odor, as well as absurd schemes and the habit of getting in the way of the normal life that Jerry thinks he deserves.

Put it this way: Jerry should leave his apartment, dump George, and forget Kramer, and he needs to find himself a girl, or seven girls, and get into a sex life. Instead of just keeping Elaine around, loved but impossible—like a wife? But *Seinfeld* famously is a show in which nothing happens. Early test audiences could not credit that a mainstream show was going to function in such complacent vacancy. Of course, the sex life would not be shown, or talked about bluntly, any more than sex was explored on *Friends* (1994–2004). Because we are talking about a show that was aimed at network television.

That chaste form barely exists now; it can be regarded as a model for an American assurance before 9/11, Abu Ghraib, the rise of gay life, and Black persistence. I am not putting all these innovations on the same level, but I am trying to portray an old empire in its final days, the mood in which "we" were expected to watch the same shows and bow before the same commercials and feel that, once the bogey year of 1984 had been passed, we were in the clear and set on our way. I am talking about organized idiocy, and that is getting back towards the social criticism in a show like *Our Friends in the North*.

Seinfeld worked. It acquired its briefer title. The original character Kessler was renamed Kramer in case the show might seem excessively Jewish. (The history of how successful people worry is in the DNA of America. It is how the radical project turned reactionary.) The main sets were arrived at: the apartment and Monk's diner—yet again a place a real Jerry Seinfeld would not frequent. A grumpy, bumpy linking score was hired in from Jonathan Wolff. Seinfeld and David presided over a corps of writers, but no one really ascribed the scripts to anyone but them. And it was noted that David insisted that Jerry and Elaine be together without being together. Equally, he never flinched from the feeling that George was very like Larry.

David also delighted in the fusspot wordplay in which the four characters are engaged. *Seinfeld* had not just endless, literate, clean talk, but characters who were unhinged by the meaning of words and the thread of communication. One cannot live with *Seinfeld* without becoming obsessed with language. Talk is its action. Even so, I have sometimes tried attending the show with my eyes closed, reveling in the radio of the lines. It does not work. Those actors worked as hard as all good actors to animate what they were saying and how they were listening.

And so it produced 180 twenty-three-minute episodes.

Reports say that the show shot slowly, with a live audience expected to behave, to get its interactions precise. As much happens as it did in *His Girl Friday* or *Bringing Up Baby.* Conclusion: *Seinfeld* was always tending towards being old-fashioned because it appreciated the modes of screwball comedy, in which a man and woman on screen can be in a relationship and suffering from it. So Jerry and Elaine are more like Cary Grant and Rosalind Russell in *His Girl Friday* than they resemble the loveswept couples in *Friends.* And I'm not knocking *Friends.*

The matter of stuff happening on television is of significance, and it touches on mystery as much as the conjunction of René Magritte and the need to defend against sleep apnea. Television has always had an aptitude for nothing happening: it is like the nothingness when you turn the light on. The trial of O. J. Simpson, to pick something from the *Seinfeld* era, was months of nothing, albeit a nothing of fruitless disputation, and audiences were as hooked on following it as if they were watching extra innings in the seventh game of a World Series. I put it that way because O.J. and baseball were still big in those years of *Seinfeld* and *Friends,* and baseball did get into Seinfeld when George joined the managerial staff of the New York Yankees.

Sport—

Yes, I know you'd be insufferable without it, but truly that endless male suspense is a pain in the neck.

In February 2022, Chelsea played Liverpool in the final of the Carabao Cup. The game had no score after regular time. Another half an hour of extra time still produced no goal. So then there was a penalty kick shoot-out that reached 10–10 before the Chelsea goalkeeper Kepa Arrizabalaga missed his shot. He booted it way over the goal and into the crowd, as if offended that goalies were expected to score.

So Liverpool had won. Which is OK. The tense match was full of action: he kicked to him; him generated space; there was a foul, a header, a bold tackle, a ridiculous miss. I can feel the sway of emotions as the game passed by. Yet nothing happened: twenty-two men in colored kit, red and blue, went back and forth across the green, striving mightily in a riot but getting nowhere. The sit stayed secure—and millions of people were watching it on television as if their lives depended on its silliness. That is the essence of television, and it was a mark of simple-mindedness that no one at first recognized the same purposeless frenzy on *Seinfeld* that was marked by "inactivity." Although I have a limited capacity for it, I can see that *Succession* is nothing more or less than a board game that might go on forever.

Still, it is a bored game in which I cannot find a way to like the Roy people who are reduced to the level of spiteful actors. Whereas on *Seinfeld*, the misbegotten foursome are endearing, and their loyalty to their impossible situation turns them into pilgrims. So Jerry and Larry did not need to talk or think about the compulsion that held them together.

Seinfeld did poorly at first. Linguists and philosophers picked up on the show, but big audiences were wary. It was one of those series that had to teach us how to become its audience. But in its ten years on NBC, it took its initial viewership in the high teens per episode into the thirties. We are talking millions, and admitting the colossal imprint of network television when one venture could still grip a portion of the audience larger than *I Love Lucy* had managed. America was together then, and that was gone in the age of the Internet.

But we were told that would bring us together.

Lucy and I talked about what we were seeing. It was always the case that the show provoked conversation on the couch. We agreed it was still very funny. That is a matter of the talk and its timing and how the actors possess their roles. But Lucy complained that it was too tame now, that Jerry was too safe, or too deaf to deep dismay. He can't be hurt, so the viewership stays intact, and this was a show targeted at young men and their purchasing decisions. Jerry is telling himself it's a funny old world and not a lugubrious hell in which he is trapped.

Lucy's right, and the show now feels perfumed in a self-confidence that rises above George's discontents, Kramer's derangement, or Elaine's hesitation. These characters cannot lose sight of being in a hit show, nominated for Emmys and prizes and being some of the best-known and richest people in the world. As if to say he was simply Jerry, a nice guy—right? The show ran from 1989 to 1998, and you can fill an evening with listing the concurrent events it overlooked, just as it never touches the experience of people of color or begins to explore the fresh powers and same-old problems in being a woman. It may be because of Larry David—seven years older than Seinfeld— that the ethos of the show is from Hollywood in the '30s, '40s, and '50s.

The more you watch *Seinfeld,* the easier it is to see Jerry-Elaine as a new version of the comedies of remarriage, in which a broken couple drift back together again, in wisdom and forgiveness (or is it just helpless familiarity?). In effect, Jerry and Elaine are divorced, and half-reconciled.

Still, the charge of tameness is profound and it's very noticeable now (and even encouraging for some) to see that *Seinfeld* could function without "bad" language or situations that might offend sections of the audience. A recurring motif in the show is the comedy of men and women misunderstanding each other, and spending their life puzzling over that predicament. But the stance of the show was still unduly kind to men, and timid about addressing the self-satisfied attitudes of a moribund society. So Elaine can be sarcastic and edgy. She gets annoyed sometimes. But if she ever tipped over into rage then the 1990s show would have lost its traction and its ad income as some viewers wrote her off as literally "mad," or that other word, "hysterical." *Seinfeld* was a smash for so long that it thought it was addressing biological and social reality, but it was actually making the world cozier for guys— white guys.

Kramer is eccentric, yet not ready for therapy. George is a creep, but Jerry's creep. And Jerry himself is so self-admiring that he doesn't need a mirror. The cutaways to his stand-up act were plainly meant to keep the "comedy" level of the show prominent. But they are also vital to Jerry's neurotic urge to perform, an energy so often denied to him in that crummy apartment.

That is meant to sound critical, and it may be that I am so lost in being a white guy that I can stay with *Seinfeld* all night long, confident that if one episode falters, another is coming up fast. It's like watching soccer, adoring the motion, patient for emotion. It was a brilliant show, simple and then very complex, and one of the most important ever done on television. I doubt that any show has inspired more excellent critical analysis, often academic, but a sign of how far TV was generating more searching commentary than movies from the same period. Why not? Television was closer to the national pulse. But *Seinfeld* had to be the end of the sitcom as a viable network staple—a universal passion, like love songs, movies, driving, and soccer. If you feel that's going too far, just consider what *Seinfeld* would be like if Elaine had been played by . . . some less conventionally appealing actress, as a woman who might have scared Jerry away. I could suggest women not of the '90s— Barbara Loden, or Lena Dunham, Alana Haim, or any Black actress. (Do you realize how dangerous it still is for a player of color to be un-nice?) That could open the door on the sham and the slick shit in Jerry. That's where Harold Pinter might take over.

So who's afraid of Larry David?
I know I am, and I suspect Jerry was.
Which is a way of believing that we could never have had *Curb Your Enthusiasm* if *Seinfeld* had not happened first. That's not just part of the scheme of success in which the first show let Larry bluescreen a future for himself, and his always vexed and vexing persona. It's a way of feeling that one perfect marriage had to be redeemed by separation, and David's querulous raised eyebrows at that Jerry having been just a pretty guy wild about being liked. Isn't it central to Larry David's bristling ego that no one—not one soul—dares like him? That territory is left for Larry alone, like every creative aspect of *Curb Your Enthusiasm*. Never forget that first disciplinary verb; I don't think it's playful.

I have stressed that Larry was older than Jerry when they met, with Jerry farther ahead in the comedy game. There was no hint of years together, putting their timing in place and talking out some future show. Neither was there any record of hostility when they set out on *Seinfeld*. But the concept of that show was irrevocable: it was about Jerry, founded in his powers at stand-up and his palpable likability. David was quickly identified as a conceptual mind, a great writer and a visionary in social awkwardness. Everyone took it for granted that Jason Alexander's George was modeled on the neurotic, insecure tyrant lurking within Larry David. And David was a writer who haunted the set, rewriting sometimes and timing its timing. He might have been a pain if he hadn't been so smart. And if he'd been as daft good-looking as Jerry, well . . . get out of here.

They shared in the success, if not equally. While both made a ton of money from *Seinfeld* as it went into syndication, Jerry earned more. Of course he did; he had to: the show had his name, he was on screen in every episode, and people loved him. They thought he was like them. They got an Emmy together for the show (and Larry was an executive producer ahead of Jerry). But the only individual Emmy for the pair of them went to Larry for writing the episode "The Contest."

Why would anyone take umbrage over Jerry's passover? Especially when everyone knew Larry was the smart one in the odd couple and a pain in the neck. I'm not saying that with a catalogue of evidence, or in a metaphorical sense. What I mean is just study Larry's neck and the way he holds his pained head, and how he looks or doesn't look at people. You don't have to be as smart as Larry to realize he is the interesting one to look at. When would the world catch up with that? And get over Jerry being so passively adorable? While recollecting that Jerry never won an individual Emmy for the show—not one—so much for being pretty. Michael Richards's Kramer won three as supporting actor.

It's not clear what David wanted from *Curb Your Enthusiasm,* beyond more recognition or enthusiasm for himself. He teamed up with HBO, which had only recently ended *The Larry Sanders Show* (1992–98), with Garry Shandling, a clear forerunner for David's mock reality. The situation Larry presented to HBO was of a successful screenwriter helplessly like himself, living in Los Angeles, with a wife, and no children. That minus was very important: it's hard to think of the show's Larry being paternal, warm, or unselfish.

He is the baby in his house. It was plain that he would turn the situation into a narrative, not in Larry's pursuit of more screen employment, but in getting into misunderstandings that act out his narcissistic alienation. This Larry is neurotic but invulnerable. If he upsets his wife or his friends, he doesn't really care. He is either into Asperger's or pretending to be as a way of avoiding emotional candor.

David generated the storylines and then liked to get the cast together to improvise scenes derived from it. This was a way of working reminiscent of how the English director Mike Leigh fashioned his material. It meant that David was writer, lead actor, and effective director of every show. I say lead actor, but his role is more than that: he is the human force that determines everything, rather as one might think of Chaplin. And as with Charlie, it is Larry's mindset (his aggressive self-pity) that requires the stories. Everything is there to illuminate the notion that Larry doesn't quite get it—the way life works—and declines to see that as his error or shortcoming. Indeed, *Curb* contains a vision of how life should be that is bleaker than you would expect in a show called a comedy.

Curb Your Enthusiasm is funny, but in a direction that reaches beyond *Seinfeld.* Larry David never excludes the possibility that Larry is disturbed and too hard to live with—or considers any way of treating or healing that defect. For several seasons, the edginess of the show and of Larry was mollified by his wife. As played by Cheryl Hines, she was patient, understanding, and fond—she was eighteen years younger than Larry. How she put up with him, or why, was not always clear or plausible. But Hines radiated kindness and good humor; she tenderized Larry. Many worried when she left the show, and I don't think it recovered from her absence.

Curb Your Enthusiasm has been a great show just because it wrestled with the tortured crossed fingers of Larry—and it's not going too far to suggest that the show's Larry might have gone into therapy, or some more complete rest. He is a comic—like W. C. Fields, Jerry Lewis, Don Rickles, or Ricky Gervais—who challenges us with his need to be unlikable. I admire this for exploding the medium's craven wish to be pleasing. Why not a season where David goes to one shrink after another, a serial patient, and they all collapse in his wake, devastated, depressed, and lost to any thought of healing?

What this ecstatic misfit allows is laughter, tireless embarrassment, and true pathos. Larry David is an astonishing artist, desperate to seem casual, trying to ignore his own loneliness. But great humor takes proportional risks in denying itself relationships—and their ruination—such as we encounter in life.

But it's gone on too long. Starting in October 2000, *Curb Your Enthusiasm* has run eleven seasons and 110 episodes, with Jeff Garlin as Larry's agent and best friend—it is odd in show business for an agent and a client to be this close, and it's stranger still that this agent seldom gets into the deals Larry might have. I'd love to see Larry whining over huge sums of money and subsidiary territories. David is seventy-six now and his age sometimes seems as much of a drag as it does with Joe Biden. His situation feels repetitive without getting into crises where we have to decide about Larry. There are even times when I find myself longing for the lyrical boredom of *Seinfeld*, with Jerry wondering, Don't you love me? Geriatric shows on television seem too removed from the national energy. Larry needs a nap, and he might take it if he weren't afraid of being woken.

It's a measure of Larry's fascination that he tends towards the dank and the forbidding. He trusts no one and expects the same in return. One wonders at Los Angeles letting his disruptive shadow wander in its sunny malls, an accident in loafers. All of a sudden he can seem so out of step or old fashioned he could be an unemployed serial killer. Then you wonder, how could that job go out of fashion?

It's too much to ask David to come up with a brand-new show, with Larry exposed to family life or political demands. In life David has been a supporter of Bernie Sanders, but on screen Larry is the ultimate in detachment, closer to a Howard Hughes—one role he might take. And I think he is more revelatory of America now than Sanders or so many other public figures. If asked to nominate someone in television who helps reveal the split personality of the country, both self-pitying and hostile, Larry David is hard to top.

The present-day Jerry Seinfeld would provide little competition. He seemed to retire after *Seinfeld* closed and his several returns have felt vague or incidental. Not long ago, Jerry was in late-night talk with Stephen Colbert. The subject of Bill Cosby arose, and Seinfeld had been on record over the years saying what an influence Cosby had been. Now he said that Cos's comedy was still very funny, but Colbert admitted he couldn't watch it anymore. Jerry seemed bewildered and out of it, someone from a different time, wrapped up in a myth of show business fellowship. Larry David has always known that idea was a snare and delusion. It's easy to see him as another invalid on his couch, watching us watch him.

The sitcom is a model for stability: a group of us together laughing trouble away. Year after year, until there is no way to avoid accepting it as a frame for the ads. So in being present we consent to do our bit, consuming the American product, ignoring consequence. Entertainment exists to distract us from critical thought.

Our bank failed yesterday—did you see?

No, I'm staying cheery. I'll write a comedy about a bank. *The Bank Around the Corner?*

15

Larry All Alone

Didn't I see you doing Larry David this morning?

What are you suggesting?

Up and down the corridor, with his odd way of walking.

Is that a nice thing to say?

I can't help it, or get Larry David out of my head. I have to keep thinking about him, if only as a way of not being afraid of him to a point of panic. The surreal charm of his show, the ongoing tension of *Curb* and *Enthusiasm* at opposite ends of its construct, suppression and abandon, is the presumption that this querulous jerk can stroll around his privileged part of L.A. looking for a faux pas to suffer. I think we are agreed that his capacity for misunderstanding and petty disaster is not Larry's bad luck, or even his Asperger's, it is the mechanism he calls living. He prowls the streets, the lots, the salons, and the marts looking to be misunderstood.

And I can't get that nagging intimidation out of my mind. Not that it's personal so much as abstract. No matter the chilly outburst of mirth David can put on, he has a depleting gaze, as if summing us up and failing us. Will it be enough to have his scrawny hands like claws reaching out to strangle us, or should he go to his deep pockets and let the .38 have an outing? Don't you realize he's set to get us? That is the revenge he is nursing, the grave resignation to his not being absolutely alone, like Robinson Crusoe or Howard Hughes.

Has your author gone mad? Not a bit of it, a good part of him was there already. I told you, if you live lying on your couch long enough you're going to end up quietly disturbed. If you can kid yourself that quietly is the way to do it.

Is this taken from life? Or has imagining won the last battle with reality? You see, the matter of fact is that Lucy and I have had the habit in the time of plague to wash up after dinner and then go to what we call the TV room, as if that otherwise pleasant and promising place had been occupied by that function, the way the Germans occupied France. There are two sofas at different angles to the TV, and we take one each with blankets to save from putting on the heating. More or less we agree on something to watch, either from lists and flawed memories we are always assembling, or just grasping at an unknown attraction on the platform sites. Then we watch and listen for sounds from the other couch that may indicate one or both of us have fallen asleep. Don't knock that escape: it is a device, like a cut or a dissolve, that offers the magic of a few waking seconds when you don't know where you are and have to find current in the stream.

You can chuckle over this domesticity, but truly if we are victims of dull habit we are also adventurers ready to take off. Lying on a couch you may seem helpless, but the posture is also close to feeling you are flying. So there is humor in the juxtaposition of a fine book on Magritte and a CPAP machine that may need replacing. You can see the humdrum side of it, but Lucy and I are over forty-five years on our couches, and that has acquired not just a legend of sweet engenderings but passages of howling rebuke and proclamations of hatred. What else did we expect?

As if we hadn't guessed there would be a Larry waiting for us one night. I am reminded as so often of the Ray Bradbury story "The Veldt," about two children (Peter and Wendy) who have a futuristic playroom where the walls are screens on which they can summon up any images from the complete archive of things seen. So they could behold the plateau of Antarctica, the mysteries of Stonehenge, the nocturnes of Magritte, or the stoicism of Buster Keaton. But as their parents note, in mounting alarm, they are obsessed with scenes of lions on the African plains, the veldt. And the lions seem to be coming closer as if they have caught a whiff of our stinking couches. Can the lions actually see the kids?

Sometimes it seems to me that Larry steps aside from his silly stories, just for an instant, and he looks off into the darkness that includes us. I believe he has either seen us or appreciated the theoretical possibility that we are there watching him. Ready to undermine his solitude. So he may be coming for us. Wouldn't you do the same?

16

Where's ——?

You know, I'm rather worried.

I'd be disturbed if you weren't.

Yes?

It's what you do instead of panic.

I didn't know that.

Isn't it what you have me here for? To cut the solitude?

Don't I include you?

It's your book. What do you want to do?

You see, two chapters back, as if he had been an influence on Larry David, I mentioned Garry Shandling. But now I'm afraid I've left Garry out.

But you've just put him in.

Doesn't he deserve more? He's a great man, don't you think?

Phenomenal, and lovable.

You had a thing for him?

Mad about the guy. I watched him interviewed by Ricky Gervais the other night to make sure I loved him.

Really? Let's make a note of Shandling. Put him on the list.

OK, chief. "Garry Shandling, born Chicago, 1949. Moved to Arizona so his older brother could be treated for cystic fibrosis, but the brother died when Garry was ten."

I didn't know that.

Broke his heart.

It did?

Did you ever look at his face? You want more?

That'll do for now. But so we don't forget him.

Don't say one word more: a short chapter can be like garlic in the stew.

17

Something Wicked This Way Comes, Please

When was it that we agreed to be afraid? When did we understand that our own sweet place—our home—was the begging place for that?

These days we're so ready to worry. I wonder whether Franklin Roosevelt wasn't the impresario of this mood. That talk about a freedom from fear was all very fine; I'm sure he meant well. But hadn't he laid the groundwork for the threshold of trepidation?

Picture this scene: on some uneasy night, our hero comes to a large, forbidding house. We expect him to go in and find an answer—why else is he there?—but we feel the tremor of uncertainty. The image shifts from color to black-and-white, from life to noir.

Our man is wary of what may be in this dark place, or its inner room. Must we then go with him down that narrow corridor? A photographed corridor is so visceral and erotic; it is a shape in interior space, made not of walls, but of flesh.

The music has become more brooding, with hushed strings and a bass note behind them. But our brave man ventures forward: the camera, in front of him, backs off, impressed by his courage. Then the point of view cuts, and the forward motion is carried on in a following view from behind our man. The new view suggests there might be something coming up on him. That head of his seems so vulnerable. But then something subtle or insidious deepens the experience: we realize that *we* are where an assailant might be. We're watching so intently, it's as if we are making the film. Doesn't the storyline hang on our voyeurism?

Creeping up; the stringed music is more afraid now. We did like his nerve, or hers, but in an instant we feel the opportunity of striking. You see—this is all seeing and feeling—that voyeurism effortlessly brings the gift of malice. Or murder.

Isn't this a lark!

Did you hear that noise? Lucy asks. Is this her way of telling me I'm going deaf? That gentle bumping.

The wind under the door. Come over here and hold my hand, won't you?

Do you realize how intimacy is part of this menace?

On our couches, we wait for something, a hit show or a show that really hits us. The softness of the couch, its tenderness, the conspiratorial dark of the room, and the fluttering dawn of the screen can all contribute to a feeling of safety. But it's threatened safety. Isn't that the way it is now? We are more than six thousand miles from Kyiv, and that used to be so far. But we have had live coverage coming that distance like the speed of light, and that is a polite excuse for barrage or explosion, or the shocking bloom and fallout of what might be a big one.

I did urge you to see how being stretched out on the sofa was a metaphor for being wounded. In Ukraine already there is the problem of what to do with the bodies. The arrangements can kill you as easily as the bombs.

That sounds callous, but we need a hardness to absorb all the corpses. Oh yes, millions we say. Until some image crucifies us. In Ken Burns's The U.S. and the Holocaust—*did you see it?—there is a shot of an SS officer filming a man at Dachau, or somewhere. I thought I was dying.*

And someone was filming that SS man, someone behind him—and now Ken has filmed it all again. Is that how we handle these things?

The fear can take so many forms. This week a tent has appeared on the other side of our street. Not quite a tent but a tattered silver-gray wrap, with garbage at its edges as if the campers toss out their refuse with no respect for property values. Will that be cleared up?

Isn't there some new series about a murderer? Lucy asks. *Taken from life—isn't that how they put it?*

I think so. There usually is. But I've forgotten what it's called.

They're doing a new Law & Order, *I see. Is it still Sam Waterston?*

I saw a trailer for it. He's eighty-one, you know. On the gaunt side. Who'd hire a lawyer that age?

Lucy smiles. I love her. *I thought that was your age,* she says.

Oh, he's months older than I am.

We think our lifetime has been just a minute—we hardly saw ourselves growing, or altering. So let me remind you how in the first days of television, the late '40s and early '50s, it would have been unthinkable for any show to represent a murderer as if he or she might be serious, with a point of view, or close to sympathy. Such a show would have been an outrage in which we or they might have banned the medium. A lost opportunity? In America, hired in from radio, *Dragnet* began in January 1952, with Jack Webb as Sergeant Joe Friday, confident that the facts were there to be found, so that crimes would be brought to justice, and wicked people put away. In Britain, in July 1955, the actor Jack Warner took his first shuffling steps as Constable George Dixon, a copper on a London beat. This scheme had started a few years earlier in a movie, *The Blue Lamp,* where a vivid hoodlum (played by Dirk Bogarde) had shot P.C. Dixon dead on the street, so that audiences stood back in dismay. The British faith in its police was marked by the way Dixon went unarmed.

He was a soft-hearted man, a working-class gent, patrolling his neighborhood, helping people across the street or advising unruly kids to settle down, lads. He was already sixty when the show started, and he was still doing *Dixon of Dock Green* at eighty after 432 episodes. He was as genteel as a favorite teacher so that Webb's Friday seemed ostentatiously tough and mannered. But Americans were like that, weren't they? In truth Joe and George were fraternal, doing a hard and dangerous job for peanuts, pilgrims of law and order.

How could the world get along without that partnership? Even so, in 1952 and '55 those admirable cops were like soothing ads trying to calm any helpless inclination in television to report the appalling murders and the wicked people all over the world. We had so much to suppress. It was not just the 75 million or so killed in the Second World War in the more or less lawful and orderly pursuit of justice. It was the mere six million who had been rounded up, stripped, humiliated, beaten, tortured, and gassed in the most up-to-date, efficient way efficiency could endure. And then in 1945, citizens had been burned alive, incinerated, vaporized. The newsreel coverage of such events was strictly controlled—there was official caution over alarming us—but still such incidents were an imprint of what murder might mean.

And these demons might be coming again.

Is that someone at the door? Lucy asks. *I thought I heard a knocking.*

That's just your heart beating, beloved.

Voyeurism was the religion of the twentieth century. The delicious sin. Oh, stop me watching—I shouldn't be doing this.

Do you recall how we watched Marion Crane? I'm talking about that secretary in the realty office in Phoenix, Arizona. I know, she's as likable as Janet Leigh, but Marion is more than edgy; she's falling off her ledge.

At the very start there she is in her underwear stretched out on a pitiless hotel bed for a lunchtime exchange with her guy Sam (no time for foreplay or daydreams). Not that pleasure or gratification are improper. But in the overcast of censorship, Mr. Hitchcock enjoyed staying furtive. This lunchtime affair had an adulterous air; it was a snatched pleasure because Sam and Marion were too poor to get a flight to Acapulco or Niagara. When Marion goes back to the office after lunch, her hair and her shirt have to be as crisp as new money so nobody will know what she was doing. In secrecy guilt begins. She will have to ask herself whether she smells of sex—she had no time to take a shower. Not yet.

The next thing she does—without a word to anyone, or even talking to herself—is to abscond with $40,000 of cash instead of depositing it in the realtor's bank. (The money is the sex we did not see.) As she's thinking about this, she undresses again, going from white underwear to black. Then she takes to the road, haunted by the gaze of her puzzled boss as he sees her driving away when she had said she was unwell and needed to lie down. (Did he *see* her black bra?) Her paranoia mounts. You can say a master is handling it. But Hitchcock knew how much paranoia had always existed in the medium, like current on the third rail.

Pressure mounts on the trapped woman—as it does on us, waiting to see what will happen. As she drives north on a Friday evening, heading towards where Sam lives, she sleeps overnight in her car in a lay-by and has the suddenness of a highway patrolman's dark glasses staring into her guilty soul. So she resolves to trade in her incriminating car, only to make so bad a deal it draws more attention on her. Everyone is looking at her, us included. Twice already we have seen Marion in her underclothes, and there will be once more as she undresses to take a shower at the Bates Motel. As in paranoia, everything fits.

It is in the screen's remorselessness that *we* are the something wicked that must be coming. It is because we are so fixed on watching her that Marion is doomed. She's there only for us. So she sits in her car on the way north, grilled by the loss of daylight and the rain, by the accusing voices she hears and by the close-up she cannot escape. She lacks even the ease of driving because she is locked in a back projection.

You can say this is a movie, but we're watching on our screen in our room, without a crowd, so the trap seems more claustrophobic. The old cinematic festival has come home, emphasizing the solitude in viewing. And the creative control: watching a TV screen we are close to the superiority of the editing room. Enough to share the cruel privilege in putting scenes together.

That's why Norman Bates comes as such a relief. He is the first thoughtful, tender person in the film. Long before he proves himself as a killer, we have begun to like him. Marion feels the same way. It's listening to Norman's sad kindness that teaches her the fool she's been. So next day she is planning to go back to Phoenix, return the money, and face the shame of coming clean. Time for a shower.

You're always talking about Psycho.

I can't help it. It grows like a tumor.

Psycho was the turning point, a marriage of horror and the mundane, one of the earliest instances of a killer as the most understanding person in the film, and an artful grasp of cinematic storytelling as a torture chamber, the most complete identification so far of the medium's paranoia and its sexual anticipation.

The old code of censorship (a commercial safeguard) was getting ready to crack: there would be spectacles of sex and violence coming down, so why not both at the same time? The shower slaughter in *Psycho* was a surgical fusion of antisexual violence and erotic aspiration. Before our eyes, and for our eyes, Marion would get ravished. And the killing itself, Janet Leigh alone in the shower, is an orgasm. If you turn off the shrieking sound the scene has an ecstatic religious air. Like a sacrifice or an annunciation.

In those days still, the cinema seemed so much braver than television. The hit shows of 1960 were archaic even then: *Gunsmoke; Wagon Train; Have Gun Will Travel; Rawhide*—as if good-guy sheriffs then needed their trusty six-guns to resist the new streams of racial truth, sexual liberation, feminism, drugs and rock and roll, and American murder. Put those forlorn old-guard shows against a movie world that seemed full of daring and departure. For twelve minutes, talking to Marion over a cold supper, Norman had been so discerning of human social nature, but it was not possible for those insights to exist in a television program. The movies were it, or out there, just because their business was foundering. TV was written off as a drab entertainment for homebound proles.

And Hitchcock was so afraid of *Psycho,* he made it as if it was TV.

How was that?

On a low budget, with his TV crew from the show, *Alfred Hitchcock Presents,* in black-and-white still.

You can trace the cinematic steps that followed. There's the blissful dismissal of a few rural dullards in *Bonnie and Clyde,* part of our happy participation in the self-expression of the famous couple. There's the very beautiful offing of so many figures in *Butch Cassidy and the Sundance Kid* and *The Wild Bunch,* where concentration is often shifted to the technology that accomplishes such things. And then there's *The Godfather.*

It's not so much that there are exquisite specific murders in those films, as that the practice of murder is being carried on, without any more rebuke than revenge. Michael Corleone kills two men who seem thoroughly deserving. I mean McCloskey and Sollozzo shot down at dinner in that neighborhood Italian restaurant. Michael needs to be brave and skillful to do it—we are so much on his side. After that, it's the system that removes so many enemies. Michael has his brother Fredo killed, but he doesn't have to do it himself. So we are spared and that much more respectful of his baleful purpose.

I nearly forgot another step. In November 1963, whether we liked it or not, there was a confused moment in the basement of a police station where one man went up to another and shot him in the stomach. It was badly done as a scene; the blocking was clumsy, and if we'd known about it in advance, of course, it would have been banned. But it got away with it because it was actual or verité. Jack Ruby had shot and killed Lee Harvey Oswald. The first killings on TV had the excuse of being "real life" (beyond denial, or justification): so we saw lamentable dismissals, all of them drabber or cruder than Sam Peckinpah or Alfred Hitchcock would have permitted. That cunning actuality found a way to worm into the imagination.

Almost as instructive or influential as *Psycho* was the appearance of Hannibal Lecter in *The Silence of the Lambs* (1991). Thomas Harris's fictional creation had appeared earlier—that was Brian Cox in *Manhunter*—but he's only scary there. What do I mean by "only"? Well, it's the unquestionable way in which Anthony Hopkins makes Lecter a seducer. To do that, he has to have a victim-beloved, the daughterly Clarice Starling (Jodie Foster). That Lecter is a monster, but he's like a genius and an artist who gets a soft spot for Clarice, and seduces us in the process. If you doubt that undertone in their relationship, realize that in a sequel, *Hannibal* (2001), Lecter has a suggested love affair with a grown-up Clarice (embodied as Julianne Moore). Hannibal here was a Norman Bates with a stronger libido and the eloquence and sophistication to talk Clarice into his arms. The director, Ridley Scott, admitted that Lecter was still evil, but he seemed to understand that the eroticism in his dangerous state had passed into our bloodstream. Hadn't that chemistry been apparent since the original Dracula? Bram Stoker's novel appeared in 1897, just as movies were beginning.

Norman, Michael, Hannibal—a new tradition on the screen, with unimpeded authority by the late 1980s. The easement reached much further—and I am curtailing my survey—into works aimed at the small screen where women might be killers. Much of this said it was owed to "real life," that helpless reservoir of story. *The Burning Bed* (1984), was based on a nonfiction book, but it was a TV movie, with a TV star, Farrah Fawcett, as a wife made so desperate by her husband that she responded by setting fire to the bed he's sleeping in.

And the jury acquits her. People said this was a breakthrough in the battered woman syndrome and the society of men had the tact not to complain at the example being set. Fawcett was nominated for an Emmy but she lost to Joanne Woodward facing Alzheimer's in *Do You Remember Love?*—and perhaps you don't. In 1987, JoBeth Williams was a woman in Kansas who felt she needed to do a murder in *Murder Ordained.* Three years later, in *A Killing in a Small Town,* Barbara Hershey is a wife in out-of-the-way Texas who has a buried killer instinct.

All made for television, these are absorbing routine fare, which means that oppressed female murderers were by then reckoned to be very American. Sometimes the tendency was better than routine. In *A Dangerous Woman,*

Debra Winger was very touching as a mentally troubled woman in another small rural town who is driven to kill a man she knows is a liar. (*A Dangerous Woman* and *A Killing in a Small Town* were both directed by Stephen Gyllenhaal.) *Dangerous Woman* ends awkwardly, and Winger's character may be too childlike, but it's one more film that teaches us to feel the undue emotional pressures put on women and the way they will not always lie there obediently.

I think I'll get myself a little drink, says Lucy.

The tension in small towns, TV budgets, and actresses on the downslope of their careers was blown away in 1992 with *Basic Instinct,* a San Francisco setting, the brazen affront of Sharon Stone, a harassed male lead (Michael Douglas), and a film that attracted large theatrical audiences while being talked about as trash and exploitation. As written by Joe Eszterhas and directed by Paul Verhoeven, it was an insolent, witty summary of emerging trends in which Ms. Stone played along with the story that she had been taken advantage of, while aware that it had made her an undisputed star. *Basic Instinct* was at least as acute and respectable as *The Silence of the Lambs,* and it did introduce a new camp terror in men's nervous lives—that a beloved might keep a radiant knife under the bed, as fresh as raspberries, so don't kid yourself you don't deserve it. A knife is like a gun: if it appears in a film, chances are it's going to be used.

18

BREAKING

There has to be urgency in stories: they need an inevitability to help us be good, or better—to others, and for ourselves. So we have to attend to suspense. The idea of a moral in stories was derived from the religious writing we had grown up on. Then, in the history of the novel, we entertained the possibility that we were not simply good, or cut out to be virtuous. We were tricky. Adam and Eve had been tempted by the Tree of Knowledge, that first metaphor for fiction. The tree had been ravishing; but it was a banyan tree, or a diagram of traps. As we climbed it we realized that we could not get down. So we made a poetry out of the tree.

In *Psycho,* there is this calm moment where Norman confides in Marion; we can believe he hasn't talked to a living, listening soul in years.

"You know what I think?" he says. "I think that we're all in our private traps, clamped in them, and none of us can ever get out. We scratch and we claw, but only at the air, only at each other, and for all of us, we never budge an inch."

Long before he might be "confined" by the plot, Norman is in prison.

She understands, for he is her unwitting therapist, bringing her down from her madness. "Sometimes we deliberately step into those traps," she admits.

"I was born into mine," he tells her. "I don't mind it anymore."

She is hurt for both of them. "Oh, but you should. You should mind it."

"Oh, I do," he assures her, with a smile. "But I say I don't." It's an instance of our house-proud dishonesty.

So we told stories about our improvement, even as we paid increasing attention to the lions on the veldt, magnificent and somber creatures that had no inkling of how clever we could be.

I had been surmising for a few years in an open-minded way that murder could increase. Not for the customary socioeconomic reasons, as in the struggle against poverty and insignificance, but simply because as we lost faith in our own moral being we did see the possibility that we would start to behave badly, as if for its own sake, but to break free at last of the entire encumbrance, the thing we called propriety or meaning. As if one sunny day in Westwood, Larry David decided that instead of getting into another fatuous scrape of misunderstanding he might drive his anger straight into some hapless passerby. And then stroll home, with that jaunty broken stride he has.

Can you imagine trying to explain to Joe Friday—not so long ago—the case of Walter White? He is this science teacher at a high school in Albuquerque, New Mexico. Chemistry is his thing, and he loves it like a hobby. Walter White is a pilgrim's name, echoing Walt Whitman. He is fifty-two, married to Skyler (she is forty), and they have a son, Walter Jr., a high school kid who has cerebral palsy. In addition, she is pregnant again—life and mortality intertwined.

Like many people at fifty-two, Walter is facing up to disappointment and deterioration. His cough seems to speak for his unease. He regrets the palsy his son has, and he wonders how the boy will fare as a grown man. He detects that Skyler has her own dismay, not just regret at not having made a life as exciting as she hoped for, but with an older husband who is plainly in some decline.

Not everything is bad. Walter has a job. The Whites have a pleasant house. And they have New Mexico with its light. This bursting West is supposed to be the America of continued promise, and Walter does his best to play that game. On the other hand, it is 2008, which was not a good year for promises in a country pledged to lying assurances about what was going to happen. And pushing the lies on television.

This was *Breaking Bad,* a new series on AMC, where it played with commercials. It is available now streaming, so you don't have to watch this intervening lard, in all its shitty sweetness, but when the show began the ads were no more escapable than worrying symptoms in a middle-aged man. We kid ourselves by finding a delivery system where the shows we love are minus the ads. Truly the ads are not just glue, they are blood, and I wish the show's creator, Vince Gilligan, had been asked to compose and shoot the commercials himself as well as the rest of the show. Someone has to admit how the story and the ads are integrated on TV.

We can kill the sound on commercials. We may wait for boxed sets that are without them. We pace the room in fury—and forget what we were watching. But in every situation it is a struggle to accommodate these infernal messages. Even as you see them slip by silently you resent the bald lies they tell, and the fatuous aplomb, and you feel for your innocent screen being stained and impaired as if by blood or poison. As I've tried to suggest, even with a show that has no commercials, the slipstream of selling and positive urging never goes away. You can tell yourself that *Ozark* is a description of a life you don't want to have—so bad you don't know why you're watching—but you will never escape its proud air of problem-solving and making dirty money clean again. Don't forget, it is a series about the laundry business, and clean clothes—think of clean sheets on your bed—can be as gracious as light.

So the ads deserved Vince Gilligan, as much as he needed to face the seepage of their lies. He was born in Richmond, Virginia, in 1967, the son of a teacher and an insurance claims adjuster—you can see the seeds of moral awakening and gritty realism in that parenting. In love with film, he went to the Tisch School of the Arts in New York, and he started to write scripts. That was what got him involved on *The X-Files,* where he wrote many episodes and began to function as a producer, or an overseer.

He was talented, but he did not see himself as a movie auteur. What I mean by that is the kind of independent artist figure who—we tell ourselves—created great movies, or even some that are less than great, but which were personal and revealing. When Gilligan was twenty, such American figures might have been Woody Allen, Martin Scorsese, or David Lynch. Such people were esteemed, and reviewed as if they were Sondheim, Warhol, or Didion. They seemed in charge of their movies, though they might have smiled at that, remembering how much they had had to bend and compromise to get their stuff funded. But around 1987 that stuff included *The Purple Rose of Cairo, Radio Days, Goodfellas,* and *Blue Velvet*—films of which it would be said that nobody else could have made them. This is why moviemaking seemed glorious in the era after Hollywood had subsided as a crass business enterprise.

I doubt Gilligan saw himself that way. He was a team player, quite willing to have a picture business regain its confidence. *Breaking Bad* and *Ozark* are both stories of desperate business success.

That does not diminish Gilligan. He had gone to school on *The X-Files,* a very good show and a terrific success; its audience built three seasons in a row, and got over 20 million on Fox. As created by Chris Carter, from 1993 to 2002, it had nine seasons and 202 episodes, in a fusion of horror or the supernatural with what I'll call an Intelligence procedural. (In hindsight, its imprecise ideas of conspiracy were well suited to the emerging Fox sensibility.) It lived and breathed paranoia as no series had done before, and it made agents Scully and Muldur into household figures, with Gillian Anderson and David Duchovny in the parts. It was a key step in the process by which America gave up on a naturally shared sense of reality—because we never trusted what seemed to be happening. It was as fascinating as it was scary, and it pioneered the uncertain status of our couch and our own living room.

I think I've always found TV more frightening than movies. You can walk out on a movie, breathe the fresh air. But if you turn the TV off, somehow you're still trapped, sitting there alone, knowing it's still going on in its dark screen. Streaming—it's such a visceral word.

The Twilight Zone (1959–87) had often been dark and foreboding—but it was sci-fi fun. *The X-Files* was open to a greater unease that never went away. After an episode, if you looked out at the empty street at night you were seeing the décor that the show believed in.

I love the look of empty streets at night, the sinister prospect and the moon-light. Magritte painted that silver light.

The color of a blade. And I know you are often fearful of someone coming in off the street.

You believe that too?

How does this suspicious mood take hold? Because television was ready for it—it was the dominant screen in the culture already. But then because of Carter's vision, and the group of people he enlisted to carry it out. The several producers included Michelle MacLaren, who would become a leading director on television series, without establishing a recognizable personality, and Vince Gilligan.

It was never clear to Carter or the show as a whole that it was going to last for nine seasons. That longevity depends on viewership and so it hangs in the balance, year by year, waiting to be renewed. But Gilligan saw, like everyone else, that such a show relied on a situation that could run free without dramatic climax. In the case of *The X-Files* the situation did not feel stable, but Anderson and Duchovny were still there and we were wondering how close they were going to be. That's good. The most compelling screen romances remain unresolved.

It was Carter's task to keep the unknown in order—that is a key to so much screen storytelling—and Gilligan was one of those who learned from the experience. But whereas Carter was attuned to the quality of science fiction and alien abduction, Gilligan was more grounded in what might pass as mundane reality. In his creative mind, the true aliens we encountered were the familiar people we knew and lived with. So *Breaking Bad* was set in the desert country *The X-Files* loved, but while Carter's series was entranced with the noir mood of desert, Gilligan relished the real space and colors of that terrain.

The X-Files was often nocturnal, but Gilligan loved bright sunlight. *The X-Files* wanted us to be afraid of the unknown (it really was more timely than *Breaking Bad*). But Gilligan's show was haunted by the known. In both cases the magic being aimed at was the steadiness of a situation allied to the prospect of how dramatically it might change from week to week. This is a way of indicating how long-form television had taken over our imaginative center from the movies. Walter is doomed; but he gets to live in a movie about an underworld he once thought was fanciful.

He faces not an Area 51 of the soul but an American reality: lung cancer. Not that cancer was a common subject in TV fiction, where the audience was being fed constant recommendations for elixirs and medicines. But Walter sees his illness as the last straw, the way he will revolutionize his life by giving up on being a decent man. This was the departure of the show. Instead, he will redirect his skill and knowledge and start to manufacture crystal meth for cash to pay for his own treatment and to ensure a future for Skyler, Walter Jr., and the baby on its way. Because he knows he will die—to that extent *Breaking Bad* had a built-in terminus.

In making the drug, against his educated instincts, he enlists one of his own failed students, Jesse Pinkman (Aaron Paul). Jesse is a flake and lowlife, but he will find some redemption and integrity in what happens. Yet Walter trades away his honor and becomes a cold killer who admits that the criminal life has fulfilled him, as if for decades he fantasized over films like *The Godfather* and told himself he could never do that. This transposition of Walter and Jesse is well done, with as much comedy as tragedy.

Breaking Bad became a landmark, the kind of show other showrunners aspired to. (*Ozark* is one of its offspring.) It ran five seasons with sixty-two episodes. It gained and held an audience: it did what TV has been meant to do—it made a lot of money. It won prizes (two Emmys as outstanding drama series) and earned the reputation of being an epic novel told through television. After all, it was a movie that ran over fifty hours.

This was not like novels of the twenty-first century. It was closer to the reach of Balzac or Dos Passos, teeming with action and characters, and feeling like a portrait of America at large, where intimate family stories were set against the storm of outlawry and disorder. Its plotlines were furiously imaginative but plausible. The need for suspense was allied to the question of how far Walter would go, and whether the admirable Bryan Cranston in the part could keep our sympathy. He won four Emmys as lead actor in a drama series. Could we understand that in our America a decent man might turn into a monster if only to allay his own fears? And would that other version of ourselves—the audience—ride along without falling off the vehicle, or abandoning it in the desert as un-American? It was for television that story gave up the impediment that our central characters had to be likable.

Were we grown up enough by then to see ourselves in outcasts and demons?

A key in that dilemma was the growing distrust between Walter and Skyler. They were not united, like the Byrdes in *Ozark*. Walter was lying to her for so long, as if pretending to be secret, isolating his malignancy from the world. He revealed his obvious cancer, but not the one in his nature. So some audiences became angry with Skyler's apparent disloyalty, and criticized the actress, Anna Gunn. In a sidelong way, *Breaking Bad* became a rueful portrait of a lost marriage.

It was a lesson in our wretched nation that Anna Gunn was so attacked.

Agreed.

Agreed doesn't butter any parsnips.

What did you want?

Well, if Saul can get a spin-off series—which is fine by me—what about what happens to Skyler and the kids?

It was true: *Breaking Bad* couldn't be done without a handful of robust supporting characters and an outer circle of cameo parts. Walter was haunted by his brother- and sister-in-law, Hank (Dean Norris) and Marie (Betsy

Brandt). But then there were career villains, like Gus Fring (Giancarlo Esposito), Mike Ehrmentraut (Jonathan Banks), and the irate but silent Hector Salamanca (Michael Margolis) whose tiny bell tolled for all of us. Then there was Saul (Bob Odenkirk), the louse who became our louse. The casting of actors in even small parts was as important as managing the scripts so that we didn't lose touch with the smaller roles.

You can call this organization, but it is a higher skill than that word conveys, and it takes us back to the vivid narrative enterprise of nineteenth-century novels. To run a show is like managing a large theatrical company, making sure people have screen time, adequate pay, kiss-ass attention and lives to play, and a proper place in the story. Then the organizer must generate the story itself, the characters and the possibility. The show. I think it is as true as it was for *The Godfather* that in doing a criminal story, the peopling of it was so engaging that we wanted to be part of it in our home. This is fantasy, of course, but it is how fiction has always operated. A high achievement of shows like *Breaking Bad* was to carry us back to the movie companionship of the '40s and the '50s. How could actual movies, made in the age of *Breaking Bad*, compete?

There was a vivacity in *Breaking Bad*, despite its dance with death and destruction. The work must have been very hard—long-form television is the old studio system brought back to life—but it was plainly fun, too, and that primed our loyalty to the show. We didn't want it to end, but Gilligan played fair by lung cancer and the old hope that great series need to conclude. So I'm not sure whether it is sufficient to say that *Breaking Bad* was simply dark, tragic, and despairing. All those strands were there, but that did not spoil the exuberance of weaving them together. Gilligan is not a natural pessimist, and he always liked the courage and resilience in Walter White. The show was like any masterly production—it might have been *The Importance of Being Earnest* or *Götterdämmerung*—because we came away with satisfaction.

And vindication—it said, yes, this is like us.

The actors in the show may never have the same chance again. Bryan Cranston became a leading American actor, inspiring and exemplary, but when the system tried to use him again, in *Your Honor,* developed by Peter Moffat from an Israeli show, the result felt ungrounded or fabricated. There was a delay after its first season before Showtime said they would do another. Cranston was good still, but a compromised judge was not as winning as a dying chemistry teacher. Concept is delicate and vital in these shows; would *The Sopranos* have worked without Tony on the edge of anxiety and needing a shrink?

All of which is a reminder of the longevity of, say, Gillian Anderson, a revealed star on *The X-Files* but then a star again in such different shows as *The Fall* (2013–16) and *Sex Education* (2019 onwards). Anderson (in her early fifties now) does theatre and movies, but she is best known as a television chameleon. She has done Miss Havisham for another *Great Expectations,* the Duchess of Windsor in *Any Human Heart,* and a Margaret Thatcher in *The Crown* who could have made the iron lady envious. Basing herself in Britain was a wise move for Anderson.

The shabby star emerging from *Breaking Bad* was Bob Odenkirk, whose Saul Goodman became a hangdog fixture pitched between fraud and chutzpah. This very modern American got his own spin-off show, *Better Call Saul,* in the way long ago various players on *The Mary Tyler Moore Show* (1970–77) got series to themselves. It would emerge that Odenkirk was as desperate as Saul: the actor had a heart attack while working on the show. But carried on. Don't we expect commitment in our actors?

19

Where Is Carol Anne?

I have given up on wondering whether fear will ever go away.

It was some nights later. I woke between three and four and I stole out of our bed so as not to wake Lucy. I walked around our place in the dark until I realized that as well as the seepage of moonlight in the house there was a flush of milkiness at the end of the long corridor. I wondered, had I left the television on the night before, and I went to the room to turn it off. This is what I found.

Lucy was not in our bed. She was on her knees before the television, and she was attending closely to what I thought was the snow of static—as if the set was on, but without a program. She seemed to be looking into that haze with reverence or some trust that there was something there, a something I could not detect. Then I realized there was indistinct sound within the static, a rustling with variations, like a faraway wind or the muttering of some prayer. And Lucy was reacting to this noise, in ingrained call and response. I could not hear words or any urge to communicate, but she was swaying with the process. I felt she knew who or what was there in the recess of the screen.

I put a hand on her shoulder and whispered that she should get some rest. She did not resist. But she did not seem quite awake, though her eyes were open. She stood up and knew the way back to bed. When I was sure she was secure again and sleeping I returned to the television. I studied it for several minutes but found no pattern or persona. So I shut it off—begone!— and felt an extraordinary relief as if a pressure had abated.

Of course, the film scholar in me half-recognized what had happened. There *is* a movie of this situation—without a need to decide whether it is good or bad. Had its stream leaked into our house? Don't you sometimes feel the shows are curled up in the wiring, like spirits or fragrances?

In that real movie, the Freeling family live in Cuesta Verde, a carefully designed but unnatural community in Southern California where all the nice houses are as alike as TV screens. This is building on the Vegas plan. The father works in real estate. The mother looks after him and their three children: a teenage girl, a boy of eight, and Carol Anne, who is five. They seem pretty OK, if you know what I mean, but Carol Anne is in a relationship with the TV. She sits on the floor before it, and worships its fluctuation. She accepts the primitive force of the medium, while we have taught ourselves to be blasé.

Then one evening a fierce storm tears up a tree outside, and Carol Anne vanishes into the TV.

This is *Poltergeist,* from 1982. That film is so crystal a wow it surpasses questions of worth or substance. *Poltergeist* just is, but with a further cloud of mystery. The direction of the film is credited to Tobe Hooper, who had made *The Texas Chainsaw Massacre* (1974). But its story and its script bore the name of Steven Spielberg, among others. It was a Spielberg production, and there have been stories that he directed some of it himself, or was there, a force, leaning on Hooper. This is not as uncommon as it might seem. The "directed by" credit in cinema can cover a multitude of unclear influences.

Lucy and I had not looked at *Poltergeist* for years, but we had seen it together when it came out, and we had been thrilled and amused by its vision. And its implications—I think that would have been the word.

At the same time, in the week or so preceding that half-past-three in the morning, we had been exploring what I want to call the complicity in some television shows, and the insinuation that there might be a continuum between the safety of our couch and the turmoil in the TV picture. A way of getting from one to the other without crossing state lines. This is what we had been seeing:

Parts of *Dexter*—do you remember that one? It was a series on Showtime, from 2006 to 2013. Dexter Morgan is a disconcerting fellow. He is a kind of investigative scientist who assists the Miami Metro Police in looking at bloodstain patterns in certain killings. This doesn't quite fit: Dexter is a highly skilled technician, a creature of laboratories, but the actor who played him, Michael C. Hall, was what you might call a hunk—good looking, big and strong, maybe a football player. But there was more. Dexter had also been enlisted to murder and dispose of certain killers who had managed to escape the law. You could say he had a vigilante purpose, but the clash of investigation and execution was stranger and deeper. It suggested a profound conflict inside Dexter, and if you were so disposed you could interpret that as a manifestation of our own confusion, or complicity: wanting to have mortal crimes discovered. But also inspired to commit those crimes. It doesn't have to be half past three for that *Psycho* pattern to seem striking. And intriguing.

There is something else in the show. Dexter is the adopted brother of Debra Morgan, who works for the police too. They are not tied by blood, but they work in that medium, and they are caught up in an affinity or complicity, hardly addressed directly, but a version of being in love. She is a good-guy cop, and he is her ambiguous aide. The unaddressed pressure in their feelings took a strange turn, for as the show went on so Michael Hall and Jennifer Carpenter (Debra) fell in love and married. It did not last long, but I think we tend to overlook the underground attachments between actors in a show, or between ourselves on the couch and characters contained in the bright box.

Dexter was derived from a novel, *Darkly Dreaming Dexter,* by Jeff Lindsay, and it was set up as a TV show by James Manos Jr., though others took a hand in it later on. Eight seasons and ninety-six episodes, a hit series, with several follow-ups. And not entirely nice. The show had that feeling of going off in directions, or coming up behind you, in ways that might be sinister or foreboding. You felt a little unclean or undermined watching it. But people were hooked, as in being reluctant to miss it. Those were the days when an episode appeared every week, before the whole show or a season was there saying stream me. So under that scheme the waiting was more precious and scary, and it left you with a lot to think about.

There was another show that had a similar complexity, and I've mentioned it already. I mean *The Fall,* in which Gillian Anderson is Detective Superintendent Stella Gibson, who is seconded from London to Northern Ireland to look into a series of unsolved killings. She is a bold, glamorous figure—Angie Dickinson's *Police Woman* (1974–78) is her only screen rival as an authority cop with a sex life, and Anderson makes Stella loftier or more austere than Dickinson was ever prepared to be. Stella needs a sex life the way a superintendent expects a car and a driver. And so she gets to work in Belfast, that part of the United Kingdom that is not confident about being part of united. Equally, while Gibson seems like a decisive and very smart detective, we begin to appreciate that she is hiding from something in herself.

There is not much doubt about the murderer she is tracking: he is Paul Spector (played by Jamie Dornan), a chronic killer but very intelligent. And as time goes by a degree of symbiosis unfolds between Stella and Paul. And with us, or our watching. It's not an emotional latency, as with Dexter and Debra. But the two leads begin to see how much they need each other, and that interaction is like our own habit of watching murderers on the screen, working them out as in detection, when in life the blood and its splattering would pitch us into nightmares or those séances that can occur between three and four. Let's just say there was a chemistry between Stella and Paul, and as Walter White could have told us, there are laws and conditions in chemistry uninterested in moral explanation. Seeing and being seen are as much a part of us as atomic structure. So much of TV is founded in blandness or reassurance. But the medium knows we will watch terrible things and come back tomorrow.

The Fall is one of those shows contemptuous of the old English puzzles according to Agatha Christie—who done it? *The Fall* is going to the heart of the matter: not just why it was done, but why we need to watch. If you get that far, you may start to wonder why the show is called *The Fall*. Who is falling, and how? Is it Stella? Or could it be us? When the series ends, Spector is dead after nearly killing Stella. Is that what she wanted: does the detective yearn to be found out? The energies being released are disturbing. *The Fall* was created by Allan Cubitt, just three seasons and seventeen episodes— a taste for shorter series was advancing in Britain. Cubitt did a lot of the directing himself and the show is as icily calculated as Hitchcock, our godhead of paranoia and watching. Anderson was also an executive producer, along with Steven Knight, one of the more interesting writers around. He wrote and directed the astonishingly simple *Locke* (2013), which is ninety minutes in a car as Tom Hardy drives from Birmingham to London, talking to people on his phone. With us just there soaking it up. Wright was also creator and writer on a lot of *Peaky Blinders*.

Do you remember Poltergeist? Lucy asked a few days later. Out of the blue. I hadn't mentioned her early hours communion with the screen.

The child in that film, she wanted to know, *what's her name? Is she rescued in the end?*

Carol Anne, I said. Yes, she's saved and the family quit their house. They go to a motel.

Where the father rips out their room's TV connection?

Quite right, I say, so the audience can feel better about themselves.

Did you know? says Lucy. *The teenage daughter in the Freeling family. That actress was Dominique Dunne.*

I had forgotten.

It was soon after Poltergeist *that she was murdered. Only months later. Her lover strangled her.*

It's coming back.

The trial was a scandal. Somehow the killer claimed it was a crime of passion. And he only got six years.

I looked this up, and Lucy is correct. The verdict was a travesty. The killer's name was Sweeney.

As I recall, says Lucy, *that man has been free for years. The murder was in 1982. It was a shocking thing.*

This is a matter of record. Dominique's father, Dominick Dunne, wrote about it. Her mother formed a relief group.

That Sweeney is out there, she said. *I believe he may be in these parts.* She looked at our surrounding evening, as if to say, *I told you so.*

Not long after that, we did a binge on *Killing Eve.* We hadn't got into that show at first, but now the overlap of investigator and assassin seemed to mean more. I still don't count myself a fan, and I think the show fell off a lot. But Jodie Comer was intriguing as the killer, and you felt she longed to be found out. That first season of *Killing Eve* was all written by Phoebe Waller-Bridge so I am reminded of how she broke on the scene with *Fleabag* (2016) and her decision to talk to us, as if the complicity had to be owned up to and made part of the show. And Phoebe was funny, and affectionate.

She took our breath away. But where's she gone now?

20

All Our Sad Detectives

In movies, from the outset, there has been a game of search and find. There does not have to be a crime, much less a murder, but we are required to follow a story, to assemble its clever clues. The whole enterprise presupposes a solution, or a destination. At the end of *Citizen Kane*, when the journalists say they have given up on finding an answer to "Rosebud," the camera stays behind as workers start to feed the Kane possessions into the furnace. Then the camera travels, as with a life of its own, and it fixes on a laborer who has picked up a childhood sled. And we go with it to the threshold of the fire.

We have been detectives, and if the inquiry was a joy there will be a touch of sadness when the "mystery" is solved. Isn't there a more profound unknown—the hope of storytelling—that lies behind all the mystery stories? Isn't that what makes us think of story as an answer or an alternative to helpless existence?

I remember, says Lucy, *at the National Film Theatre in London, there was this woman, she came to many films and liked to sit on the end of a row. Time and again, five minutes before the end of a picture she would get up and leave.*

To catch her bus home? I wonder.

I think she could not bear to see the story settled.

I like that, I say. In the early days of surrealism, a gang of them would go to the movies in Paris. They would enter, twenty minutes or so into a picture, and they'd sit there not knowing what was happening. But then as soon as they had worked out the story situation they would get up and leave.

And go to another cinema? she guesses. *I wonder what it is like to be in love with a surrealist?*

In Britain, in 1962, *Z Cars* began. It was created for the BBC by two good writers, Troy Kennedy Martin and Allan Prior, and it would last until 1978, or 801 episodes. The nation knew it was different, after the homilies of *Dixon of Dock Green.* This show was set in the tougher north of England, just outside Liverpool, with two-man patrol cars going after reports of criminal activities. The cases were often sordid, and the treatment was startlingly naturalistic. The show gripped the audience and it coincided with reports in the news that real coppers might be bent, corrupt, crazed, and at the end of their tether. In a changing society real policemen often proved very conservative, and angry at what they were seeing. As if these truths had always been known, the British audience accepted a more mixed view of life.

Even so, the cops in *Z Cars* were likable characters, doing their best, and suffering under a blustering, bullying chief inspector, played by Stratford Johns. There was one episode, written by John Hopkins, about a sex criminal, a child-killer, and a policeman who loses control in interrogating him and kills him. It was so strong it became a stage play and then a movie, *The Offence* (1973), directed by Sidney Lumet, with Sean Connery as the cop and Ian Bannen as the pederast. But somehow on the big screen it seemed tidy after being raw and shocking in our living room.

A rival to *Z Cars* in its first years was an American series that crossed the Atlantic. There was a general feeling that most American cops were too uncouth or melodramatic for British audiences to comprehend. This show was *Naked City* (1958–63), and it was prompted by a 1948 movie, produced by Mark Hellinger and directed by Jules Dassin, that had been shot largely on the city streets and which included reference to New York as "a naked city" with five million stories (it became eight million for the TV series). The TV show was devised and often written by Stirling Silliphant, one of the most adept and productive of screenwriters.

It was solidly dutiful and it had a gloss of the real, but the cops were good or unshakable guys: John McIntire and then Horace McMahon as the chiefs, and James Franciscus and Paul Burke as their juniors. It was movie-like still in that it intended to have us like and trust these policemen. That trust was not just personal. It was institutional, for it told us that everything was going to be all right, a creed that hardly prepared us for the wildness in Texas in November 1963, and in the rest of the country since then. That is not to attack Dallas or Texas, or to add to conspiracy theories. But it is a way of attesting to the common experience that—as much as any of us—cops could be dishonest, brutal, and incompetent. All those things were now more likely to be observed and recorded by video coverage on the streets. What did we expect? Sherlock Holmes? What had Officer Derek Chauvin expected in Minneapolis in May 2020? Didn't he watch TV? Didn't he understand a nine-minute shot?

Z Cars and *Naked City* stayed episodic, without a streaming storyline in which we saw the characters develop, though Paul Burke in *Naked City* did have a girlfriend (played by Nancy Malone) who seemed an attempt to get a female audience. Little suggested that cops might crack under the strain, might break down, might yield to the complex political pressures that affected police forces on the job. As yet, few understood that policing was an instrument of power in a society where new liberties were battling reaction. Order was always a political concept. I say that to recall how the police aspect of the story in *Our Friends in the North* was an attempt to track the place of corruption, and the police's own diligence in hushing it up.

A comical version of that insistence on immaculate integrity in cops can be seen in *Columbo,* where Peter Falk became endearing for his dirty raincoat and his slovenly personal habits while unfailing in his job and as serene as Galahad. *Columbo* ran from 1971 to 1990 and it was all "personality." It was set in Los Angeles, to have easy access to guest stars. The formula was fixed: we were shown a murder and the murderer, and then homicide detective Columbo entered in his shambling way, an apparent street person going up against spick-and-span celebrity villains. It may surprise you that an early idea for the show was to have Bing Crosby as the detective. Yes, Falk worked far better, and it turned him from a fringe actor known for originality and daring into a household star imitated by kids—such a radical and ironic shift might have driven him mad or pushed him into his own act of murder, killing Mrs. Columbo, perhaps (often mentioned, never seen, or not until a sequel, where Kate Mulgrew had the part), thus allowing a finale in which he would be called in to investigate himself—the one case, with scratched head and many sighs, he could never solve.

The show was created by Richard Levinson and William Link for Universal Television and NBC, and it may have reassured the bourgeoisie about every dastardly murder or break-in being solved—so long as they could tolerate having this unwashed, mumbling vagrant in their house. (Falk wore his own clothes for the part.) To be a star in Hollywood, especially a star in semiretirement, and not to have done a *Columbo* episode, was a mark of ignominy. The very talented Patrick McGoohan (creator and star of that surreal paranoid classic *The Prisoner*, 1968) was a hired-in scoundrel four times on the show. Unable to develop his own projects, he also directed five episodes. It is worth adding that the very first episode, "Murder by the Book," was written by Steven Bochco, and directed by someone named Steven Spielberg. That was 1971, just before Spielberg directed *Duel*. Falk died with four Emmys for *Columbo*. He was very rich by then, but he had his own dementia.

In this survey I have passed over dozens of routine police or crime shows—*The F.B.I., Mannix* (a private detective), *Hawaii Five-O, The Streets of San Francisco, Kojak,* the aforementioned *Police Woman, Starsky and Hutch, Baretta, CHiPS*—all of them episodic, built around alleged star presences and single-mindedly devoted to police probity, courage, and prowess. But there were stirrings, convinced that many cops had difficult lives as they grew older in a society increasingly troubled over defining liberty. There were notions afoot that a police station was a site of community, well-intentioned, but confused and often distraught over the job. So many basic functions in

American society—even being successful and happy—were under examination. Could television match up to this uneasiness?

Steven Bochco was born in New York in 1943, and educated at Carnegie Mellon. As a young screenwriter, he had worked on *Ironside* and *McMillan & Wife* as well as *Columbo*. In 1978, he joined MTM Productions, the company led by Grant Tinker that focused on Mrs. Tinker, Mary Tyler Moore. (To think of Mary is to appreciate our lost confidence.) It was an outfit that understood family, community, and humor. So maybe a police station could be funny sometimes? Prompted by Brandon Tartikoff, the production head at NBC, MTM gave Bochco and Michael Kozoll the go-ahead to develop a new kind of police show, *Hill Street Blues,* the start of so many possibilities.

Hill Street was in an unnamed American city, and it had characters with unresolved lives that weren't shelved in the name of catching crooks. There was a better than TV-normal racial mix; there were women in view; and there was a hell of a lot going on, all at the same time. That was the originality of the Bochco-Kozoll approach. So many cop shows had been built around elderly stars who said the same thing every week. *Hill Street Blues* was emphatically a group show—and that variety made it hard to grasp at first. In its early seasons the show seemed a disappointment; maybe the regular cop show audience preferred set attitudes, repeated plots, and clichéd dialogue. Such shows had enjoyed a solid male audience, working class, from the hinterland, not unduly educated or cool with the manners of screwball comedy. But *Hill Street Blues* was funny, and willing to puncture old male stereotypes.

The lead, Captain Frank Furillo (Daniel J. Travanti), had an ex-wife and a new lover to negotiate, and his lover was an attorney he might meet in court. A lot of the other cops were offbeat or eccentric—with a cast that was a gallery for supporting actor quirkiness: Bruce Weitz, Joe Spano, Michael Warren, Charles Haid, Kiel Martin, Taurean Blacque, Betty Thomas, and James Sikking. It was no mean feat to keep them all in play, to tell case stories, while letting their lives unfold. So it was clever to have a desk sergeant as a kind of traffic cop for the show. That was Phil Esterhaus, played by Michael Conrad, and as that actor faced his own death so the character became beloved. There was also a stupid and none too honest chief in view, played by Jon Cypher.

Esterhaus was a dreamboat, like the sergeants in old war movies, but cool as Bob Newhart. I could have stood being cautioned by Phil.

Once you got the hang of it, *Hill Street* was a pleasing show—witty, humane, unexpected, written and acted more in the spirit of movies of that time than according to the rubber-stamped process of a *Mannix.* The camera was handheld sometimes, in the action instead of organizing it as tableaux. The audience grew and it was a new crowd for a police show: they were more liberal, better educated, and more open to what was happening in America (and *Hill Street* was the early '80s, as stuff was coming apart). It attracted a group of writers who would do good work on television for years. The critics loved the show (and they enjoyed the new respect for television criticism); in time it would win four Emmys for drama series. Many of the players won awards, too. Betty Thomas was nominated as supporting actress in every season, with one win. This was a TV version of ensemble acting such as had been evident in some movies by Robert Altman. The show ran from 1981 to 1987 (146 episodes), yet it was never in the top ten—*The Cosby Show, Dallas, The A-Team, Dynasty,* and *Murder, She Wrote* did far better. But something serious had occurred: an audience that had preferred movies in theatres realized that television could keep them home. There were even tentative hints of a degree of sex and violence that was waiting for cable and the legitimization of a less than universal audience.

That said, on going back to *Hill Street Blues,* I felt nostalgic respect, but not quite excitement. Of course, television has always said it wants us now, and not forty years later. Still, I have more fun now with a short-lived show that came in the last years of *Hill Street Blues.* It was *Crime Story* (1986–88).

By the mid-'80s, Michael Mann was a promising movie director. He had made *Thief* and *Manhunter* and had been the driving force behind *Miami Vice,* a television cop show more interested in the sheen of Miami, the design of clothes, and the pulse of music than in anything else. But the show was such a success on NBC, and it so appealed to a young audience with spending power, that the network told Mann he had a free hand with whatever he wanted to do next. He was not timid in taking that offer.

Networks traditionally had looked for long marriages—why not seven seasons?—but now they were sniffing quick affairs. To make a series for television is generally to assume a long view. It has assembled scripts, crew people, sets, and actors—it is a campaign, with budgets and forecasts. Against that, a lot of feature films still felt sudden or headlong, with sensational, ravishing, but destructive couples, like Bonnie meeting Clyde, so we have to go with them, we have no defenses. *Crime Story* was like that from the plangent wailing of Del Shannon's "Runaway" as its theme music and into the notion of an existential blood feud between a Chicago cop, Mike Torello (Dennis Farina), and a young gangster, Ray Luca (Anthony Denison)—though Torello the cop carried himself with a gangster swagger.

I wanted to go where Runaway *might be going.*

The setup was not plausible, but such thoughts were swept away by the story being a clear-cut serial. At last the medium had decided to let streaming stream. Thus, in two seasons, the pursuit moved from the Midwest to Las Vegas and a desert where nuclear weapons were being tested. The plan was to be impulsive, violent, and sexy, a graphic novel brought to life. It refused to be a regular series. There were lovely and reckless women played by Darlanne Fluegel and Patricia Charbonneau. There was a genuine sleazeball in Pauli Taglia (John Santucci), the sort of wrecked guy who didn't normally get on TV.

It felt as if the show had been invaded.

Crime Story had not just fans but punk cultists, all of whom guessed the show was doomed. It would be lucky if it finished two seasons. But it was a blast and it had a feeling of a dangerous America that foreshadowed *Breaking Bad* and *Ozark*. Somehow Mann and his collaborators reckoned the show had enough of us by the throat, so the storyline took no prisoners. You had to watch every week. In that failure to be businesslike a true frenzy was unleashed.

I always wanted more Ray Luca, says Lucy.

Like salted caramel, he made Torello seem vanilla and humorless. As if lawfulness had turned quaint or historical.

You wouldn't say no to a weekend at the Mirage with Ray.

That place opened just a year after *Crime Story* closed.

The year we visited the Nevada Test Site and the guy said not to worry because all the radiation was at the bottom of the crater.

Why did you like Luca?

Trash, I guess.

And you wonder about having an affair with a surrealist.

Steven Bochco was not just a personal success from *Hill Street Blues;* he was a model for how an ingenious and hardworking writer might become the operational genius in TV. Genius can have quotation marks or not, depending on what the person does next. Before *Hill Street* was over, Bochco (with Jeffrey Lewis) had created another series, *Bay City Blues,* about a Minor League Baseball team, another ensemble show. Only four episodes aired before cancellation, and Bochco was fired from MTM.

He bounced back with *L.A. Law* at NBC, starting in 1986, recognizing that a law office was another kind of police station. The principle was building that no country can understand its police force without being prepared to face the compromises we use in the practice of law. That show ran until 1994, so it overshadowed the aberration of *Cop Rock* (1990), a police show force-fed into being a musical. That was a lesson in how far surrealism could not go.

Cop Rock seemed outlandish, and it died after one season. What was Bochco thinking, industry wisdom asked, when he had come to understand network needs so well? One answer was that he was chronically rebellious, no matter that he loved team setups. Another was that he might have been transported by a six-episode masterpiece from the BBC in 1986, a show that blended noir archetypes with old popular songs. It was produced by Rick McCallum and Kenith Trodd, directed by Jon Amiel, starring Michael Gambon, and a cast that included Jim Carter, Patrick Malahide, Bill Paterson, and Joanne Whalley—*The Singing Detective*. That show had alarmed the BBC, and it upset many British audiences with its sexual undergrowth, but its greatest threat was to standardized TV. In that "error" it was one of several works that let the writer Dennis Potter loose. When it appeared, many viewers said it felt like a movie, with dreams and reality in competition, a musical and a tragedy, without noticing how few movies were like that anymore.

There was no way a *Singing Detective* could work in the 1980s on American television. But that tells us more about the system than about the madness in Potter.

Whatever, Steven Bochco reassembled his businesslike reputation, and he was persuaded to repeat what he had done before: a cop show, an ensemble, and he called it *NYPD Blue* (though it was largely filmed in Los Angeles). It was instantly understandable as a concept, though there were innovations. Network television was already shamed by or envious of liberties being taken on cable, often in matters of sex and violence. In all of this, Bochco was helped by a new collaborator, David Milch.

Milch, born in Buffalo in 1945, had been to Yale as a student and then a teacher. He was writing fiction as he drifted to TV and became a scriptwriter on *Hill Street Blues* and then on all the other Bochco shows. He was brilliant and difficult, and as much an original as Dennis Potter. He also shared the English writer's reliance on illness. But Milch was friendly with a real cop, Bill Clark, who would become a producer on *NYPD Blue*. And it was Milch who had the instinct that some cops might be self-destructives and psychotics.

The new show began with partners, played by David Caruso and Dennis Franz—officers John Kelly and Andy Sipowicz. The pairing was telling. Caruso was or believed he was cool and handsome, a man on the edge of a big movie career. Dennis Franz was none of those things. He tended to be overweight and balding and in any casting contest he was a natural as a villain and lowlife. The two characters were fond of each other, but the show could not quite contain them. Milch suffered a heart attack in an argument with Caruso over a script direction. Soon, Caruso left the show—he would find himself in the endless *CSI* series. But that was only after Andy Sipowicz had become the sour heart of *NYPD Blue*.

It was true to the Bochco-Milch partnership that Sipowicz would come close to a rogue cop who needed to be fired, or indicted. He was alcoholic, foul-mouthed, and right wing; he cut corners and was edging into corruption; he was a disgrace. And Franz flowered as if he understood that we the public were responding to him just as we had come to adore the Corleones and Hannibal Lecter. *NYPD Blue* became a hit—twelve seasons and 261 episodes—and Sipowicz ended up married and a dad. If only all awkward cops could be so rehabilitated. Franz won the lead actor Emmy four times. At its peak, the show had about fifteen million viewers an episode. That was more than enough, but it was way short of the top ten. This hardly mattered in a climate that insisted on a higher and nastier reality weighing on its policemen.

Several affiliate stations refused to carry the show. It was a starred case in arguments that TV standards needed to be reinforced. Ironically, local abstinence arose in parts of the country where the police might be the most free from restraint. That argument was often offered on high-minded moral grounds, but a deeper fear was that a shrinking audience meant less advertising revenue. *Breaking Bad* started in 2008, only three years after *NYPD Blue* ended. And that cable show managed on an audience of about three million, rising a good deal higher for its last season.

It was telling that *NYPD Blue* had pursued Sipowicz to a point of breakdown, or indictment, and then reined him in in its recovery system. One could imagine in the emotional framework of *Crime Story* that Sipowicz would have collapsed or become impossible as a network figure. What would happen with Walter White was the medium's way of admitting the pressure can be too much—a good man is growing darker every day. And in subscribing to the cable stations—taking that package—America was going along with this new, bleak contract. In fifty years, television had abandoned the pursuit of happiness on which it had seemed to be based. So cops were now less convincing as guides and guardians than as rueful warnings of our downfall. There was a way television had turned on us as if certain we had been guilty all along.

The guilt is profound and pervasive and we will have to get to it later—unless we need to agree to abide in that state on our couch. But in 2014, the first season of *True Detective* had an average audience of about 2.3 million on HBO. Perhaps it reached 10 million in DVDs and streaming reruns. But that was on a population of 300 million. In the early '50s, with a population half what it is now, with TV only in so many homes, *Dragnet* averaged 15 million a show. So *True Detective* hardly seems like a mass medium—until you *realize that 2.3 million sales for a novel would be extraordinary.* And *True Detective* was in the running for the best work of American fiction for 2014.

One could write a short book about its implications, or a short history of lost authority. It was the story of two detectives in rural Louisiana, Cohle and Hart, and the way they are haunted by memories of a sex crime they never solved. Spanning two decades, with the guys being interviewed for a later investigation, the show was filled with uncertain memory, the occult nature of the killings, and the contorted sex lives of the detectives. The third lead character was Hart's wife, with whom Cohle would have an affair. The wife was played by Michelle Monaghan. The detectives were Matthew McConaughey and Woody Harrelson, and their wavering presence and fervent talk held the characters in place, no matter that the plot could be elusive. It was more like reading Faulkner than going with an episode of *Columbo* or *Hill Street Blues.* It was a study of broken American manhood, and that may have played a part in driving the grotesque rage ahead to make America and its masculinity great again.

Two other seasons of *True Detective* followed, and they were nowhere near as compelling. But the first season, all written by Nic Pizzolatto and directed by Cary Joji Fukunaga, had achieved what seemed impossible—to find an equivalent of *The Singing Detective* made not just in America but in the back country of Louisiana. The filming of that landscape courted a beauty that television seldom entered into—as if beauty might upset audiences being sold tidiness and glamour. It was the work of cinematographer Adam Arkapaw, who had also shot Jane Campion's *Top of the Lake* (2013), another study in bereft landscape (in New Zealand). In *True Detective*'s network of conflicting stories, the overcast weather of rumor and folklore, and the proximity of supernatural yearnings, one felt America as a lost frontier or a forlorn wilderness that the Western had been afraid of treating. In its mournful view of open ground, we felt how we had betrayed nature. *True Detective* 1 was as honorably pretentious as it was beautiful, as desolate as it could be piercing. And in that pause you recognized that television had always been intimidated about reaching for poetry.

I used to love listening to those sad men storytelling.

Actors as well as cops.

Unreliable and adorable.

That gets it just right.

Reminds me of you, my surrealist.

What does that mean?

Just because you're the author doesn't tell me I have to trust you. I've got my eye on you.

21

In the Prison of *Law & Order*

I've done my time, governor, honest I have. Lying patiently on my sofa, watching all 459 episodes, without anesthesia.

I am ready to speak on your behalf if there is a parole hearing.

Doesn't good behavior count for something? I've been a model prisoner. You'll never find a better one.

We were talking hardcore *Law & Order,* that heartfelt penitentiary experience serving a twenty-year sentence from 1990 to 2010, and still echoing down the corridors of syndication. You have to appreciate Lucy's point of view: there's something clammy in the servitude and longevity of this show and its claustrophobic reassurance. Here's a show where the fun is so enclosing it is a kind of solitary confinement. You might think it's tough enough being with a surrealist, but having to watch that show over and over again . . .

I've seen you watching Claire Kincaid episodes over the years.

Which one is she?

Dick Wolf was born in 1945, and he became a copywriter in advertising. But he wanted to write more creatively and that got him into television, doing a few scripts for *Hill Street Blues* and *Miami Vice.* Coming up on 1990, he had the idea for a compartmentalized show in which the cops on New York streets made an arrest, and then that case was turned over to the district attorney's office and brought to trial. The episodes would run no more than forty-five minutes, so a lot of story would have to be crammed into every cell. And there would be terrific, punchy music by Mike Post, with a ker-chung motif that could sound like your cell door closing.

I've heard you go ker-chung at the weirdest moments.

Wolf talked up the show but many places turned it down. They said people were jaded over cop shows, and never grasped how jaded might be the medium's oatmeal. Where would the stories come from? Wolf was asked. He had an answer, from the daily papers—rough urban incidents. The real thing, the real things on the inside pages? He made a pilot, but there were still no takers. Then Brandon Tartikoff looked it over, and surprised Wolf, who believed anything turned down once would always be refused. Tartikoff said NBC would do it. Dead at forty-eight, in 1997, Tartikoff was an executive beloved by creative people (and network shareholders). Over the years he backed so many successful shows, not just *Law & Order,* but *Hill Street Blues, The Cosby Show,* and *Seinfeld.*

At the start of *Law & Order,* Chris Noth and George Dzundza were the cops. Dann Florek was the station captain. Michael Moriarty was the executive district attorney. Richard Brooks was his assistant and Steven Hill was the crusty seen-it-all DA, a man named Adam Schiff—there is a serendipity in TV if you wait long enough. Hill had the bearing of a man ready to quit, but he kept that sourness up for ten seasons. Early on, it became apparent that *Law & Order* was a meal ticket, utterly reliable and bearable. It felt already as if it had been running years.

As time went by, there were cast changes: the cops turned into Paul Sorvino and Jerry Orbach—Orbach would do twelve seasons as Lennie Briscoe, suffering from the prostate cancer that would carry him away, and seeming so caught between boredom and a wisecrack that a degree of hokey naturalism was ascribed to him. Or was he on automatic, another ker-chung?

S. Epatha Merkeson was a station chief, Van Buren, from season 4 to 20. As a rule she had a couple of weary knowing lines in a scene, as if to indicate she had seen it all so often and was not entirely invested in the process. No more than the doors on the cells. It was in season 5 that Sam Waterston came on board as DA Jack McCoy, an aggressive lawyer who would sometimes push the spirit and the letter of the law. He was the first person on the show with ego and his own convictions. He could seem liberal and then conservative; this made him the most complicated but essentially upright lawyer television had ever had. Later in life, McCoy did think about getting into politics, but he realized he was too much of a loner.

The show was a hit before Waterston appeared, but he codified its structure and made it clear that we should be more interested in the lawyering section of the show. So often, it was the attorneys who faced the best challenges, and who exercised skill in trapping the guilty parties. It was there, too, that the guest stars—the perpetrators or the victims—got a chance to shine. Invariably they were depicted as liars, but our regulars were straight arrows. We never saw the cops' or the lawyers' homes or their domestic situations. But Jack McCoy did drop passing details for sleuths watching the show, enough to put a case together. He had been married twice and divorced; he was estranged from a daughter. Was he a workaholic? Isn't that what we expect in a DA? Yet it did seem to be the case that Jack was into having affairs with his assistants.

Don't forget that chorus line, or the one in the puce blouse.

Is that Claire Kincaid?

Don't you know her every line, ker-chung?

Sometimes a writer has to rise above the heckling. It became apparent that the show was prepared for a tradition of attractive young female assistants to the DA. So for season 4, actor Richard Brooks was replaced with Jill Hennessy as Claire Kincaid.

She was all detail: with too little to do as her character, she favored every sidelong glance and off-kilter walk. She did three seasons and then moved on (not to be typecast or imprisoned?) and was replaced in succession by Carey Lowell, Angie Harmon, Elisabeth Rohm, and Alana De La Garza. It felt as if our law schools had resolved to supply the courts with smart, cool, well-dressed lookers. How did legal assistants afford those clothes? But none was at the Kincaid level, and hints along the way suggested that she and McCoy had had a fling (though she had also had an affair with a corrupt judge her office was pursuing). Then, Claire was badly injured in a car crash caused by Jerry Orbach's character. He gave up booze because of it and then later it was reported that Claire had died. Jack McCoy was what you had to call cut up. There *had* been something between them, something never said. It's one of the unopened boxes on TV.

I admire the way you're being judicious about this.

Maybe that is the influence of the show, with its stress on evidence and reasoning, and—

A puce blouse beneath a gray jacket.

Your honor, I'll speak candidly; I'll come clean. *Law & Order* was a level-headed charade, a trick by which the true role of justice in society was traded away for a hit show so that elderly people in Scarsdale or Los Altos could take some comfort in how the vagaries of society and the unruliness of American justice could be constrained or smoothed over by loyal supporting actors and the homily that, more or less, everything would be all right. Go to commercials. We'll be right back.

Law & Order had good writers who learned how to tell tricky short stories quickly while keeping in touch with all our favorite characters. It sometimes drew upon real cases in which the law had been stretched and revised because of new technologies and hitherto unappreciated depths of iniquity. The guest players often had a ball, and fought for Emmys. Jane Alexander, Barbara Barrie, Shirley Knight, and Julia Roberts were all nominated for guest shots, and Elaine Stritch actually won. Roberts was in a 1999 episode about a man who died from overdosing on a sexual-enhancement drug. She did not play the man. The "incidents" in the show pretended to be from newspapers, but they were seldom that dull or commonplace.

But the speed and polish of the prison cell did not hide the confinement of the concept. This was less justice or the actual workings of law than stereotyped TV, in which the full, demanding turmoil of case studies was turned into a set of tidy boxes and the easy conclusion that the model was working. Would that that were the case. If only the quandaries of justice could conform to 45-minute episodes. If only our real cases were played so swiftly and with such aplomb, instead of being subject to delays and financial shortcomings and the different degrees of skill in lawyers who reached beyond the show's pretty women and nifty clothes.

There was another implicit lie smothered by that ampersand: that every ugly incident was detected and brought to some verdict. But in actuality the police often draw a blank, and losses and resentments are discarded because no one can afford the proceedings or live long enough to see them through. Countless offenses in everyday life, trivial but wounding, go unnoted and uncorrected. The law (lowercase) has learned to live with its limits, and yet the public are still suckers for capital-letter Law, and the pipedream of virtue existing in splendor.

No matter how often in your tired life you watched the show, wistful over Claire Kincaid or the cop played by Benjamin Bratt, the cases that came up for public attention ignored the impoverished imagination and cruel impulses of so many people who regarded justice as once the Irish, the Germans, or the Russians thought of America. Never mind the Blacks.

Law & Order was a very tidy diversion masquerading as real: that's how it ran twenty years, and launched so many spin-offs. It filled the hours for lonely people and left Dick Wolf with $500 million in net worth. Why not? If you can keep fifteen million of us attentive—and maintain that hold for decades—you have served a significant purpose without ever telling us that the unfairness in our society is outrageous, and might be within the scope of reform. Ker-chung is the sound of a slot machine, a swallowing, or a bullet in its chamber.

Law & Order is a big title and it means more every day than war and peace. But in the show it all came down to bread and butter.

Oh, that's cool and grand. I can see that Claire Kincaid giving you a demure grateful eye.

There is a merriment in watching together, and it can be at its height with a show one has absorbed without ever quite admiring it. So we watch *Law & Order* by talking back to the screen and its prim routines: McCoy bristles—Adam Schiff groans silently—Claire Kincaid wants to say something acerbic, but bides her time. So it goes, and that can be more calming than the latest broken-up reports from Ukraine. It may be as hard to conceive of a responding attack in that pained country, a refusal to take it, as it would be to hear Kincaid telling McCoy, "What the hell is going on, Jack? Are we playing *I Love Lucy* instead of owning up to ourselves?"

Sometimes you have to leave a show and forget its silly sweetness.

22

The Night Of

Detection is a version of writing and watching. It needs a nose for in-trigue, or the urge to turn untidy, wayward life into a thing called plot. It presumes there is something worth solving, a Maltese falcon or some double helix of happiness. Often the writer is in the dark, too; he or she simply doesn't know what they are looking for. Once in a while, the discovery comes to the authors and to us the watchers at the same time.

The Night Of (2016) is an alluring title, with signals of a police proce-dural that could sink into the extra depth of night or noir. The series opens with black-and-white views of New York at night where darkness is brushed with overcast or fog—or is it the imprint of doubt or malaise? It's a while since New York has been wonderful, or exuberant, a place for young people to go "on the town."

The ways to photograph that city now are as a labyrinth, or an inescapable place. So The Night Of *begins like an old movie about existential atmosphere.*

But we wonder at the title breaking off in midair and being left cryptic. What will happen on this night, or did it happen in the past? Are we left wanting to know what occurred, without any thought that it was good or bad? Or are we drawn to the implications in that unanswered "of"? Who owns or runs this night? Is it ours, or are we just homeless in the nocturnal grid, without a chance of ownership? Are we following a story or absorbing a condition? Is this mood the creation of New York, or of television?

I don't think that question is going too far—it's in the title—that this story may have a mystery that exceeds our simpleminded estimate of the shape of things and the sheltering sky of law and order. From the start, the music (by Jeff Russo) knows more than we do. Don't expect to find some tidy satisfaction just because you're watching TV.

But it's promising in its credits because *The Night Of* is created, written, and directed by a special partnership: Richard Price and Steven Zaillian. That seems like a threshold to narrative accomplishment as well as a gut feeling for seething street life. By the time of *The Night Of,* Zaillian had done the screenplays for many pictures, including *Schindler's List, Gangs of New York, American Gangster, Moneyball,* and *The Girl with the Dragon Tattoo.* A class act, and a director, too, on *Searching for Bobby Fischer, A Civil Action,* and *All the King's Men.* It's true, none of those films he directed was at the level of the films he wrote for other people. But one respects a writer who wants to be a complete movie author. More than that, one of the eight episodes of *The Night Of* would be directed by James Marsh, an Englishman who had directed one part of *Red Riding* as well as the extraordinary essay film *Wisconsin Death Trip,* derived from Michael Lesy's photographic book on shattering events in Black River Falls, Wisconsin, in the late nineteenth century (one of the first instances of noir pathology in U.S. history). Marsh had also directed the documentary *Man on Wire,* about the man who did a high-wire walk between the Twin Towers of Lower Manhattan in 1974.

You have to tell people to hunt down Wisconsin Death Trip—*it is one of the great films.*

Beyond that, all of *The Night Of* was written by Richard Price, one of the best realist novelists of street life and the author of *The Wanderers, The Breaks, Clockers,* and *Lush Life.* He had always been in love with movies, so he worked as a screenwriter on many films, notably *The Color of Money, Sea of Love, Night and the City, Mad Dog and Glory, Kiss of Death,* and some episodes of *The Wire.* You can't count on credits in advance, but this was a prestige lineup that was hard to resist. In addition, *The Night Of* was derived from a British TV series, *Criminal Justice,* that had been created by Peter Moffat. James Gandolfini was listed as an executive producer, but sometimes that means no more than that he came to dinner once. Gandolfini was dead three years before *The Night Of* played. But he had been ready to act in it in 2013—would he have been the lawyer (John Turturro) or the detective (Bill Camp)? Or some other character we don't know?

None of which mattered once we fixed on the pale face of Naz Khan surrounded by the night. Decades of track records come down to just such a hesitant image and the presence of an actor like Riz Ahmed. Naz was maybe twenty, a cautious but eager outsider who yearned for romance and the chance of getting laid. So this promising college student goes out one night, without permission, taking the taxi his father drives. He will go from Queens, where they live, to the mythic Manhattan and a big party he's heard about. It's the kind of thing a timid kid on the edge does, especially if his parents are earnest and respectable immigrants from Pakistan, a country Naz has never seen.

So he's driving in a city he hardly knows with a taxi that has a *for hire* light he can't turn off. Then a young woman gets in the cab at a light, expecting to be driven. Naz goes along with this because she's lovely, with an odd, still calm, and because he wants to be taken over. Her name is Andrea (Sofia Black-D'Elia); she's white and rather listlessly available. You could fall for her, and you feel that she has been chosen, or cast. They drive, they talk, they sit and look at the water. It's one of those movie passages where two young people are sinking into each other. She takes him to a house, the place where she lives. The house is empty but unexpectedly grand. They have a drink together; they play risky games with a knife; they do a few drugs; they have sex. It's like a dream for Naz—and for us? Film has always been like this.

Have you noticed how these days there are sexual situations on screen— maybe sweet and romantic—where there is a hint at violence to come? It's in the way of filming sex, a slight touch of it being illicit. I think it's the influence of pornography. Isn't there a hint in that genre that the guys might murder the women?

Naz wakes up in the kitchen of the house; it is still night and he realizes he needs to leave. He goes looking for Andrea to say goodbye, and finds her corpse on the bed they had shared, wreathed in the blood from twenty-two stab wounds. He panics and runs away, but it's not long in a tangled procedural before he's picked up by the police who find the knife he took from the house. Before the night is over he is a murder suspect.

This has been a riveting start, a plunge from romance to terrible violence. The cops talk like real cops, or in what I trust is Richard Price's ear for sharp language. Andrea was beautiful and obliging, and then she is savaged—though all we see of that is her bloodied body. The house is mysterious, or like a character. Then there is Detective Box on the case, the one and only Bill Camp. And there is the face of Riz Ahmed, not actorly or explained, but wounded and afraid. He is the sort of utterly present but withheld actor movie has always fed on. We care about Naz—we are interested in him, because of the face as much as the script placement. You can't ask for more, and it's liberating that he is not explained or laid out in full. To remain mysterious after eight hours requires depth in an actor.

This has made a great first episode, with seven more to come. The shape and prospect of a series sets in, and we start to wonder how the misguided but innocent Naz is going to come through this great test. We agree with ourselves to be back for HBO at the same time next week. The arc and context of "the night of" seems clear, like a ballgame just beginning. We feel glad about it because we trust how such things operate.

Then it relaxes—tactfully, creatively, with the steady application of talent, in a style that has so many things to keep you watching. But as things slacken, the show becomes an intriguing mess, enough to make you think those several talents never quite agreed on what they were doing and left the responsibility to the face of Riz Ahmed. Naz becomes older, a little harder or more suspicious, waiting for his trial on Rikers Island, maybe the most effective finishing school in the United States. As the "story" moves on, we come to see that "the night" is metaphor for a wider moral confusion in the city.

Naz insists he didn't kill Andrea; his story has been shaped to have us believe in that. And there's never any doubt about how taut and frightening a story can be if it involves someone we like who is being falsely accused. We appreciate Bill Camp's detective because he won't shrug off his instinct that Naz did not do it.

We will meet Naz's parents; they are decent and sympathetic. Naz's case is picked up by a hapless lawyer who acquires clients by hanging around the police station and the courts. This man, John Stone, is played—brilliantly—by John Turturro, and Stone is hampered and humiliated by a serious case of eczema in his feet. It's not that one has no sympathy for this malady, but early on we've had enough of it already—so we start to wonder whether Price and Zaillian intended it as a significant metaphor, something that was going to pay off in the end, or be part of our noir overcast. (Note: Richard Price suffers from asthma; and Peter Moffat, the original writer on *Criminal Justice,* has eczema. Does any of this help *The Night Of,* or end up less bewildering?)

So here's a point that takes us into the structure of extended television narratives. It may be irritating that so much time is devoted to Stone's feet when neither he nor Bill Camp's detective wonder about Andrea's life. That fatal house, on West 87th Street, sighs with money. This aimless girl owns that big house—valued at $10 million? That should prompt Stone and the detective to think about someone else killing Andrea—someone who knew her better than Naz. She was stabbed twenty-two times, and she was twenty-two years old. Do you see how composing a story can draw you into fragments of motive or causation that you may call clues, or rungs on the ladder?

It takes too long for investigation to put together a stepfather for Andrea (not a nice guy), a financial adviser to her life (no better), and the framework for a fuller reading of the case. So people who knew her wanted Andrea dead; did Naz simply blunder into that situation to be sent to prison for many episodes? The perfunctory cops on *Law & Order* could have worked this out in half an hour. There is a way in which the acuity of cops meshes with our acquired acumen from decades of watching thrillers and believing that some-body must have dunnit. Of course, that's hard on actual cops who have a clearance rate of about 60 percent.

Did the show want to say Rikers Island should be closed; that we should be more sympathetic to immigrants, or not wake up in the kitchen after good sex; or that there may be a darkness behind faces as begging as that of Naz? There is early advice from Stone that cases and trials have less to do with "the truth" than how things are presented. There are hints of a storyline in which innocent and impoverished young people (especially those of color) can get trashed by the system, even where Bill Camp plays a decent and sensitive cop—he listens to classical music on his car radio, and he is about to retire. (In fiction, don't we know that retiring cops are facing trouble?)

There is also the subtext of a thoroughly nocturnal or warped world. That is the outlaw version of our well-meaning society, the power-game on Rikers Island, where nearly every inmate is of color. Naz is properly afraid of con-ditions in that prison, but quickly he is taken up by Freddie (Michael Ken-neth Williams), a sultry boss in the joint and someone who is drawn to Naz because of his intelligence. I'm shy of putting it that way or suggesting that Freddie has no other reason for making Naz his boy. The homosexual feeling in this setup is not explored—but maybe HBO (that H stands for home) concluded that that would deter a lot of the audience they wanted (though the sex between Naz and Andrea was permitted, and lively). Better still, if Naz begins to fall for Chandra, the young Indian lawyer who starts to work on his case (she is as pretty as her actress, Amara Karan), then isn't the whole show "humanized" a little? Or is that too tidy?

Don't misunderstand me: week by week the unwinding episodes hooked audiences and delighted critics. At every turn, there were fresh, unconven-tional roles to attend to: Jeannie Berlin as a sour and sweet district attorney; Glenne Headly as a calculating lawyer; Chip Zien exquisite as a learned pathologist; and always John Turturro fretting over his damned feet and his inability to get an erection because of the medication he's taking. Turturro is a treasure to behold at work, but he was cultivating a dead end. At one point in the story, on the subway, a woman sitting next to Stone moves away from him when she sees him rubbing at his ulcerated feet. I felt the same need for distance; while Turturro was presenting a fascinating outcast in the New York legal system, I didn't want to know. Though I did recollect the greater pathos or torment of Michael Gambon's skin disease in *The Singing Detective*. There is itching and there is mortification.

The Night Of went eight episodes, and it ended up with a hung jury and Naz as a free man, though it was apparent that his misadventure had hardened him and cut him off from being a son his parents could trust. In fact, the show went further: there are hints that the young adventurer was doing drugs on his own before he met Andrea. And there is still the vestige of a plot line that he might even have killed Andrea. As if Price and Zaillian couldn't bear to exclude that possibility. Even now, the series nags at a closer viewing, and Naz admits to being not quite sure what he did, or how he woke up in the kitchen. At Rikers, he has assisted in the killing of another prisoner—he *is* capable of such things. In short, *The Night Of* is an anthology of its own prospects, increasingly frustrating as it fills its time with "irrelevant" material but growing into a fuller portrait of its night.

This is a frequent dilemma in TV story construction where often the creative team is not quite sure where the vehicle is headed. In that uncertainty, authorship doesn't like to exclude other promising arcs. No matter that we get too much of Turturro's Stone, I wanted more of Camp's detective and Berlin's DA.

I think those two had an affair in the past. You can't put Camp in a show without getting us to wonder about what else. That's the actor he is. And some of our supporting actors seem like the happiest people around.

There may have been a chance once in the story conferencing that naïve Naz could become as dark as the night. But the show and HBO didn't care to go that far. So in a disappointing way, the night turns into décor while the story is muffled and evaded. But we agree nearly all the time that *The Night*

Of was a terrific show. It won prizes (an Emmy for Ahmed) and its audience built by a factor of four.

It's easy to be critical in hindsight, or to feel part of the writing team, never quite satisfied with the show. But "gritty" material often goes gently on itself in the name of noirishness. There was one more arc available, or there is now. In September 2021, the actor Michael Kenneth Williams (Freddie) was found dead in his Williamsburg apartment after a heroin and fentanyl overdose. He had been renowned as Omar Little in *The Wire,* a sad-eyed gangster living off addicts in overheated Baltimore. People had been drawn to Omar's enigmatic point of view; it was clear that he was unashamedly gay. It is likely you remember him. Years later, his Freddie was immaculate, a suave master in the hell of Rikers. As if he was home being there. But the character was doing drugs all the time—and in what seemed a credible way. When Freddie smiled at his smoke what was Williams thinking? Could we the audience handle a searching multiepisode series on the irony of an actor who wins fame as a dude but can't quite live up to it? I came away wondering whether Williams might have been richer than Naz as a subject.

Imagine him lost in the dream of acting out his self-destructive destiny, like the early Naz transfixed by the look of Andrea in his rearview mirror.

23

The People on TV

More or less, we still want to be decent people. Doing what was once thought of as our duty. Doesn't the vague communal air of TV hope for that?

You feel something benign is in charge. On MSNBC, Rachel Maddow is as jolly as a nice head of school. Yet she's aware that school is in chaos. And sometimes she seems weary.

But that attachment, or even the sense of our part in life, is shaken or diminishing. Is that the drug or the elixir that hides in the cushions on the couch or in our horizontal posture?

Why are we watching? What are we looking for? Are we killing time or are we hopeful of becoming better?

I was talking with a friend the other day about the "best" documentaries up for Oscars in March 2022. "Documentary" is now a rather archaic branding of the truth or the real—and "documentary" is not offered to the large TV audience; it has become as elitist as foreign film. But it is the chance of seeing our country and ourselves. And we have let this seem esoteric.

This is strange when actuality is compelling. We watch January 6 over and over again. And 120 minutes of that Chelsea vs. Liverpool game is classic (the penalty kick melodrama). Raw surveillance footage of an underground car park can be hypnotic; mere watching can seem alluring. Or think of rough combat footage from Ukraine. The last of those would be painful yet not even recognizable because filming warfare accurately is beyond a filmmaker's control or his nerve. Explosions all look alike and tend to be just illustrations of fear or peril. But the surveillance footage of the car park might determine whether you, or someone seeming like you in the half-gloom, put a bomb beneath the steel Tesla or stole an envelope from its glove pocket. And in the intense continuum of Chelsea vs. Liverpool, cutting from one camera to another, you could tell yourself you had followed the game. Your footage might have been employed to resolve whether Sadio Mané or Kai Havertz was offside or not.

So the real has many levels, most of which are too mundane and endless to satisfy the pressures of a feature film. Would it make a difference if that sleek Tesla belonged to Putin or Zelensky? Is the car black or silver steel? How far must context reach for the truth to be upheld? Just the other day, the daughter of a Putin supporter was killed in a car explosion.

But how can we know what happened? Or what "opposition" might be forming? Or did Putin kill off one of his own for "sympathy." All these immense words need to have scare quotes now. The news seems fake because so many of its fragments remind us of old movies. The large public is both bored by documentary and incapable of trusting it.

My friend was arguing that *Summer of Soul* should win the Oscar for 2021. It is a 117-minute documentary, directed by Ahmir "Questlove" Thompson about the 1969 Harlem Cultural Festival in which over six weekends there were open-air concert performances. About forty hours of film were shot, and they feature Nina Simone, Mahalia Jackson, Gladys Knight and the Pips, Sly and the Family Stone, Stevie Wonder, the 5th Dimension, and many others.

The performances are exhilarating and moving, the more so in that the footage and the festival were dormant for many years, taking second place to another festival of that summer, the one at Woodstock. I believed *Summer of Soul* would win the Oscar in two weeks' time (it did).

Did you have money on that?

Remember sweetheart, we have no money.

Summer deserves high praise, prizes, and audiences as a reward for the pleasure it gives. You feel very good with the film, not least because it is artfully constructed as a celebration of Black culture and a plea for its recognition.

My companion was going to vote for this film; she is in the Academy. I am not a member of that organization, but if I were I would have favored *Attica,* that documentary on the 1971 riot or insurrection at that prison in upstate New York.

She didn't like *Attica* because she felt it was old-fashioned and too dependent on talking heads. I suppose I see what she means, but if talking heads are Hitler's secretary (*Blind Spot,* 2003), or Billy Wilder chatting with Volker Schlöndorff (*Billy Wilder Speaks,* 2006), there is immense historical value in listening to the heads even if they are not recalling what happened accurately. Twenty-seven seconds of Shakespeare talking about how he got Prospero wrong could be golden.

As if we really do accuracy. History cannot come close to reliability without admitting our fallible memory, confused or fabricated accounts, and the stories we end up telling one way or another because we find it so hard to recognize events as not happening to us.

I am not saying that the witnesses in *Attica* are lying—but they could be—and any documentary needs to keep that in mind just as in life we have to look at someone talking and decide how far we believe them. The proper object of documentary is to have us question the documents. What *Attica* does deliver is the behavior of the state and local police called for by Commissioner Russell Oswald and Governor Rockefeller (with the approval of Richard Nixon). Another thing the film does is to state the first official declaration that mutinous inmates cut the throats of hostages and then demolish that with precise medical accounts calling all the hostages who died victims of indiscriminate police gunfire.

What happened at Attica in 1971 was an attempt by prisoners (a majority of them Black) to draw attention to overcrowding, poor medical services, sixteen hours a day in lockdown, and general brutality, otherwise known as the enforcement of racial differences. (Or a way of life in the U.S.) Some of the inmates felt they were treated like beasts. *Attica* is not fun or liberating; it does not give you a good time; but it delivers a fair account of what happened in that prison—a state penitentiary that is still fully employed with a similarly disproportionate contingent of inmates of color. And because this is all so long ago, we are left appreciating the endurance of prison systems. We may even be a touch less comfortable with our own cell life.

It matters therefore that the thing we call television is so central as the place where we can see such matters. We have given up on newspapers as a culture; a few of us listen to the radio; but the great majority accepts without questioning that the real stuff, the urgency, gets on television and on our phones. We call it coverage, like fitful sleepers tugging at a blanket.

That's where we go to see the shelling of Kyiv and the trails of refugees heading for Poland. But we cannot tell that they are really going to Poland—or are they coming here to camp on our street? In the same way we cannot be sure that the explosions are fresh or current, and not stock shots from the archive. Enormous commitments of trust are undertaken without much examination, just as we hear that the other side—whichever one that is—is already disseminating false information. The cry of "fake news" may be the ultimate undermining of our humanist ideals. For it has the seed of our anxiety—why are you bothering to watch? Why not go to the songs or the soccer?

Think of the millions of people you have seen on TV, such a crowd that you have forgotten most of them. Is it possible that for all the vividness of faces, the purpose of TV in history has been to teach us forgetfulness, as in a numbing terminus to humanism and the notion of us mattering?

Before we get to Armageddon, could we have Garry Shandling?

In the nature of this book there are so many left out that I no longer notice the unfairness—we like to overlook that part of our being. So I would like to make amends. Here are some people from the box, people or players who have interested me over the years, talking heads in whom I can detect some general principle of value.

Of course, in remembering a few I will have to do without so many more. It's like marriage: you can only marry the people you meet.

Or some of them. Just remember that, sweetheart.

The other day we were watching the first episodes of a miniseries, *The Dropout*. Created by Elizabeth Meriwether, it intends to be the story of Elizabeth Holmes, who dropped out of Stanford at age nineteen to develop a company proposing a revolutionary method of blood-testing. This biotechnology venture was called Theranos, and Holmes raised large sums of money on mere assertion and her personal appeal. In her twenties, she was a force and a performance, dressed in black, speaking in a low voice, like Blossom Dearie becoming Darth Vader. But then her scheme foundered because it did not work. So she ended up in court and was convicted of fraud in January 2022 (only two months before the show opened). She was sentenced in October to eleven years in prison.

You can understand why Hulu felt this was series-worthy. That decision was made ahead of the trial, so they were gambling on her guilt, ruling out the Joan of Arc angle. But ask yourself which element in the story was most pressing or important: that a bold young woman carried off a fraud; that her society had yielded to the deceit; or even that her dream might vanquish the science?

There is a subtext in *The Dropout* that ought to hook any patient or practitioner: it is the possibility that doctoring, or wellness, is becoming a discourse carried out on TV, virtually but not actually. This was accentuated during the lockdown, but it was there before it. So much of going to our doctor is a matter of sophisticated tests and referrals to specialists. If you have a good doctor then it is hard to get an appointment. You may be passed off on a nurse practitioner. And any doctor is going to require you to get bloodwork at a lab. The technology is diagnosing you.

Is it science fiction or future fact to think that one day you might insert your finger in a very smart phone and have the analysis just an hour later? Ms. Holmes proposed a mere drop of blood. Elizabeth Holmes may have been a fraud—but she is young enough to look like a visionary one day.

The Dropout is shallow and sensationalist, but that's all right. Its first episodes were directed by Michael Showalter, who had also directed the movie *The Eyes of Tammy Faye*. Amanda Seyfried is arresting as Holmes, who had worked hard to direct her own appearance and performance. She was putting on an act, you might say, and that seemed to promise deceit. But perhaps she just liked acting more than being. Still, no virtuoso work from Seyfried can help leaving us with the feeling that it should have been Holmes herself in the show, even if she had needed to defy or argue against her lines and scenes as written by others. Once we knew the trial verdict, it was redundant to have us in suspense over the narrative interpretation. You wonder whether the series could have played if Holmes had been acquitted.

The Dropout also risked mirth in having Sam Waterston, our Jack McCoy, play former Secretary of State George Shultz, one of several impressive figures who had endorsed the Theranos venture. There he is, put down at his stately desk in a room filled with books and antiquities. In his polka-dot bowtie he looks like a boy hoping to meet a pretty girl. And so an ancient McCoy tells Seyfried's Holmes that he's never met a girl like her before.

Ninety-one at the time, Shultz listened to Holmes and recommended her to some powerful friends, including Henry Kissinger. Shultz joined the board of Theranos and ignored the worries of his grandson Tyler, who was employed by the company and then became suspicious of its claims. Worse than that, George tried to suppress Tyler's objections. Was I alone finding Waterston in those scenes compromised by his past with us? That documentary element would not go away; it was a movie about Sam Waterston acting. We are talking about the way an actor can try to lose himself in being someone else for so long. That is not just a professional dilemma on its own. It is part of being seen so steadily by others that performance consumes actuality.

And yet Dropout *proved only our preparation.*

That's right, on Hulu programming one night, it took us straight into *Pam and Tommy,* a show we hadn't heard of. We stayed up all night with that. We'll come to that.

There are other actors in whom I do not feel that peril, the McCoy trap. I'm picking Laurie Metcalf. She plays an academic in *The Dropout,* someone who felt early on that Holmes was either a stupid innocent or bent on fraud. You know Laurie Metcalf even if you can't quite place her. She is sixty-eight now, and regarded in the business as a natural, and reliable.

She got a degree in theatre from the University of Illinois and became a founding member of the Steppenwolf theatre company in Chicago. In 1984, she won an Obie for her performance in Lanford Wilson's *Balm in Gilead.* So many awards and nominations have followed: for *Long Day's Journey into Night* in London; a Tony for *A Doll's House, Part 2;* and another as caretaker to the old woman in Edward Albee's *Three Tall Women.*

These are highlights in a hardworking career that also includes many striking movie performances, like her mother in *Lady Bird.* But it's her television work that is my focus here. She won four Emmys as the friend in *Roseanne*—

No, she was the sister. You need a copy editor as well as a wife.

—in which she was a bystander if you like, though increasingly felt, like a dog left out in a rainstorm garden. She did *The Big Bang Theory* and many other things, not least a role in Louis C.K.'s *Horace and Pete.* In all of this she has seemed decisive without being vain or self-glorious. There is a kingdom in supporting parts, a kind of truth we hold on to like touching wood in the dark. Metcalf goes to the core of a part so swiftly that sometimes she leaves a show seeming finished after she has done her work.

That is what I felt with her in *The Dropout.* Hers is not a big part. She is there just in early episodes as Professor Phyllis Gardner from Stanford—you can look her up. But she possesses the patient, firm, and weary authority of an expert who is accustomed to the lazy ideas of second-rate students. So there is a scene where Elizabeth Holmes follows her down a campus path trying to win her attention and support. Metcalf turns around on the kid and not unkindly tells Holmes that she has so much work to do before she is fit to be heard. Meanwhile the professor is eager to go home and have a glass of wine with her husband. Goodbye.

Someone must have said Laurie Metcalf could do that and they were right. This is not to say that Metcalf cannot act out indecisiveness when she needs to. I am confident she can do anything, and play it with an insight and a detail that would not rule out hesitation or humility in the character. She will have thought it out and she delivers. She is representative of the host of actors we think of as supporting players who keep up a level of credibility in our fiction. She is dead on, while brightly alive. That is lovely for the moment, but it works against *The Dropout* because we are left in no doubt but that Elizabeth Holmes—no matter the charm of Ms. Seyfried—was reckless or an idiot. So early on in *The Dropout,* the need for the series as a real story shuts down. It opts for the mythology of feminist courage. The fact that Theranos got as far as it did, and that it is now a show, is a measure of our helplessness in not distinguishing real life from TV melodrama. Everyone—George Shultz included—should have known better. If only our television had been tougher and a more credible forum as the place where we see people and their cases. As it is, I doubt we've seen or heard the last of Ms. Holmes.

There are these actors that I hunt for, as if feeling that they will never give up their own hunt. And television is the place where they can do so many small things, as in defining being alive. Something in the eagle eyes of Laurie Metcalf makes me think her search has to be unending. I dream of her as Lady Macbeth, especially if Peter Mullan can be her king.

That's not out of line. Mullan is Scottish, born in Peterhead in Aberdeenshire in 1959. He was poor and he became a radical, a fierce man whose anger can feel close to violence. He is not a comfortable presence on screen, and long ago if he was cast I got ready for something out of the ordinary, and frightening. How do some actors defy the immense pressure in the medium to be likable—is it because they feel something repugnant in acting, or pretending? Do they have a dream of honesty that can never be satisfied? Mullan has seldom played a character who is content with the world, or with himself. I suspect that makes him seem difficult in the eyes of some projects.

Of course, he has done exceptional work in movies, some of it not well known. If a Mullan picture is working then you can anticipate audiences feeling nervous, edging away as if having to pass a ranting homeless person on the street. He had small parts in *Shallow Grave* and *Trainspotting*, and then he won the acting prize at Cannes in Ken Loach's *My Name Is Joe,* playing an alcoholic always on the chipped edge of violence. Even in love, he is dangerous: in Mike Figgis's *Miss Julie,* opposite Saffron Burrows, he is like a rebel taking her citadel, prepared for murder. He was the Henshard figure in Michael Winterbottom's *The Claim,* a restaging of Hardy's *The Mayor of Casterbridge* in the American Northwest.

He directed *The Magdalene Sisters,* a harrowing story of three women sent to be reformed at an Irish nunnery. This was based on real incidents, but it felt driven by Mullan's anger at cruel authority. The film won the Golden Lion at the Venice festival. That was twenty years ago, and he has only directed once since then, *NEDS,* about juvenile delinquents in Glasgow. As if his head isn't filled with other stories.

He was a cuckolded husband in David MacKenzie's *Young Adam* and almost unbearable killing dogs in *Tyrannosaur,* directed by his friend Paddy Considine. Still and all, this immense actor was established on film, yet so intimidating that he seemed driven to escape into television because it is more casual and freer. Thus in the three *Red Riding* films (2009), he emerged gradually as the likely serial killer, a warped clergyman, a demon breathing salvation and sacrifice. I was frightened by his menace as I might have been by someone in life. A few years later, he was another monster in Jane Campion's *Top of the Lake*—that is one of the great works of modern television, with a detective heroine played by Elisabeth Moss, while Mullan hangs over the film like a fog full of brambles.

We might have been ready for mercy, but then he was back as a Missouri patriarch in *Ozark,* a man so in love with his strange wife that one of them might kill the other. If that sounds impossible, you have to go to *Ozark* and observe his scenes with a haunted Lisa Emery, and the weird way in which the modern story seemed to have roots in Faulkner or the Dark Ages. No sooner said than done, as Mullan became a southern landowner in Barry Jenkins's masterly *The Underground Railroad.*

If you ever hear of a Mullan film, be careful. He has earned that respect. Actors are easily typed as entertainers, but some of them are dangerous. It is said that Mullan is a Marxist and I am not surprised. He has an air of disgust with the world and an urge to be avenged. If ever there was an actor who requires King Lear, this is that man. In a moment, he can take television and make its habitual salon feel like a blasted heath.

24

You Are Not to Be Alarmed!

It was only a few days later (television is a diary), when as we watched *The Dropout,* its platform suggested that we might find similar exercise in *Pam and Tommy.* We had no idea what it was, but we acquiesced; there are times when one hardly notices the soft wind of advertising, or the way one day our programmed and sympathetic set might start to play "Our kind of thing," at the first pressure of our tired bodies on the couch.

The medium is a massage.

Pamela Denise Anderson was born in Ladysmith, British Columbia, Canada, in July 1967. Her life was plain and close to poverty, and she seems to have suffered several kinds of sexual abuse. But she grew up, and there are these available ways of describing her:

She graduated high school at eighteen and moved to Vancouver, where she worked as a fitness instructor.

She was an appealing and friendly young woman.

A lost soul, she was always afraid so she grew bold to conceal that.

She was an available babe, stacked, hot, cute (delete where inapplicable), and uncritical of the ways she was being looked at.

She was blonde and voluptuous according to the code.

To my eyes and mind, she looked not quite actual, but theoretical, as if all the roles on offer were a tangle she could not resolve. I think that is what makes her interesting.

In 1989, at a football game in Vancouver, she was shown on the Jumbotron wearing a T-shirt to promote Labatt beer. This so pleased the crowd it started her career.

In the TV series, *Pam and Tommy,* Pamela Anderson is played by the actress Lily James, who was born in Esher, in polite suburbia south of London, in 1989. She attended the Guildhall School of Music and Drama.

Lily seems such a nice young lady that she became Lady Rose Aldridge in *Downton Abbey.* She was also the secretary to Winston Churchill (a fabricated character) in *Darkest Hour,* the lead in a live-action *Cinderella,* Natasha in the 2016 adaptation of *War and Peace,* and the "I" character, the second Mrs. de Winter, in a new movie of *Rebecca.* Wasn't she indicating she could do anything in a masterpiece way?

To play Pamela Anderson on TV, she became platinum blonde (we do feel the metal). Her eyes were armored with false lashes and mascara. Her forehead was built anew in makeup and she acquired a prosthetic bosom, either through makeup devices or some computer-generated imagery. There is a scene in *Pam and Tommy* where she takes off her sweater for Tommy—all in one shot and in fondness—and the spectacle is impressive and entirely plausible, but it is like that Magritte painting of a briar pipe and its caption, "This is not a pipe." We know we are going mad and we wave to ourselves with a call-out, have a great trip.

I think it's fair and necessary to say that in playing Pam she did not look like Lily James.

So the casting and the performing had a flourish of magic and illusion that was amazing. This was only added to as the series went on in the realization that Lily was playing Pam with something we often call brilliance and insight while knowing those words are inadequate. There is a scene where Anderson, "the bimbo," is asked by a promoter how she sees herself and she has a lengthy speech where breathy cliché breaks down in admitting that she identifies with Jane Fonda. This is among the great scenes in screen acting, and it lets us share in the concept of *Pam and Tommy* that Anderson had a creative desire throbbing beneath the imprisoning apparatus of her babeness. Time and again, watching James, you appreciate that this TV show, while being committed to its own process of exploitation, is an exceptional and alarming portrait of a Promethean woman, a babe in fearsome woods.

You must not be alarmed—though I'm not sure how you can avoid it, or why I should try to protect you. This is the kind of friendly and forlorn advice authors find themselves giving. Of course, there is every reason for alarm, as much as if you were George Shultz confronting Elizabeth Holmes for the first time. But we need to assess the nature of the series, *Pam and Tommy*.

Pamela meets Tommy Lee, who is the drummer in the group Mötley Crüe. Lee had been born in Greece in 1962, as Thomas Lee Bass. He drummed the way a young King Kong might have done, trying to escape, in a heavy-metal style, and I find it hard to believe he had talent except for being outrageous. In the series, he is whiplash thin and a canvas for violent tattoos. It feels he has been swimming in the ink. He walks around a lot of the time in thong underwear, and as we will discover he has a way of talking to his penis. This is a prosthesis—isn't it?—attached to the body of the actor who plays Tommy, Sebastian Stan. This makes for good screwball chat, in which the witty dick can assume a question mark form as well as its anticipated exclamation point!

Tommy has been married twice when he meets Pam—an earlier wife was the actress Heather Locklear. He falls for Pam and pursues her to Cancún, where she is filming episodes for her show *Baywatch* (1989–99). This was a series in which she had a modest and immodest role as a beach guard, and in the process filled out a number of alluring swimsuits, often red. We see her at work, adjusting the suit so that it will show off the cleft between her buttocks. This is silly, of course, and demeaning, but *Baywatch* was so big a hit show that its reach has to be contemplated. Once we get into versions of democracy, we have to admit that hope has poor taste.

The records say that worldwide more than a billion people a week watched *Baywatch*. That is about half the number of card-carrying Christians.

Tommy and Pam fall in love.

And that collision of a bimbo and a scumbag instead of becoming a comic-book farce turns into an astonishing romance. I loved it. I could not credit how moving it was. So I was hurt when Lily James lost the Emmy to Seyfried in The Dropout.

We believe they are in love in a way that seldom happens on a screen these days and which is endearing because we guess the two characters have a disastrous future. But that is just our condescension—or mine. Just see the show and recognize how these two celebrity savages are in the real thing. You can say it is a Barbie doll being with Sid from *Sid and Nancy* but that's only a gesture at resemblance. We don't think their frenzy can last, but we have no doubt about their passion.

In their honeymoon aura, at Lake Mead—before those waters started to go down—Tommy and Pam film themselves fucking. There's no other way to put it, though the show does not reveal the tape of them together. But later two other characters look at the footage in awe, as if seeing something they know they should not be seeing, like a Chernobyl meltdown or the double jaws of *Alien*'s alien.

The footage is called "explicit" and "pornographic," and it turns into a large shady business, but many of us are so in love sometimes, or so swept away by its sex, that we want to find a way of commemorating it. Sex was a religion for about a hundred years as we felt able to own up to it. We wrote songs or poetry for it, but now the common fuckers pick up a video camera or put it on their phone. That can be innocent and exuberant, fatuous and dangerous. Perhaps the show misses a valuable opportunity in not having Pam and Tommy talk about this, because it has to do with their lyrical spirits, the withdrawal of its actuality in our lives, and the way in which we now regard ourselves as figures in a movie.

So the tape exists, Hi8, and Tommy puts it in the absurdly huge safe he keeps, which is empty but for a few firearms, souvenir clothing, and some petty cash—not the treasure of the Sierra Madre. The safe is a big plot point and a metaphor for near-empty lives.

To improve and renovate his mansion for Pam, Tommy had enlisted a few construction workers, one of whom is Rand (Seth Rogen). He is a shy, bumbling fellow, a self-conscious failure, a good enough guy, but foolish and downcast. So we are on his side when the loutish Tommy refuses to pay him for his work, and brandishes a gun in his face as Rand tries to retrieve his carpentry tools. Rand is miffed, and feels exploited by the thoughtless egotist. That's why he steals the safe as a way of getting back at Tommy. It's only later that he discovers the tape and realizes what it could be.

He remembers an old friend in the porn trade, Uncle Miltie (Nick Offerman), and together they see a way to make some money on the tape. This is in the infant days of the Internet, when they realize that horny loners can mail-order the tape, without having clearances from the two blissful fuckers. This is illegal or unethical, but the tenor of the film makes it comical and no less than Tommy deserves—until we appreciate the damage it will do to Pamela. In the same story arc she is pregnant by Tommy, though she will have a miscarriage in timing with the discovery that her body is the Excalibur or the mouse in a lucrative exploitation business.

You have probably worked out by now that *Pam and Tommy* is an intricate but uneasy comedy in which the lead story and the Rand plot are intertwined, with the storyline going back and forth in time. But the fun and the laughter only aggravate the pain felt by Pamela. It points towards the savage irony of our appetite for sexual fantasy in a show that lays on Pamela Shamela like hot butterscotch sauce on vanilla ice cream.

You're always at the ice cream. I suppose it is the American metaphor. Frigid on the point of melting. With all those flavors—the American diversity.

In short, Pam is being used both as part of a media critique and as a hard-on device. We the public can see her foolishness, but we are eating up the folly. We want more and more. We hesitate at the brink of seeing the crucial tape while telling ourselves this is a mocking moral lesson. Having our ice cream and eating it. This trick is managed in such a way that Pamela is digested and excreted while Lily James could win prizes. This is further underscored by the way on Hulu the story keeps breaking into commercials that might have been done by the filmmakers themselves.

Pam and Tommy grew out of the real events and a story in *Rolling Stone* written by Amanda Chicago Lewis. Initially, it was the project of James Franco, who wanted to play Tommy and direct the show. That plan fell through because Franco had been reported behaving badly enough to jeopardize his participation. Seth Rogen had been part of that scheme and he stayed with it as Robert Siegel took over as creator in charge of the writing, with Craig Gillespie hired to direct the first episodes.

There would be eight episodes as the story traces how Pamela Anderson more or less survived the scandal of the tape to become a *Playboy* cover model and a feature in countless reality TV shows. She's said to be a wealthy woman now. I think the daring in the show fell off fast after the first three or four episodes: it could have ended at the comic tragedy of Pamela being exposed and shamed, a bride stripped bare by her bachelors, a thin talent waiting to be fifty—she is fifty-six now and one has to imagine her declining to watch this show in the way the Queen may have lacked the curiosity or the patience to stick with *The Crown*. Or was she a fan, searching for her rosebud?

But hot series can go cold, and not many "good" series are as complicated as *Pam and Tommy*. The four central players—James, Stan, Rogen, and Offerman—are faultless and witty—yet maybe one term defies the latter, for in its deepest nature acting should be willing to make mistakes. The camera style is headlong and gaudy, self-mocking but in love with light, skin, space, and irony (it was shot by Paula Huidobro, who photographed the movie *CODA*). To watch it is to understand why two-faced voyeurism is a drug for our time, and to see how citizenship has been usurped by it. It is a great show and I would recommend that you watch at least the first three episodes in one night to get the full mad package and take it off to bed.

25

Previously on . . .

My Garry Shandling file is still open?

I bet it is.

We chatter late at night, about smuggling extras into the book, but pushing it beyond normal ideas of what "a series" can be and recognizing that TV itself is one of the longest-running shows there ever will be.

When we're all over, I Love Lucy *will be playing still in the Dakotas.*

Television is so much one sprawling series we should be careful not to draw hard lines of definition.

The Weather is a series, likewise the News, the commercials, and sports (something vital that does not matter—thus its definition).

It's as if every night when we start again, the medium whispers "Previously . . ." To have us think things are in order.

I think it would be nice to do Garry justice.

In a regular summer, here in San Francisco, 162 games of Giants baseball will be shown, home and away, boring and then not, and we nod along with it as a background, listening to Jon Miller, Dave Flemming, Kruk, and Kuip, into extra innings and maybe the playoffs. You never know, and if you are in the dark about the names of our commentators, you have your own in Boston, Chicago, or wherever. In a full season that could be getting on for 500 hours. That's not far from what Johnny Carson did in one year on the *Tonight Show.* And he did it from 1962 to 1992. From the Cuban Missile Crisis to John Gotti being sentenced to life in prison. Did Johnny ask, "What's the diff?"

Fifteen thousand hours of TV in which Carson remained familiar and reliable—he was always Johnny as in "Here's Johnny!"—but mysterious, or withheld, or seeming to say don't count on him, he might not be there. So much presence, so much absence.

Here is a Carson story. In the 1960s and '70s, when I was English, I would sometimes watch TV coverage of the Wimbledon fortnight. The camera might roam between games and it sometimes picked on a good-looking but rather indefinite man sitting in the stands of Centre Court, enjoying the tennis. No one in Britain knew who he was, or understood that a few thousand miles away he was known to everyone. So a tactful British commentator would murmur, "And that I am told is Mr. John Carson, a notable television personality." As if this quiet spectator had come down from Mars on his day off.

I can hear Garry doing that line, impersonating a dry BBC sportscaster. With Johnny looking up in horror. Could be a scene.

For all I can recall, this might have been those days in 1969 (it took two) when Pancho Gonzales beat Charlie Pasarell in five sets, before the age of tie breaks: 22–24, 1–6, 16–14, 6–3, 11–9. That match was one of the best series I ever saw on TV.

Johnny Carson did not seem disconcerted at being unrecognized on the BBC. He may have enjoyed the rest from fame. Though there must have been other Americans in the stands who knew who he was and even asked for a picture or an autograph. I hope he declined such requests politely, as if he really preferred not to, like Herman Melville's Bartleby the scrivener.

Over the years, Carson kept his figure and his distance. He grew older, of course, but that grayness settled in on him nicely because it fostered the anonymity he wished for. He could be amused and easygoing with guests he liked, but there was an unshakable air about him that he was the host or a concierge at a class hotel where discretion was served for breakfast. He did jokes; he had a worked-over monologue that opened the show. He did a few comic characters and had a sidekick, Ed McMahon, who was like a buddy at the other end of the bar who sat in grave respect for Johnny and was never a wind to shake his tree. Not that Carson was an oak or a beech—more an aspen.

You could argue that in his white dapperness, he was an ideal American guy in the second half of the twentieth century. Johnny was midwestern but mock urbane; he seemed open, yet he was conservative; he was smartly dressed—yet increasingly old-fashioned. He did warm and funny while staying heartless. He was the show for all our lives, it seemed, someone we came to meet at night. But he was alone. He made us feel chipper to be watching him; he admitted that a man could get along on $25 million a year (that was 1968), and he never thought to let on that the second half of the twentieth century really was going to be the end of ease or dapperness or doing the show every night. He had no ambition or agenda except to stay on, to be sure that the crease in his pants was crisp and that his fly was not open. He knew a vast uneasiness but it was appeased if his jokes functioned. If they dropped dead he'd make a joke of that, too. And he needed the guests to come and go without alarming the horses. He was so intent on their not being alarmed that he had actually outlawed the horses.

He might refer to his marriages and his romantic dismay, including the ruefulness of alimony and solitude. But he never gave any hint of a man who might be swept off his feet—by booze, depression, the state of racism in America, the monotony of his success, or by people he plainly liked, such as Don Rickles or Angie Dickinson. He was always there, always on, and very good at it, but in his spirit he did not want to be noticed or known. It was not just that he typified television. He was the medium, and over the years that persistence began to turn into a kind of Asperger's. Long before retirement, he was backing away. He stood up straight for his monologue and after that he sat at his desk as if it were the bridge on an aircraft carrier on a lost patrol. But in his soul he was on the couch, signaling to us that it lay in wait.

It was said that he was replaced, as late night talk shows multiplied. There were successors or pretenders, as sharp as Letterman or buffoons like Leno. But they all knew the kingdom of 11:30 was gone, so late night was now the early dawning of insomnia.

And so on.

Take a breath. You don't think Shandling could fit in here? I have the file ready, chief.

"He was born in Chicago in 1949, but the family moved to Arizona because his older brother was ill. That brother died when Garry was ten and it marked him for life. The family then moved to Los Angeles, and that's where Garry started writing. He did a few scripts—what were the shows?"

Sanford and Son *and* Welcome Back, Kotter.

So he was about thirty in 1979? And he was handsome, yet insecure and a touch goofy.

Like the best handsome guys.

He thought about getting into writing but it didn't please him, so he began to do stand-up comedy in Los Angeles, and word got around. In 1981, he obtained a spot on the *Tonight Show,* and it was an event. The audience loved him.

And Johnny liked him. He was always smart with comics.

Correctamundo. And so he was on the *Tonight Show* quite often, and then he would fill in as host when Johnny needed a break. There was a feeling growing that Shandling might take over the *Tonight Show* one day.

But Garry didn't want it. Insecure but reckless, if you know what I mean.

In 1985, out of the blue, with Alan Zweibel, he created *It's Garry Shandling's Show* for Showtime. The title was an assertion, but it left room for doubt. And Garry played himself, a neurotic stand-up comedian, whose dull life is a kind of sitcom.

A little like The Truman Show—*but that was more than ten years later.*

Shandling was maybe the first hint of Pirandello on television, authentic in mundane ways, yet absurd, too. And as if Garry felt a creaking in his bones and his lopsided smile, he started talking to the studio audience. It was staggering, as if for the first time someone had understood that the fakery of TV could be addressed. It was Pythonesque, yet there it was in the this-is-real world of Los Angeles show business. It was one of those shows that knew LA was the heart of the country. It ran four seasons, 1986–90, the end of Reagan, and it became a cult show, nowhere near as popular as *Seinfeld*. I mention the president because it was a show that grasped how the most powerful man in the world might be a used-up actor hoping to do narration on a promo. Fox took it over, smelling something new, but then they canceled the show. Nominated four times for an Emmy, it never won. But it was so much better than its contemporaries and so startling you had to hold on to your couch and your existential credit cards.

That persona of Garry Shandling was prelude to the marvel of Larry Sanders. This Larry was a national figure; he had a late-night talk show so close to the *Tonight Show* you had to separate reverence from satire. It was created by Shandling and Dennis Klein and it would run on HBO for six seasons and ninety episodes. There was a team of writers but they were doing their best to keep up with Garry (and Larry), whose improvs often dictated dialogue and situations. Larry had two regular aides—played by Rip Torn and Jeffrey Tambor—and there was a steady stream of guests, who would do their cute bit on his show and then (while we went away) talk to Larry like real, bitter celebrities bored to be there.

This was the moment in which Hollywood and the rest of us gave up on the dignity of celebrity, and respect for H'wood. Or any kind of honesty or occasion in talk shows. Contempt was in; you could feel its creep advancing with the O.J. affair. But most of the Sanders show was done with his airy good nature—as if that was Garry's own longing—while being the most scathing inversion of Don't Go Away–ism that television had ever managed.

This is great. You should have Garry on the jacket of your book.

That won't be my decision. They'll say Garry is dead now and never had huge audiences. I daresay they'll want a collage, *or* just a bold typographic cover with a short punchy title.

Your publishers are good people?

They are. They've put up with me for five books.

I must have done twenty with you. They could put us on the cover, curled up on our couches. Too geriatric?

Not on the cards.

Butters no parsnips. Garry must have won Emmys?

Shared one for writing on *Larry Sanders*.

Never did another show like that. Did not marry or have children. Had some serious illness I forget the name of. Fired the girlfriend he'd been living with, Linda Doucett, who had a part in the show. Still only sixty-six when he died. Hadn't done much for years. There are people you fall in love with, in your home night after night.

There's a documentary, *The Zen Diaries of Garry Shandling* (2018), directed by Judd Apatow, who had written for Garry from long ago.

I saw it. Broke my heart again.

26

Our History, Our Game

When did television pass on from being a toy or an entertainment, a cute extension of the movies? That pipedream on progress could not last once it became apparent that we were absorbing the world through this wicked window in our living room.

Wicked? How so?

Because the seeming window was a dreamscape. Visibility had been tricked into fantasy.

There were highlights in that education and they were thrilling, if unsettling. The outlines of a horror flick were emerging. Around 1960, when it was clear the movies had lost their industrial heft or confidence, TV ran an election in which a movie star figure seemed ready to dispel the dullness of politics. That guy was then made vivid in murderous circumstances that defied understanding and accelerated fiction. The close-up of his smiling head was blown apart.

I was too young to know that Jack.

But you call him Jack, as if he is a hero in your head. What was it like? It was a moment when our history turned into a show. That was TV, when history became our melodrama.

Like Las Vegas instead of "our town"?

There would be more assassinations and they became like a rhythm in contemporary history. Some felt conspiracy in this mood, but perhaps it was only our own urge to set fiction above fact. Conspiracy was a new rapture, a modern religious habit, and our screens were altars or becomings. This was long before Twitter. Fragments of war movie came back from Vietnam, in which heroes and decisive battles had no place. Other ghosts of men walked on the Moon, while dark space stared back at us unimpressed. So much was happening and only the derided and inert television screen had a chance of saying it was pointless. Just progress. It was clear, yet unspoken, that "democracy" had gone to sleep. So to smother any unease the machine repeated frantic mock poems on our prosperity, commercial gospels on what we could purchase and how that would transform us in the God-supplanting pursuit of happiness.

Meanwhile a desolate unhappiness kept quietly building. Few movies dared to grasp this. But the TV screen stayed on and available. At first the window had closed down for the night, but then it realized we were not safe alone. And in its chaos—for those brave enough to face tumult and tedium together—the ongoing history was grinding us down. It was no wonder we needed couches to support our last nights.

There had been a first thought that television was made for factual reporting, and a survey of our busy world with gestures about our being united. We have failed in that, of course. Our News now has despaired of reporting: it settles for "breaking news" instead of its explanation; and it fills its hours and years with disputes and invective over what the news means. It collects talking heads who would not know the field if it surrounded them, with horses or lions grazing in the distance.

I am not writing this to be partisan. You can guess my allegiances, and feel nostalgia over such inclinations, but the honorable Rachel Maddow and the hideous Donald Trump are only point and counterpoint in our spitting images. Their value systems may be in conflict, but conflict is the show. They are people on television, and kindred in their empty noise. The medium is the message and it will be ready for a battle of the century even as transmission closes down.

Still, I am drawn to television series in which there is a sense of grandeur, a feeling that yes, we can tell you human stories that may be sad and funny (*I Love Lucy* in a ruined city), but we'll set them in the larger context that TV has always confronted. It's not that there has been a tradition in such shows, but I have harped on the model of *Our Friends in the North,* that BBC series that thought to follow a few lives over thirty years as small footprints in the larger march of time. So Gina McKee and Daniel Craig grew older in that show (more or less), and Britain gave up a few illusions.

Our Friends was far from faultless, but it is pretentious to look for perfection in television. Nor do I mean to say that the three shows I am going to discuss now are pinnacles, looming over less ambitious programs. Indeed, I'm going to start off by saying that *The Plot Against America* is not very good. But its idea was unavoidable: America was overthrowing itself.

The novel by Philip Roth was published in 2004, and it is an enticing mixture of the old-fashioned and the innovative. The novelty consists of the narrative conceit whereby in the presidential election of 1940 Franklin Roosevelt is defeated (massively) by Charles Lindbergh. And so a new America moves forward, resolved to make terms with Germany and Japan, to "reeducate" its own Jewish population, and to sink into the fascist hesitation that faced the world in 1940. And is still here. This surprise development is told as a weather system falling on a Jewish family in Newark, New Jersey. But it is an old-fashioned book in that it feels no pressing need to offer a narrative style beyond what this family would have been able to read in 1940—or even 1840.

I like the novel well enough, though the writing falls flat on the pages as I read them. Roth's book is stubbornly prosaic in its delivered experience when I know two comparable works that radiate another possibility. I am thinking of Dos Passos's *U.S.A.* (1930–36), with storyline, newsreel passages, portraits of luminaries that would be worthy of the Kane papers, and even the sketchy drawings by Reginald Marsh. The other novel I'm thinking of is *Ragtime* (1975), by E. L. Doctorow. There is a movie of *Ragtime* and it's very poor. It never grasped the elated dynamic in cutting from one thing to another. Or Doctorow's calm instinct that human stories and their value were all swept along on the rhythm of ragtime and change. Long before the concept became current, *Ragtime* was a rhapsody to streaming.

The Plot Against America began for television in the minds of David Simon and Ed Burns. Simon (born in 1960 in Washington, D.C.) was a journalist in Baltimore who wrote a book, *Homicide: A Year on the Killing Streets,* in 1991. That became a very good TV show, and that led Simon and Burns to create *The Wire,* an exemplary and groundbreaking show, another portrait of Baltimore and a study in how that community was remade by the drug business. It was an absorbing show, very good on race and urban gridlock, that ran from 2002 to 2008. But it was overshadowed by *The Sopranos,* because Simon lacked David Chase's sardonic identification with his family or his caustic humor. Simon followed it with other good works: *Treme,* one of the best series about race, set in New Orleans after Katrina, and then *The Deuce* (written with George Pelicanos), an examination of the business of pornography and Simon's funniest show.

Simon is a key figure in modern television, but on the screen his series can feel subdued or too thought out. The idea of *The Plot Against America* was presented to him soon after the novel was published. But he demurred, or he was too occupied with the shows in hand. He got excited about taking on the Roth book only after the election of Donald Trump in 2016. That fateful nudge. He and Burns wrote the six episodes, talking to Roth as they went along. Was there too much respect being paid to the great man? Minkie Spiro directed the first three episodes, and Thomas Schlamme the last three.

Everyone did good work, and then there was the cast. Morgan Spector plays Herman Levin, the ambitious insurance man, Zoe Kazan is his wife. Winona Ryder is her older sister, John Turturro is the rabbi drawn into the fascist movement, Ben Cole is Lindbergh, Billy Carter is Walter Winchell. I have no complaint over any of them. Nor do I dispute the care taken with the locations, the period props, and the clothes. I feel I am there, and I got the point of that re-creation. But I had it after fifteen minutes as the Levins drive past an open-air gathering of Nazi sympathizers who are drinking and singing and waiting to watch Jews.

To read about Houdini, J. P. Morgan, and Evelyn Nesbit in *Ragtime* is to be carried away by the interaction of so many strangers. You feel a great throng at the edges of the page. But on television *The Plot Against America* never frees itself from the careful assembly of naturalism and production values. Few things held TV back more than the wish to keep its fiction plausible or authentic—when the wings of great fiction wait to rise above that discipline.

More than that, as it played in 2020, to good reviews and sinking ratings, *The Plot Against America* was in helpless competition with what every network and channel was haunted by: the election of 2020, in which sound and fury culminated in January 6 and its demolition of hope. That was not David Simon's fault. But no representation of Lindbergh had a chance against the profuse, lyrical ugliness of Trump. "Profuse" and "lyrical" can be read as favorable words, and they denote the way we have been living in the dark light of a television genius, a man who speaks to live rallies only to be seen more widely on our screens. No, I do not give him credit for that or hate him any the less. And I am not ashamed of that anger. But one cannot come to terms with Trump without realizing that—in his mindless, impetuous way—he had intuited the fearsome dynamic of this medium. He is a reason for terminating television, all of it, and taking away the poison of advertising.

Yes, that sounds naïve and comic. It can never happen. But that does not mean we should carry on as our own doctors without knowing that in taking on television we destroyed its potential by determining that it should be paid for through advertising. So its every attempt at argument or evidence would be betrayed by flagrant lies. We were doomed then. No going back.

And so on.

Overlooked doom has a tradition on TV. As early as 1954, the BBC dramatized George Orwell's novel *1984*. Nigel Kneale wrote it. Rudolph Cartier directed. Peter Cushing played Winston Smith, Yvonne Mitchell was Julia, André Morell was O'Brien. The result was frightening and disruptive. Can you imagine its outrage in 1954? Some said the production was riveting. Others felt it was so scary it should not have been shown. There was even talk of television itself being a malign force, as if that took precedence over the dangers Orwell was trying to describe. So the medium said, let's keep doing it, as in *previously, on TV.*

The Plot Against America should have been a similar storm, but it was sedate and admirable, bland as a book at bedtime, a sedative or Ovaltine. Think instead of *Babylon Berlin,* which seems to me the best show in this book.

It was derived from novels by Volker Kutscher that center on the last years of Weimar, 1929 to 1933, as Germany struggled to emerge from economic downfall and political demoralization—or to inhabit it. It would be a collaboration of German Public Broadcasting, of Sky in the United Kingdom, and of Netflix, which would play the series in the United States. The show was created as scripts and then directed by Tom Tykwer, Henk Handloegten, and Achim von Borries. It was said to be the most expensive production ever undertaken in Germany. (That was 55 million Euros—or about half the cost of Scorsese's *The Irishman*—720 minutes against 209.) It was launched as two seasons together, in 2017. And it has since had a third season, or twenty-eight episodes in all. And it has not yet got as far as 1933, though its sinister atmosphere has so many hints of what is coming to settle the confusion and dismay of that Germany.

I still find smart people who have not seen it yet, so the most valuable thing to say earnestly is that you have to see it. How can I finish this book if you are still, amid Ukraine, in the dark on *Babylon Berlin*? Perhaps you are daunted by having to read the subtitles. Or you have tried it enough to be intimidated by the teeming plot with action and intrigue worthy of the cold-blooded visual imagination of Fritz Lang. In *Metropolis, M,* and *The Testament of Dr. Mabuse,* he was the great director of the late Weimar period.

It is a police story, with one of the saddest of detectives. Gereon Rath is a police inspector played by Volker Bruch, guilt-ridden from the war, a drug addict, one of those policemen with outlawry in his head. He has a companion in his pursuit of crime, Charlotte Ritter (Liv Lisa Friese), impoverished, trying to support her family, a whore sometimes, but eager to be a police inspector herself. She and Rath are like lovers who cannot declare their love, and in episodes 15 and 16 of the show they join in what is one of the last sequences in romantic cinema. No, I am not going to spell this out for you. You must go and find it.

But you should not just dive into its cold water, as you can if you are streaming a show. You have to get there as part of a long swim. You must live with the large supporting cast—Leonie Benesch as Greta, Peter Kurth as Inspector Bruno Wolter, and so on. You need to be dazzled by the locations and the sets, by the color and the hallucinations, and the music—this is a show in which the music is like fire, creeping beneath the doorsill. I am trying to emphasize how, in being true to 1929, this show is energized by the crazed action of German movies from that period. Fritz Lang would have saluted this show, though never in his life did he know how to make characters so adorable and unreliable.

Are you still here?

The adventure of *Babylon Berlin* is ravishing; its cinema drives you wild. But it cannot be watched without feeling the Nazis coming—in fact, I don't think the show needs to get to 1933, or the footsteps on the stairs we can hear. So one cannot watch *Babylon Berlin* without keeping an ear cocked for our own time—

Didn't you hear that noise outside? asks Lucy. *Wasn't there a noise?*

She hears things—don't we all? That anticipation has turned to dread. So we chatter in the night together, hoping to preserve calm.

I have a third series, but I have such mixed feelings over it. I realize now that those feelings are a helpless part of being English. The first large television experience of my life was in watching the coronation of Queen Elizabeth II. My parents did not have a television set in 1953, so I biked over to Grandma's house to watch the great event on her new set. Therein, the young woman, she was twenty-seven, sat patiently with the heavy crown on her head, with the anointing and the anthems. It was four hours at least on a rainy day in June, and Grandma had neighbors in to watch the crowning, with egg sandwiches and lemon barley water.

I supported this theatre in my heart. At seven or eight, I had been shown pictures of Elizabeth and Margaret as children my age. They seemed pretty, if unduly tidy. I was told stories of how the Windsors had stayed in London throughout the Blitz, instead of going to Canada. Wasn't it natural to be loyal to them? That young woman was Queen because her uncle had given up being Edward VIII to marry an American woman who had been divorced. And Elizabeth, at ninety-six, was still alive but very stooped. I had deplored her existence over the years, but I was touched by her duty. It is not just that she seemed dull, or hardly there. I believe she was the only dull woman I have known.

The Crown is a shameless trick, a way tacit republicans can be droll enough to extract every drop of *Downton Abbey* from their project. I mean the stately homes, the furniture and the banquet tables, the protocols, the furtive behavior swimming in our sea of wide-eyed tourism, and the insanity of this decrepit epic setting. So *The Crown* has an I-Am-a-Camera young woman presiding over the frazzled ineptness of so many ignobles as her country drifts from hollow iconography to tabloid humiliation.

The Crown is the creation of Peter Morgan, one of the most cunning screenwriters around. But as Morgan might defend himself: the show is the farewell treatment of a part of British culture and history, the tender insistence that this fuss has to come to its closure.

More telling than *The Forsyte Saga* (which begins with the funeral of Queen Victoria), more pained than *Our Friends in the North* or *Till Death Do Us Part*, the British original that prompted *All in the Family*, *The Crown* is a story of a family lost in the stream of change. It was always a canny TV enterprise, a large investment with enormous bounty, and the assurance that even if the monarchy is crumbling, the aristocracy of British acting will survive.

If only the royals had had a fraction of the personality and the verve in the players. Vanessa Kirby restored the reality of Princess Margaret—perhaps she invented it—when that sad sister had become a cartoon character. Later on, Helena Bonham Carter and Lesley Manville did an older Margaret like a Maggie Smith in waiting. Matt Smith really educated us about Prince Philip. Josh O'Connor made a Prince Charles to be envied, chiefly by Charles himself. Emma Corrin was the best posthumous Diana we will ever have (the original retired undefeated). Jared Harris and Alex Jennings brought George VI and the Duke of Windsor back from the dead. In all these players one felt something like reverence, as if the casting had been a benediction.

That is just the family, leaving room for supporters: John Lithgow as Churchill, Gillian Anderson as Thatcher, Pip Torrens as Tommy Lascelles, Stephen Dillane as Graham Sutherland, Jeremy Northam as Anthony Eden, Michael C. Hall (the former Dexter) as John Kennedy, Emerald Fennell as Camilla Parker Bowles, Anton Lesser as Harold Macmillan.

Claire Foy was Elizabeth for only the first two seasons (Olivia Colman and Imelda Staunton followed on), but those were the best seasons—the subsequent story gets to be plodding and morose—and many of the other actors may have trusted Foy's intrepid shyness in a production that could never escape the possibility of poor taste. Foy seemed to understand the public grandeur and the crushed intimacy in Elizabeth. For that woman had always been on television, since before she knew what the medium was. Lillibet Windsor had no aspirations to divine right or greatness. She was simply a young actress delivering the set lines and attitudes who helped teach us that the Queen, her majesty, was a player, or even a pretender—an impostor— imposed as history.

If one tried to imagine the Queen watching Claire Foy, one was into the mystery of how a television show could revive a defunct institution in just the way Rudolph Rassendyl took over for Rudolf V of Ruritania in *The Prisoner of Zenda* (published in 1894).

But by season 5 of the show, as Charles moved from prince to king (deploring a misguided fountain pen), there were doubts raised. Had "they" gone too far in making an ice cream story out of forlorn facts? A strange double team arose—former Prime Minister John Major and a sometime Queen, Judi Dench—to say some of the cliff-hanger stuff was rubbish. The way an American president might be off his rocker.

Is that what The Crown *achieved?*

Maybe it made it possible at last for the desperate royals to go away.

Where would they go?

To the wilder parts of Scotland, to Nova Zembla, or to northern Nevada . . . somewhere where they have good reception.

Poor souls.

27

The Watchers Watched

Wordle is tricky today, said Lucy. *I only got it in five.*

We played Wordle in those days. It was what we did to check in with our media, and ourselves. It was odd to realize we were wizened people hunched over small screens, tip-tapping our way towards ALLOW or MOVIE or SLAVE (please complete the poem). And feeling vindicated if we beat the puzzle in less than six guesses. We hardly credited other items on our phone in the morning: they were "breaking" flashes where the ads were either glue or some spinal fluid leaking into our organism. But Wordle had priority over damage in Kyiv.

They say everyone's doing it, said Lucy. And isn't there comfort and union in that sweeping proposition? With so many of us fixed on MAUVE, VALUE or VISTA, with Vs for Victory. And there's a fresh puzzle every day, as if some benign and playful agency—the *New York Times* or the infinite "they"—seems to authorize the phone. The force that is doing it all. The presence that legitimizes the day. Just imagine a continuum where this they has vanished in the morning.

Turning on the tube and nothing flows? No line to get help. How long before panic sets in?

In the light of the last chapter, I had been thinking about shows that might have managed to tell human stories that moved us or made us laugh, but which recognized the totality of the world's stories all going on, and knew that we were working out our history. Like *Babylon Berlin.* So why not a series that addressed the state of our American being as an enterprise that decent people might be involved in?

Imagine some Babylon, Berlin *for America after its fall. A struggle between authority and resistance fought in Four Corners country.*

Do you remember *The West Wing?* I asked Lucy.

I had forgotten it, she said.

It wasn't so long ago, and some people still refer back to that show, not just for its craftsmanship and the detail, but nostalgic for a White House fit to be in charge of us all. A respectable house and home. Of course, the enthusiasts are older than they think. *The West Wing* ran from 1999 to 2006, seven seasons on NBC, 154 episodes, and four Emmys for Outstanding Drama Series. It was a mercy and a flag in what were thought of as bad years. I am thinking of the standoff in the 2000 election, and the rumors of a betrayed process. Then there was 9/11 and all the wild reactions in a country that for the first time was hit by warlike gestures. After that, there was the criminality of war in Iraq, along with Abu Ghraib and other outrages, as we waited for the heart attack that would overtake our cholesterol economy. Watching the worst conscientious president we had ever had. I know good people who clung to *The West Wing* in that time, who reckoned its standard of lively decency was a model for all of us beyond D.C. It was a show that said there was a "they" worth believing in. It recognized how far television had a duty for being good for us.

Don't misunderstand me: it was a good, addictive show, as well as a memoir to that American entertainment mode in which smart, feeling characters talked their heads off and the conversation was like sunlight on the water. I regretted in the previous chapter that *The Plot Against America* had lacked verve or glee. I was not waiting for the next line or another revelation. But *The West Wing* had knockout moments that reminded one of Frank Capra, Preston Sturges, or Howard Hawks. You knew that Aaron Sorkin had grown up on *Mr. Smith Goes to Washington, Meet John Doe, The Lady Eve,* and *His Girl Friday,* and it felt good to be back in that swing.

Sorkin created *The West Wing* and wrote much of it himself, as if he could not stop himself doing dialogue. He was born in New York City in 1961, and he had wanted to be an actor: that energy and yearning has always spurred his writing. He wrote a play, *A Few Good Men,* in which the idea of being good is a smokescreen for everyone being a terrific talker. It became a hit film, and then he wrote a modest movie, *The American President* (1995, with Michael Douglas as the widower chief drawn to Annette Bening), and that prompted interest in a serious Washington show. Sorkin is a chronic, self-delighted writer with several other valuable TV credits, like *The Newsroom,* another ensemble piece in which the idea of a team is a model for America and movies that made us feel good. Sorkin is far from a fool and he is an authentic liberal, but his urge to feel good himself, or successful, can carry him along through thick and thicker. The marriage of being smart and feeling good was integral to American illusion, and disillusion.

Some D.C. spectators marveled that a TV show on NBC had got the White House down right. Others said it was too wholesome to be true. It raised the level of talk on our talk shows about politics, and it fostered a notion that healthy interaction was a lifeblood to the Constitution. Just as we had hoped. All of this was palatable, and it was quite easy to believe, watching it, that there was a they watching us, at least as considerate as a network, and that we were all on the same side. Networks, like the BBC, believed they had a certain responsibility. You heard intelligent people saying in 2008 that we would not have had Barack Obama without *The West Wing*. That wasn't just acknowledgment of matters of color. It was the larger hope that good talk, high ideas, and a degree of fun could still save the country (or the networks threatened by cable). But it would soon seem as tendentious as the wishful thinking over how TV coverage of Vietnam had hastened the end of that conflict.

Chances are you loved some of the people on *The West Wing,* and would have voted for them. In a way we did, the business way, for as many as fifteen million of us tuned in for new episodes. Martin Sheen (as President Jed

Bartlet) had always seemed destined for this role. It's a stray thought, but wasn't he more electable than Michael Douglas—if a shade less interesting? You could follow Rob Lowe, John Spencer, and Bradley Whitford as believable workaholics and rounded figures. Many of us favored Allison Janney, who started out as press secretary and became chief of staff. It was a measure of her spreading scope that she won two Emmys as supporting actress and then two as a lead.

The show was written as if Aaron Sorkin was playing every part as he skidded across his word processor. And I say that in the awareness that American television in that era was at last being made clear as a writer's medium.

The West Wing seemed exemplary, a landmark in the line of our "great" shows, the ones fit to be a mirror for looking good. This wasn't so long ago. The show had been the moment and the rage before Obama crystallized the racist feelings in the country, before the economy reeled in horror at how money people behaved, before the fullest realization that climate change was our terminus and that it was already too late to make amends, and that the infernal screen had taken us over. The talk in politics after that became cruder than Sorkin would have passed, more hostile, dishonest, and demented. It is fanciful now to think of anyone in television trying to repeat a *West Wing*.

Today it feels as benign as *Mr. Deeds Goes to Town,* and as worthy of nostalgia. But in the late 1930s—a very bad time, as *The Plot Against America* knows—it was possible and proper for America to offer optimistic fun with a tough edge (call it ironic realism) that let us feel we were on an insider track. Now we know that the machines we are watching report back to some heartless headquarters where we are organized as purchasers and even voters. We once spoke of "Hollywood" as a friendly force in our lives, and now we refer to "the media." Neither of those institutions has turned out in the way we hoped. They were always fierce contests for success and power, but lit up by talents as recognizable as Howard Hawks and Aaron Sorkin. But now the "they," the idea of personality in the machine, is so precarious and vulnerable that we guess we are its likely victims.

Twenty years later, it looks as quaint as *Hill Street Blues*—and that is praise. But now the White House has been reduced in committees of inquiry to the map in a drunken game of Clue—as to where Trump was lurking and in what silence as people stormed the Capitol, where he flung food at the walls, and made it hard for his assistants to avoid the odor of a beast let loose in the home.

At the same time, the talk shows have uncovered and created so many geological layers of perfidy that the Sorkin ideal of government seems outlandish. In the past six years, there have been so many exposé books—often as good as they are scary—that now the White House stands in the company of those decrepit houses of horror that owe so much to *Psycho* and 1960. We are looking at our national chaos, and realizing that we inhabit it. In terms of genre, it is easier to see this taking a pass on mere drama and going straight to civil war. Why else is the country so armed? How can the system rescue itself? How long before the West Wing wonders what Congress is for when it is driving TV?

That's why we play Wordle every day, that and Spelling Bee. You know, I realize that I play those games, not for diversion, but as the sane central part of life. Do you think Donald ever plays those games with his young son?

28

Our Sporting Life

There's a point at which a chance of rightness in our life (some modest virtue) is in peril of becoming just "the right stuff," a brand instead of the imprint of unique experience. I'm talking high theatre, and no games have so taken over our consciousness in adapting to TV as basketball and soccer.

This whole thing was an excuse to talk about sport?

If you've been to games lately, you know the conundrum in being in the stands, a hundred feet away from the ball, trying to see what happens, and then turning to the Jumbotron video screen to get a clearer understanding. I was at the old Boston Garden, long before it was the TD Arena (named for the Toronto Dominion Bank). I was so high up at the old arena it was like being on a hillside, and all I knew of Larry Bird was the flash of his blond hair below. There was no live screen to turn to then.

At an arena—whether in Boston or watching Chelsea at Stamford Bridge— you don't see the action as well as if you are at home with your TV. It's better like that—even if it lacks the cigarette smoke, the rain in the air, and peering through the mist to see Jimmy Greaves dancing over the mud.

Watching close-up soccer on plasma, you can see which player shaved for game day, while tracking the pearls of sweat sliding down the lean faces. Those guys are playing to their close-up: they know where the cameras are as well as they know their opponents' defensive lineup.

That's why live events are so subordinate to looming screens that have the TV point of view. When we see the crowd at basketball we are seeing the first few rows of courtside revelry. The people in those seats know they are on, and they have a kind of glamour or privilege that can afford those prime seats. They dress up for the night and don't need to be directed extras; their performing identity is natural and diverting, and often more exuberant or naked than the players in their cool zone. Up above in the stands, you would have to pay a minimum of $200 for a rafters seat at the Garden. It will cost thousands courtside if the Warriors make it to a championship game. That's when the theory of a commonplace right stuff gets strained. It was a neat thrill to see the Moon, a JFK scenario, but remember what that show cost: modern estimates, poker-faced, admit to $177 billion.

Not so long ago, sport was a theatre for kids and their dads. It was a manageable entertainment. In 1987 Lucy and I walked in without advance tickets for a Warriors playoff game, and still got decent seats (we were *there*, in the arena—in the café before the game Lucy went up to the then owner of the Warriors and asked was he really Franklin Mieuli? She was on a new dress if he wasn't. He was, but I believe she got a dress anyway. It was a village then.)

That Mr. Mieuli was a nice man. I told him there was a bet on, and he agreed not to be himself. But the people with him were laughing, and he was the only person there who wore a deerstalker hat.

That was over in Oakland, when the Warriors belonged to that less lustrous city across the Bay, and when there were Black people in the crowd as well as on the court. But now the Warriors venue has become the Chase Arena in San Francisco, and you know what the Chase means for the right stuff. (The Chase National Bank was named after Salmon Chase, Treasury Secretary under Lincoln, then Chief Justice, 1864–73, though he had no link to the bank. His name was used as a brand.)

There's new ownership at the Warriors and a fresh awareness that sport was invented for money. The smart Bay Area set no longer has to encounter shabby Oakland, which has also been abandoned by the football Raiders (gone to Las Vegas, no matter that the NFL "disapproves" of gambling—these compromises can always be finessed). So the Bay Area is jaunty in its liberalism, but at the same time Oakland is being put out of sight or mind. Didn't Gertrude Stein warn the place long ago that there might be no there there? That aperçu has dated a little: it's hard to make the wit convincing for the homeless in their tents.

Here's a useful story: in 1960, the Jimmy Greaves I mentioned was a light in English soccer, "a genius," and he played for 20 pounds a week—like every other player. The end of his career overlapped with the start of Johann Cruyff's, just as Cruyff edged into the time of Diego Maradona. That Argentinian rogue might have played against Frank Lampard, and Lampard was often on the field with Mo Salah. This is in one lifetime: some of us watched them all. And Salah has just signed a new contract with Liverpool for 400,000 pounds a week. If you're interested, just know that for Paris Saint-Germain, Lionel Messi and Kylian Mbappé are both on close to 1 million pounds a week.

I'm not asking whether they deserve this. But it should be clear that football has an actual show—the men on the field with the ball, and a large live crowd—but only to sustain sport as a television event. So the crowd at the game are like extras hired in for the larger show. But whereas they once were working-class men who could just afford a game, most of them standing to watch, the crowd now sits in affluence and has become the model of a much larger audience for which poor kids (like Jimmy Greaves) just can't get in.

Lucy told me, as I came back to the room after a cheese and chutney sandwich, there had been this guy in the parking lot at the Chase Center in San Francisco (that arena opened in 2019 as a new monetizing home for the Warriors). He had a camera to snap people coming to the game—that old huckster routine. But he was wearing a T-shirt with the large words MEM-ORY MAKER stamped on it. And you sort of felt that MEMORY was available like ketchup on your fries, or a power supply you could plug into. Memory was being propositioned and codified in advance of anything worth remembering.

Last night, at that ultrasophisticated Chase (you should ask about the luxury boxes—starting at $35,000 for a playoff game, room for ten in the box—your food will be on top of that), the Warriors took the Denver Nuggets apart, as the old routine of the Splash Brothers (Steph Curry and Klay Thompson) was supplemented by the youthful Jordan Poole in a three-guard lineup that was too swift and inventive for Denver. On the radio (KNBR—"your sports leader") there was busy chatter about what to call this new setup. It seemed to require a nickname or a brand—though caution urged that Poole was not proven, or magic, yet.

Till recently the Splash Brothers were part of "the Death lineup" because that is what they (with Draymond Green and Kevin Durant) had often done to other teams, as Golden State won a couple of championships. But now exploitation wanted to look beyond that. So "Death Pool" was being offered, or Splash Pool or even 3G—you could see that as a logo on sports gear, or on the body of your beloved, as a tattoo smile on a flexed midriff. There has to be some catchy new version of "Magic" to let us know we're aces, an emphatic Right Stuff. This heightening, and taking the fame out of ordinary reach, is part of what television has done to us in the name of monetization—as in "Show me the money!" Even as the 2021–22 season ended, a one-shot cutaway appeared amid the run of commercials: it was a close-up of Earvin Johnson, just grinning at us and sighing "Magic," as if that covered everything because it was promoting fame and advertising, like a call to prayer.

In a game at Denver, everything in sight and every speech bore the cry and the logo RELENTLESS. It was meant to say these 0–3 Nuggets weren't going down lightly. The slogan was there on T-shirts, on the uniform of dancing girls, on the parquet floor, and in the air. It was in the rhythm of the noise. The slogan consumed its real bearers. The fans were no longer distinct difficult actuals; they were advertisements for themselves and their transactional function. They would MAKE NOISE and be ecstatic, and in that commitment so much of conversation or reasoning was gone. They resembled all sports crowds—what is for now our best expression of unity and valor—but they looked like the Capitol mob on January, another frenzy that needed to be on TV to scare the shit out of democracy. The passion of being there and being involved, of being seen in the war cry, had eclipsed every subtlety of what might be a game itself. If you doubted it, there were clowns and mascots with their placards—MAKE SOME NOISE and GET LOUD. It is a culture in which advertising's assertion has supplanted thought and observation. We are being scripted in plain sight. There is a mob waiting in America.

I daresay there is still a feeling that it is the job of television to transmit sport to a larger audience than can attend the site of the contest, and what might have turned out rather boring. In which case, TV is a blessing for sports fans, and one more sign of how technological progress is improving our life, and organizing our history. So there!

I tell myself I saw Bob Beamon live on TV jump 29 feet, 2½ inches in Mexico City in 1968, when the seeing stretched credulity (it was *two feet* more than anyone had jumped before). This was Icarus. Beamon collapsed when he heard how far he had gone—after all, he had not seen the arc of flight as we had done.

I had seen England win the World Cup in 1966—I witnessed those three Geoff Hurst goals (in black-and-white). And when I saw the home run Carlton Fisk hit at Fenway in 1975 in the bottom of the twelfth inning, that was after 11:30 p.m., ensuring a game seven in the Red Sox–Reds World Series. Fisk urged the ball, waving after its flight, to stay right of the foul pole. I speak of these famed events as if they were apparitions, or phenomena where the media coverage has colonized the real event.

This distancing seems obvious and banal, but we overlook the way real actions have been turned into small movies, or things that have been represented for us, like items in our filing system. They are what they are famous for, and no more. TV surveillance will go on and on until something sensational or "memorable" occurs. This is a useful functioning principle, but it is interfering with the full range of memory, or any faith in a life deprived of highlights. A life fit for ordinaries.

Seen again those events might seem quaint or archaic—though always up-to-date as a must-see-now, TV coverage goes old-fashioned overnight and picks up a humble integrity and a hallowed status—like going sepia. That is too much nostalgia and too easy an evasion of the weirdness inherent in me, in West Sussex in '68, watching Beamon go endlessly through the air, and crying out in wonder. It seemed more astonishing or moving than men on the Moon a year later. To see such elevation felt miraculous. But the longer you feed on magic the more distant you get from all things mundane. And in the breath of life that carried Beamon, just two days earlier in the Mexico City stadium, John Carlos and Tommie Smith had signaled their success in the 200 meters with Black upraised fists so that some were made very angry at the "intrusive" gesture. As if Black Power had any chance or needed to be attended to? Athletes may stay RELENTLESS, but let them be wary getting into steadfast thoughts of their own.

What we are watching tonight is *Winning Time: The Rise of the Lakers Dynasty*, on HBO, though you might guess it came from Showtime, for the ball hurries up the court with the bounce and aplomb of Los Angeles Lakers' showtime basketball in that era of Magic, Kareem, Michael Cooper, and Pat Riley, the moment when basketball took over from the movies. So this new show is wild and garish, sexy and corrupt, but for all that theatre it feeds off the lost theory of documentary—feeds on it like vultures. That is how TV has grabbed the action and attention today. *Winning Time* is trash and essential, shame-making but addictive.

There is one season of the show so far, a merry extravaganza that traces the Los Angeles Lakers, in purple and gold, from 1979 as Jerry Buss (a doctor in physical chemistry and basic flim-flam) bought the team. But it has to cover the championship glory and even the moment (1991) when Magic— aka Earvin Johnson—learned that he had fucked around so much he was HIV positive. There were rumors that maybe Magic was gay, or that he had been dirty-needling. But there were other answers: we recollected that Magic had an ancestor in an earlier Laker, the Wilt Chamberlain who scored 31,419 points, 23,924 rebounds, 4,643 assists, and in the area of 20,000 women.

It's not just that this basketball show's secret message is erotic (at a time when that energy seems diminished on our screens). It grasps the sexiness in the absurd commercial venture that Dr. Buss began, when he could not afford the team he had bought, and when the streaming new fluency of the game might seem intensified by the liberation of young Black men, the reglamourizing of Los Angeles, and the creaming known as *mo-ney.* These kids could bring the ball up the court and put it in the basket. They could endorse a shoe, and become celebrities enough for us to understand that movie stars had been superseded. When Earvin Johnson, the son of an assembly worker and a janitor, from Lansing and Michigan State, was reinvented as "Magic," a thread in racial anger in America was retired. But a few Black superstars will not end racism beyond the highlighted arenas.

Winning Time is "appalling," if solemn criticism is your game—it worships a culture of gratification and fame, dunking, and the three-point shot (introduced in 1979)—but the show was irresistible. Lucy and I grew downright bitter when we realized HBO was letting it out only one episode a week.

I want to see what happens next, she shouted out. I told you, she can get angry.

What do you expect?

Just don't throw the remote at the wall.

Of course, *Winning Time* was also a nonchalant disgrace. It trashed the new idea of women, the grail of education, or reflection, and it was a mockery of Black emergence, for it did not bother to disguise how the elevation of

Black athletes was also a new iteration of slavery. There were white guys getting their chain pulled—from Buss to Riley, and the fans like Jack Nicholson—
and white sharks in suits cleaning up. But I can't think of a series in which
so many Black guys are having such a ball and doing it with the childlike
greed of the rest of America.

Look at those guys!

Why not? For all the uncritical bimbos, stretched out on couches at the
Playboy club, strutting at the games in Laker Girl routines, or just naked
beside the pools, tanning in the indolent male gaze, there were raptures over
Black dudes in the locker room or in the shower, getting set for a full-frontal
layup.

I've got to tell you, lover, I have never seen butts like these.

It was called *Winning Time* just to be clear that nobody was up for losing. As in Las Vegas, anyone can win so long as everybody else loses. Do you
see what a model for progressive suckers this is? This is politics, too, and part
of another TV melody, the codification of a religious need, identified in
money—that followed the greased slipstream of the ads. The show was derived from a book by Jeff Pearlman, and it was finessed for TV by Max Boren-
stein (he was hot from Godzilla movies) and Jim Hecht. But some of the wit
and chutzpah, the insolence of the show, could be credited to an executive
producer and the director of the pilot, Adam McKay. In a few theatrical films
(*The Big Short, Vice,* and *Don't Look Up*), McKay had found a way of turning
recent history into acid pulp, with a cartoonish flourish and joyous contempt.
This reached a pinnacle with Margot Robbie in *The Big Short,* an odalisque
drinking champagne in a bubble bath, explaining how rigged mortgage scams
were shit, and then telling us to fuck off if we were slow in getting it.

McKay had felt drawn to "characters" stepping out of story and speaking to us directly—because he knew that the whole charade depended on our
off-camera presence. In *Winning Time* he had made Jerry Buss into an em-
peror of crassness, a warped intelligence mocking his own decadence. So he
stole the time and the camera and gave us notes, while searching for a mirror

to check his wavering hair. That lifted John C. Reilly from an endearing supporting actor to be the satyr for our ruined time, a mix of Puck and Falstaff. The effect was as startling and funny as Phoebe Waller-Bridge's *Fleabag,* and for all their differences those shows shared a germ of creative revelation: if we had always talked to the stupid TV, why shouldn't it talk back and tell us to grow up? Didn't we know yet that America was a noir farce? One year after 1979, Ronald Reagan was elected president. Not long thereafter, Donald Trump was riffing on his own lines, as if performance could bury the lies.

Winning Time did something long-form television had gloried in for years. It gave us a wealth of supporting actors, along with the illusion that a society fond of these "small" people would be dedicated to human ordinariness or "regular experience." So Adrien Brody played Pat Riley as a disconsolate nobody slowly growing into his helmet hair style and being a coach out of Armani. The writer-director Robert Towne had wanted to cast Riley in a lead part in his film *Tequila Sunrise* (1988). (He settled for Kurt Russell.) But Riley had come to life by being on TV.

Tracy Letts was a jeweled study in neglected genius as the coach, Jack McKinney, the man who designed Laker play but then fell off his bike and scrambled his head. McKinney never knew how to be famous: fame's antic instability perplexed him. Jason Clarke was a spiral of comic anguish as the Jerry West who became the logo of the NBA *and* a neurotic wreck. The real West asked for a retraction after he had seen the show—but how do you retract TV? Gaby Hoffman was elegantly fatalistic as Claire Rothman, the manager who ran the Forum (the arena where the Lakers played) and had little life of her own. Quincy Isaiah was close to noble as the Magic who learned to stop smiling, while Solomon Hughes caught the odd withdrawn majesty of Kareem. It seemed that all these life models had "adjusted" to the show's way of using them as live cartoons. Point guard Norm Nixon was even played by his own son. No one said whether rights deals had been negotiated, or was the show long past a need for clearances? These dude athletes all wanted to be actors playing themselves. That's what they had in common with Reagan.

Winning Time is unreliable as history, but history is bedridden now as a public enterprise. That's how the show's gloss and pace are true to showbiz gossip and the gloating TV of the period—like *Lifestyles of the Rich and Famous* (begun in 1984), and *Entertainment Tonight* and MTV (both launched in 1981). Under a guise of news or reportage, these were all advertisements. That feels an embalmed tone now, but there was an innocent age in the airwaves when being known for being famous was creeping in. This was a new heartlessness, deadpan but luxuriating in lying glamour (it was Warholism), and it sighed over an end to fact and diligent documentary. If you want to reclaim the dry grip of research, raw footage, and open-mindedness you should devote eight hours to Ezra Edelman's *O.J.: Made in America* (2016), done for ESPN, one of the best American films of this century, and so full of patient awareness it hurts. That is documentary, lodged in the old faith that an actual America exists, wilder and sadder than the curse of what we call reality TV.

But the defects of *Winning Time* are part of its charm, and the sleight of hand where knowingness supplants knowledge. It also helps to reveal why so many American "stories" now depend on live footage. Being on TV was the clinching proof of existence. It would be absurd and too late now for anyone to attempt *Donald Trump: Made in America.* One cannot imagine Ken Burns doing Donald. The gap between those two—with hallowed analysis trying to contain scumbag improvs—is like that between Jekyll and Hyde. Trump was all about self-gratification *now,* while Burns longs for posterity. Donald did his show every day, endlessly photographed, always talking, never meaning anything, with less interest in his country, his job, or history than in his hair. He was fixed on being on. When the leader lied, that only rallied his base in rapt fantasy. It was in the lies that everything was about him. Under cover of his catastrophes, he let us see that we had given up on provable realities and coherent existence. Just disinfect your lungs—and millions of bobbleheads nodded assent in a stupor, ready to inhale. In his four years, public candor and national purpose turned as archaic as Easter.

There you are, she said. Like Donna Reed, our Mom, she had delivered a deadpan bowl of salted caramel ice cream, just conjured it up while I was making angry notes. *I thought this was our ticket.*

How so?

Well, it's delicious, isn't it, simple and perfect, but you know it's not good for you. Like this show. Cocksure but empty.

I told her I liked the idea of capsule criticisms in terms of what you should eat to match a show.

Do you remember that Warriors game we saw, when Sleepy Floyd scored 50 points. I loved Sleepy.

Fifty-one. That was against the Lakers, in '87 maybe. Magic and Kareem played that night.

And Sleepy ran rings round them. You know, that Easter line could get you in trouble. We had a pizza that night, pepperoni with anchovies. We were something then.

29

On and Off

Do you see a pattern in all this, or a test pattern? If not a clear form, then a tendency; not so much a staircase as some awareness of a height that needs to be negotiated. That fateful urge in Icarus to soar may be the last dare left, once there is no longer a rational way of expecting the mechanism to save us.

The mechanism? Call it narrative structure, or simply being on; available for its light. It's not that we have to "get" or grasp a show, or remember the details from one night to the next. Still, we assume it will be there for us, to take the edge off our evening dismay. You are welcome to think of this process serving you, like a well-arranged hotel. But be on guard: the tin tray of "dinner" pushed in your slot every night is not just immaculate service; it is a part of the lockup system, as iron and steel as the screws and bolts on the door.

In being on, it's not that we need to be ready at an unforgiving 9 p.m. on the East Coast, a fixed starting time with the thrill of a new now. You can relax; punctuality is over. At whatever time you want it, the closure to *Ozark* will be there for you—the last body taken out, sad but a given. Yes, it will be exact and climactic—a big finish, or a slap in the face—but its nature is climatic, too, or as indolent as dull weather. So many million individual strangers can count on it in the same way as you. Its digital existence is universal but notional: whatever the knockout ending, the system couldn't care less. You may tell me this vague condition is not really relevant, so much as a technological convenience. Take care, it may be our identity as audience that is edging into insignificance. Don't rule out the chance that television's function is to smooth away the last wrinkles of human differences.

Once upon a time, our collected movies were ranks of solid, labeled canisters, stored in warehouses, as costly as cubic footage of real estate. Those cans were then trucked across the fields of the republic to pretty theatres glowing in the dark like campfires. The transportation was real! But for a long time now that inventory has been infinite yet immaterial. We can try to think of every episode of every series ever made being stacked up behind the flatness of our screen. That archival theory is amusing but fatuous, legendary, and it was the onset of a fatigue that understood the shows and the episodes did not exactly matter. If we can't get the last of *Ozark*—you can kid yourself that every "print" is being watched somewhere else—why, we can go elsewhere, and try #133 of *I Love Lucy* while we're waiting.

Those men always told us, "Don't go away," Carson or Cronkite. They hated to be alone.

But they never cared to think where away was, or what could happen there.

Let's agree: when this medium began, around 1950, and now as we resume transmission every night, we have nursed an idea that the experience could repair us, enlighten us, or lead us on. We would call it "fun" or relaxation, but might it not be good for us, like relentless improvement? This was natural and positive; it didn't even need crossed fingers. Television had a childlike sense of us all having a good time. The meaning of the ads was that we're so happy we could let them be.

It has been nice to think of television in that warm way. We forgive the silly assurance of the medium, as an alternative to entropy or being downcast. But as I spell it out, I feel doubts creeping in.

As we went along, we kept up the theatrics associated with education: that the light was a beckoning ready to lead us out of darkness. And that white lie let us ignore the steady return of the darkness. There is a pattern such as I am talking about—that every night when the TV light subsides and retreats into its originating pinprick, the dark is still there, and so loyal it must be ours. How does it forgive us, for all our protestations about enlightenment? The old test patterns seemed worthy of jokes, but we may begin to realize that whatever else is on it is the assurance that yes, there could be a pattern. If that makes you feel better.

It was a day like any other. At our stage of life that is the regularity we hope for, though we were extra alert then because we had just begun on the last episodes of *Ozark,* the delayed culmination to season four, its winding up, with the risk of maybe being disappointed. Not that season four might not be good enough, but just because the momentum had elected to stop. *Ozark* was ending. A part of us resents the binge taking a break—that's too like flatlining. The courage of our attention rises to match the medium's rhythm of going on forever.

In this valor and stamina, I may have led you to regard Lucy and me as a comic variation on those Ricardos from the 1950s, a modern couple who can't help harking back to the follies and exhausted affection of that fraught union. I believe that is how I try to see things myself. But we are also old and broke, holding off dismay.

Dependent on different stories every night, the anthology of our episodes, we cannot help but be numb figures in a gallery of fiction's history. So, in a corner of our room, leaning in the angle of two walls, Lucy could be a pensive Lady Macbeth, a Chekhovian sister wondering whether Moscow was within range, or Winnie from Samuel Beckett's *Happy Days,* half-buried in sands. We make a polite custom of not drawing attention to the burial mounds of our companions. So in this production, the sands acquire new life and suffocating stealth like all the accumulated paper we have been unable to throw away. The letters, the statements, the proposals, the versions and the corrections, the reminders of things long since forgotten, the texts and the texture of dry paper, the drafts and drafts of books, like waves in a sluggish sea.

Are you all right? I asked Lucy. We choose to say something, as if one line might start a poem.

Oh, this is a happy day, she says in that way I like—is she speaking to please me with words like wings that brush my face? Or some such metaphor.

She was looking past me, at the screen, and in a half glance I see that it is pornography playing there, as ornate and fanciful as *Game of Thrones,* yet as calm or drab as an endless loop recommending bundled insurance schemes from several years ago when insurance was still in vogue. You probably remember that point in the business cycle where it was admitted that insurance was a myth. It seemed like a crisis then, but have you noticed how crises pass by now like summer afternoons? On the screen, the man plods in and out of the woman's anus, like a piston, and she affects a trembling distress that is the turn-of-the-century stylistic of masked pleasure. She needs to be in at least the theory of pain. This is not exactly sex, you see, but the intimation that sex has always been pretending, a show we run.

Sorry, sweetheart, she sighs, and she flips this imagery out of sight with the remote that could be embedded in her hand by next year. She has no need to say sorry. None at all. We have never made love, let alone had sexual intercourse, in this screened way, imitating the action of a tiger, but there was a look on her face watching it, anxious and dispassionate, like a conscientious scientist encountering evidence of alien presence, though unsure as yet whether this was a warning or a promise.

Better not mention this, she said, nodding at the screen. *It could upset people.* You notice how she cares about you.

But everyone watches pornography so much, I said. The viewing numbers are comic and increasing. It has become the film business, which helps explain why the old official mood—that great romantic wishing—is now so listless.

We don't care to be seen seeing it. You may have readers hurt to think of me in a trance over that repetitive insertion. It's not quite Lucille Ball, they'll say.

This in a land where porn has been legal and rampantly imaginative for decades. Attempts to identify and ban "obscene" particulars have given up in despair. This is a culture where children can see porn so easily and be instructed by it. Whatever children are these days. In the history of television, do not forget how the unspeakable and unbearable have become automatic.

Like seeing Helen converted to blood and membrane in Ozark.

What I am trying to suggest is that this intercourse of ours with a screen is not just a pastime, an evening entertainment, a diversion to keep us going. It is the engine and the energy on which we are bound, the wheel of fire, unable to escape.

She looked at me; she is so forgiving of my verdicts, though they may be more damning than cutaways to gasping porn, where cries hang in the air, torn between mercy and further inducements.

Do you think Wendy and Marty still have sex in these last episodes of Ozark?

Unlikely, I said. They seem bound together now in broken faith.

But is it sentimental needing to like people to have sex with them? Or what we call "relations."

Are we so nervous about sex? Hasn't porn taught us that it's just a matter of course, the old in and out? Like jogging and breathing. Of not quite knowing the people in the bodies.

I seem to recall the Byrdes did have sex once in the beginning of the show. How many years ago was that?

Twenty-seventeen. When they were excited to get a fresh start in that pretty Ozark country. When they seemed alive in their own ad. We had tourist views then of the spectacular lakes, but the show has given up on them as the country settled into harshness.

But hasn't there always been a suspicion of desire between Marty and Ruth?

She is one person he is fond of. Sometimes it seems he wants to talk to her.

But they never do it, never touch or kiss—to keep the prospect precious.

So to stay in love you should never really do it? As if staying home means you can't go out? Once upon a time in TV they would have been an amour fou.

The purpose of the screen is to impress you with wonders you cannot have. To offer you a treasury of realities—insurance bundled with amber shampoo, a new limousine poised on a Utah precipice—while withholding them. Until you begin to give up on reality. Television is a torment fixed on the theme of impossible possession.

The perfect advertisement.

The denial of satisfaction. Beautiful despair.

Perhaps you have felt this insight coming on yourself. My topic is what this process, this dedication to the screen, is doing to us, and whether we can hope to be what we imagined before the Ricardos. It's a matter of trying to decide whether it has all been such fun, part of an enslavement? This operates in all forms of slavery. They are odious, of course, but they offer one wicked comfort: we are being looked after, and nothing is more fearsome—this is coming up, like a cartwheeling crash we see on the road ahead—than the feeling that we are alone and uncared for—without parents or loved ones, and without any solace in the larger state of affairs. So a German in 1943, a citizen of the Reich, might have known what a terrible world it was, with slaughter at hand and aromas of decay on the spring breeze, but he or she could shelter from the dread at every waking by being counted and medicated by some enveloping police state. Of course, that sounds bad—and you guess the reality may be worse. But there is a despairing ease in it. If we turn ourselves on, they supply the juice—*please don't stop.*

The secret pulse in fascism, and in the TV being on, is that at the worst of times we all hear the same "once upon a time," in the certain knowledge that we are not brave enough to run free and be at liberty.

If that paradox confounds you, just look at the last of *Ozark* and see how Laura Linney had arrived at a face for Wendy Byrde cast in the self-hatred she could no longer suppress. It would be tactful to call this fine acting, but we are at a point where it is fanciful to hope that our players keep a safe distance from what they are pretending. How are any of us handling that trick?

A moment comes where Wendy's performance in life burns off like mist—

hear her rapturous lying telephone calls, "*Claire, it's Wendy!*" Staring into the camera in a matter-of-fact way, she slams her head against the structure of her car. Despair and self-loathing. A trickle of blood comes out of her hair. Was that a carefully placed sachet or had the actress's pursuit of naturalism dispensed with such fussy toys?

There is another shot in one of the last episodes of *Ozark*—and it was directed by Linney herself (her first such credit)—of a camera backing off as Marty rushes towards it. He is at last in a storm of desperation, as if his wish to stay cool has finally broken, and he is screaming at the implacable grip of his condition. He had been brave enough to go back to Mexico, and he survived there while torturing and killing an innocent man, when some similar unkind treatment might have been served up for him. Marty has given his whole being to staying in charge, assuring himself that the tangle of his compromises is still a textbook knot he can untie. But now he knows the tangle is an aneurysm, or a brain, as crowded as such organs can be before they burst. His enterprise was standing up for order against the chaos, but his scream admits the failure of his insane idea of control. And it might as well be us roaring.

So what did we expect from *Ozark*? What had it left us waiting for? This was not just the conclusion, but a delayed finale (the rest of season 4), and hadn't we been left hanging over what happened in that car crash at the start of 4? That seemed no small collision; it was as spectacular as a dream, a radical upending. Months later, we were there to see the four occupants of the car slip free from the wreckage without any significant injury, and without the vehicle turned into a fireball. No one was hurt, or even bruised? And yet, there would be an intuition that the crash had been a harbinger or foretelling of fatality. Was that so? It's still a kind of rule in the game that I am not supposed to tell you this, as if there is something sacred in endings, a way in which suspense equates to our spiritual aspiration—as in we should not know, or tell, how our own demise works out.

But the show has to shut down, and it's in the way of making the story or watching it that we expect a satisfactory conclusion. What does satisfactory mean? Well, it ought to seem credible or deserved, or a proper completion of elements we have followed. Five years of pursuit! With those Byrde children growing older. Doesn't that deserve a payoff? But shouldn't it be a surprise, too? That's a test of play-making, but it can lead to the kind of ending in which the last bow is tied too tidily or prettily. As if we hear the several storytellers chuckling in elan and shame as they vanish into the darkness or their next project.

It's spoiling nothing to say that *Ozark* had been leading to a terminus where the ingenuity of the Byrdes should give way to catastrophe. This need not be as balletic as car crashes or as pretty as poppy fields on fire at night. It need not be a last tableau in which executed bodies struggle to find room to expire and still have their close-ups. But it did not seem out of order if the culmination of the show, the infernal way in which money and murder overgrew love and family, was close to saying, well, of course, this is the Midwest, or this is America.

That need not be spoken or identified. It could be there if anyone cares to construct it, without undue underlining or a fortune cookie motto, let alone a last line where someone declared a curse on all your houses, or tried to whisper the words to "America the Beautiful."

Even so, *Ozark* leaves us to reconcile the thorough demolition of American space, its social structure and its purpose with the clear evidence that the show made a fortune and inspired a tranquil envoi from Netflix in which Garner, Linney, Bateman, and so many others said that doing it was the best time of life they had ever known.

There are dead bodies at the end of *Ozark,* but there had been such décor from the beginning. How many would be killed? You may have entertained creative ways of removing them. "Murder" may be our song in the shower, a way of coming clean. You do not need to feel aggrieved or at a loss for the fallen, though I can think of two characters—women—who had it in them to do great service to the *Ozark* storyline, until they were taken out. You can imagine conference rooms of seasoned writers swapping obituaries and future arcs back and forth, while calculating the loss to audience support if this or that actor was gone forever. Ruth was an unlikely character, you felt, until Julia Garner so established her that there was no writing her out. It's a version of life, I suppose, but actors get to be lively just to earn more paydays and residuals.

Laura Linney delivered the most disturbing performance in *Ozark*. She was the show's daring and its chance of being demented. So Linney rode the risks with a fearsome serenity, until her very face seemed to alter. Yet she did not win an Emmy for that work. Can we wonder why? Is it some answer that she played a wife and a mother in the process of going mad? And whereas Julia Garner's Ruth was spectacular and transporting, an adventure for voyeurs waiting on her every punctuating "fuck," Wendy Byrde is as close to home as a tumor in your mother's brain. Maybe Wendy was so deeply discomforting that the prize-giving missed her out. (Don't forget that among the many things not mentioned in the original Constitution—the book for our show—there is "women.")

It was my feeling as the years went by that the Byrde children—Charlotte and Jonah—might lay their young hands on power and weaponry, and either rescue their exhausted parents or bring closure to their wickedness. What does Charlotte feel about Wendy?—that angle was not pursued. Yet this is a show where we realize how often dear ones may put an end to us. Would that happen at the end of *Ozark*? I'm still not sure, though there were gestures towards some violent stirring in the young as their parents slipped into madness.

But would the ultimate challenge be grasped—I mean a way of seeing this regional story as a model for what was happening to couchland, or the United States? There was no doubt about its instinct for money and greed eclipsing the heartland—and there the setting was crucial, for we like to think that hills, lakes, and forests bring us closer to our nature. Along with poverty, narrow prospects, and perfunctory education. The Langmore family were mavericks and deadbeats, beholding the kingdom of commercials with contempt. Ruth was the face of ridicule in our mirror.

But how could they expose American Byrdeland? The storyline made minor concessions to political reality, like a reference to vulnerable voting machines. But it never dared tread on the mania for making America great again. It saw the threat coming from Mexico, in the old-fashioned Navarros; it never admitted that our homeland bogeymen, the liars on TV, could be more damaging. Nor did it explore the mesh of money-laundering and our greased political machines. Not that anyone doubts the chronic resource known as fundraising and the way state careers in government are inseparable from its graft. Our own cartels marry revenue and idealism every day without blushing. We like to warn ourselves about Russian oligarchs, but that helps excuse our homegrown moguls. It is time to realize that to study organized crime is to describe how society operates. But *The Godfather* dodged that chance, too, and laid down the model for making such crime a crowd-pleasing ticket. Don't forget that Netflix—the makers of *Ozark*—is among the precarious players in so many dark games. Netflix profits off sagas of crime, and striking coups of violence, but it is not the most obvious source of autopsies on capitalism.

Ozark took care not to pin down political allegiances for its characters, no matter that Ozark country is a model for Trump's sway in rural Missouri. Wendy had been vaguely involved in progressive politics in Chicago once, but did that still show in her? Would developing that line risk alienating some of the impoverished conservatives a show depends on? Very likely so, but that knocks up against a barrier in our affairs. For the diagram of corruption laid out in *Ozark* leads us to the brink of sociopolitical interpretation. Thus anyone watching the show for years, tracking their own pinched financial status and their attempt to be citizens (premium Netflix is now $19.99 a month), might realize that while we are all Byrdes in the trees, organized crime has the best lawyers and birds of prey. And the land of the free so yearns to be organized that it is ready to turn fascist.

If that moment comes, TV can handle it—it has learned so much from afflicting us with ads. It knows we cashed our honor in so long ago. It's tempting to think that the couch transports us. Isn't its winged state a means to change and improvement? Isn't it pretty to think so, but are the wings quietly folded, in the pious hope that real change is more unsettling than educational? In which case is our couch better seen as the scaffold for our finale, or the operating table on which we observe ourselves being dissected? Live on TV—your death. Don't go away.

What are we waiting for—greatness or demise? As Ruth Langmore might put it when facing down the somber Camila Navarro, who is holding Ruth at gunpoint, until the young woman from Missouri roars at her, "Well, are you gonna fucking do this shit or what?"

In Julia Garner's pale-skinned, foul-mouthed, razor-sharp being, Ruth was a waif in the hinterland who never had faith in being saved. She was born and raised knowing she was as close to a mistake as so many million Americans. I say mistake because her outcast liveliness lacked the faith in planning that deadened Wendy and Marty. Ruth's feral energy cannot believe in direction. Though she has a perpetually discontented edge, she has no idea how or where to go. Throughout the show, even when she gets money, she keeps living in trashy trailers, an untidy camp for indigents and itinerants.

Ruth cannot believe America is for her—and such bleak visionaries are rare on our TV. She is always a wild girl, without a chance of being a woman. Her only goal is to be the next Darlene Snell in an "impossible" romantic relationship. But Darlene is from an earlier era and a rural mood, one that so cherished love she takes the death of her beloved Jacob into her own capable hands. The Snells and the Langmores are deeply buried in Missouri history; they came there from England and Scotland, trained in poverty. Whereas the Byrdes fell off the Monopoly board known as Chicago by running into trouble with nasty Mexicans.

Ruth's tough girl act is observed without the least pathos, in us or herself.

The one time she puts on a good dress—a white cocktail sheath—she takes a bullet and a bloodstain for vanity.

In a medium that is avowedly egalitarian, open for everyone, she lets us feel how so many everyones are aimless and lost. And she offers not a glimmer of hope for the base or for any of us so arrogant to think of educating it. In the culture of advertising, and the frenzy to be great, we are all falling away, like Icarus.

A mere seventy-five years after television began in its wish to be agreeable and encouraging, here is a show, a palpable hit and prize-winner, that says, without moderation or humor, that there is no way of living in this country according to its hallowed ideals.

Except by watching every night.

30

After Golden?

As a customer and historian, I can look back on twenty years or so and believe we had a golden age with our television. From the start of *The Wire* (2002) to the end of *Ozark* (2022), we gathered for many evenings in high expectation. But some corruption was under way. I felt a first hint of it far from Ozark country.

There's a town named Shaftesbury, in Dorset, in southern England. It sits at a modest height in a gently undulating terrain that could easily be dismissed as flat and pastoral. Yet it is one of the most lovely places in the country. Some people go to Shaftesbury just to gaze at what is called Cranborne Chase, a stretch of meadows and woodland that reaches over twenty miles. The prospect seems not just ancient but providential, like a source of feeling.

There was some settlement there in the ninth century. The place then had other names, and it was known for unexpected healings—miracles, they thought—so that King Alfred began to build an abbey there in 888.

You talk of 888 as if it was part of your experience.

It was a vexed time as the Saxon chiefs in England fought to resist Viking invasion. So King Alfred—also known as Alfred the Great—fought bitter campaigns against the Vikings. He was said to be a gentle and learned man who believed in education and law, and in being Saxon.

Who said that about him? I can't say, but folklore credited his greatness. In the late 1940s when I began to collect nuggets of English history, I heard the story of how Alfred, on the run from the Vikings, was taken in by a countrywoman for shelter. Thus she told him to watch some cakes she had baking, while she went out. A simple duty. But Alfred was so preoccupied by his problems with the Vikings that he forgot the cakes and they burned.

For all I know, this travesty of academic history is still passed on to children. Can you see Alfred as a Basil Fawlty misfit, his head full of huge matters, but tripping on a carpet and bringing the house down? I am guessing those cakes started as a joke, because so often humor lasts the longest.

As England resisted the Vikings but then yielded to Norman conquest, the place we call Shaftesbury developed. It was set in farming country, and seemed indifferent to industrial revolution. It has never quite lost that rural mood. But Thomas Hardy saw it—he called it Shaston—and in his novel *Jude the Obscure* (1895) he lamented how its quality or atmosphere had come close to ruin because of progress. By the twenty-first century, it is a famous "beauty spot," sought out by cultivated tourists. And they gather at the northeastern corner of the town, near the ruins of the abbey, to look out at the landscape.

There is a café on top of the slope that becomes a steep street—it is a good location for business that serves cream teas (£5.50 per person).

On one side of the falling street there is a high wall, a protection for the abbey and its grounds. On the other side there is a curved row of cottages, some from the late eighteenth century. A few of them are thatched. You can tell yourself that Jude Fawley or Sue Bridehead might have lived there. And there are people living there still. This cobbled street is well known now—it is called Gold Hill—and that is because, in 1973, the director Ridley Scott used the hill as the setting for a television commercial for a type of wholemeal bread, called Hovis. The ad shows a boy from long ago wheeling a bike up the hill loaded with loaves. Then he freewheels down again, having delivered the goods.

The idyll uses passages from Dvořák's *New World* Symphony, as played by a brass band, and it has an old man's rustic voice as if he is the spirit of that boy from the past. This is all very effective (Scott was at the start of his career—in a few years he would make *The Duellists,* a pretty advertisement for the town of Sarlat in the Dordogne). Yet his proficiency with Gold Hill and brown bread can turn your stomach over every scheme of effectiveness on a screen. There are those who feel he ruined Shaftesbury.

Hovis used to be a decent loaf; perhaps it still is. The name came from the Latin, *hominis vis,* the strength of man. It's as much a tribute to bread as Mr. Scott is to filmmaking. There is a model loaf at the top of the hill in Shaftesbury, made of plaster and the size of a steamer trunk. Gold Hill (as it's called now) has been impaired or bought off; it is a quotation and a cliché, a brand, and a usurping of nature, the more potent in that many viewers will not notice what has been done. It's not that it spoils the far view of Cranborne Chase or the potential of countryside as a place where we might think of being. It's not that you won't be glad you went there and saw it. But you cannot move on without the certainty that in our vanity and ingenuity human beings have surpassed nature.

There was another television commercial that played in the spring and early summer of 2022. It amounted to a series, for it was repeated so much during the basketball playoffs. My friend Phil and I live only a few blocks apart and we were e-mailing every day, arguing over the merits or not of *Winning Time,* as the Warriors advanced on their real championship, with series against the Nuggets, the Grizzlies, the Mavericks, and then the Celtics in the finals. But we did not see each other in that time, and we regretted that in a gentlemanly way, while resembling two old guys made timid by Covid.

The 2022 commercial was promoting Corona beer, and it featured two men on a magnificent beach somewhere. It felt like a kingdom. They were Andy Samberg and Snoop Dogg, the one an actor and a comedian, the other a sometime rapper but more significant now as a role model. The two guys are hanging out in an amiable way, though Andy is unsettled and nervous over doing nothing. Snoop is none of those things. He wears a florid dressing gown that has a regal splendor. They sit beside an iced barrel of bottles of Corona.

Andy is anxious to know what they're going to do. He wants to have a structure to the day. He holds his cell phone as if it is a heart condition. So Snoop takes that phone, drops it in the ice barrel, and gives Andy a bottle of beer. "The best plans," he tells the white guy, "are no plans at all."

Andy is calmed; he sees a new life, like a religion. Whereupon Snoop Dogg confers a right and an absolution on him. "Just call me Snoop."

It's only thirty seconds, and I may have seen it a hundred times in a season: that adds up to a fifty-minute movie, an endless loop, and it was one of the most intriguing things on television in that time—and that includes not just the Warriors' championship, but the war in Ukraine and the hearings of the House Committee investigating January 6, 2021. You may be smiling at this, or in despair, at the recklessness ready to dump our fears over catastrophe in some cultural ice bucket.

Is that reading too much into it? Is it humorless to be so intent on what is a flicker in our air and our sensibility? Too late now: the rhythm of this book has all along been drawn to looking closely at every thirty seconds that passes by.

Andy is youngish, white, and edgy. Snoop is Black, languid, and philosophical. More or less. He seems effortlessly rich and casual, whereas Andy is more tied up in what makes Andy run. So it is that Snoop takes over the kid, not with beer, or even a sunny day on an empty beach, but with the theory that, once nothing matters, why plan anything?

Of course, that indifference is not what Corona is after. Like most ads on TV this is a calculated parable that demands close scrutiny and enhanced beer sales. Corona knows the numbers. Nothing is more misleading than the ad's casual air. But this is an uncommon storyline in having a Black man mentoring a white in how to live. Not that Snoop is Sidney Poitier, or Clarence Thomas. He makes a raffish figure, good-natured, but secure in indolence and detachment.

Some viewers will know that Snoop Dogg (real name, Calvin Cordozar Broadus Jr.) has had a checkered career. He has been a very successful rap artist, singer, and songwriter. That gives him a louche celebrity over which he seems unimpressed. His trick is to make ultimate coolness warm and amiable. Dogg is being paid for the ad, and for its every play, but he affects a sense of being his own master. He wants to be seen as a free spirit, and Corona is doing all it can to enhance that distance. But a fix is in. Snoop has had several incidents in his life involving cocaine and marijuana; he has been apprehended at airports for carrying weapons; and there have been charges of sexual harassment leveled at him. Corona does not mention this record, but the overall ease of the ad speaks to Snoop's detachment from, say, the conservatism of Clarence Thomas or the wholesome citizenry of Sidney Poitier.

But Snoop is not just selling beer. There is an attitude beneath his bearing and his brief lines that suggests the virtue in being willing to abandon plans. This is closer to the stereotype of a Black dropout than to the standing of Thomas or Poitier. It is not a role model that Black parents or educators might want to be associated with. They could say that to be a useful and remotely happy American citizen (able to buy a beer or a beach), some planning is a necessity. In the same way, in confronting America's "problems"— from race and poverty to global warming and the inequities of the world—it is frivolous to advise a life without planning. We are where we are, on the edge of ruin, because that rationale has been too often neglected.

There's no reason to think that Corona and its advertising arm were unaware of these subtexts. They are too thorough for that. They have the metrics on our responses. Still, the decision was made (by some latter-day Don Draper) to advocate the place of beer in a life of indulgence and willful emptyheadedness. No ad would risk endorsing drunkenness or torpor, or let Snoop seem homeless and derelict, but where else is the ad going? His idleness is based on wealth; he has been chosen for the ad because he sustains the legend of success—while affecting indifference to it. His Black character is superior to or more understanding than the white guy, but is he really being proposed as a mentor or as part of the larger scheme of all advertising in offering to educate us? It's not too big a leap to see that Corona is being classified beside marijuana and the larger code of dropping out, or giving up one's addiction to the cell phone. Maybe Andy will be less of a worrier if he takes Snoop's lead. Will he be happier? But then wonder what these two guys are going to do on the beach all day, day after day.

I'm sounding censorious and prim. But I take the substance of this small film seriously. In being drawn into the mood of the ad I could see that it is not so far from sentiments possible in the late afternoon light at Shaftesbury, watching shadows creep across the land and feeling something like contentment as well as mystery. Though I'm not sure that meditation suits Corona's purpose. The fix is in, so embedded that something like crucifixion is in effect. In Shaftesbury and on a fine beach there is an implicit urging to live without advertising or TV itself, and to open oneself to . . . I'll call it nature. There is a revolution lurking in the balmy light, and if Snoop likes to think of himself as our jester, and his own role model, there is reason to reach far deeper and to admit the merciless planning in the ad and its theory. And the slavery that grips Snoop Dogg.

Television was designed and developed to make our life seem easier, or less problematic. Yet somehow that gift has grown harder and more tiring as the problems have become like dragons. You may have been affronted at first by the suggestion that our being on the couch watching is a kind of masked invalidism, but consider that possibility carefully. The medium that offered to bring you the world—to make you better informed, more aware, and altogether better (that was the inherent ad in the system)—has turned us into helpless spectators. We have no authentic politics because we have been taught to enjoy the point/counterpoint of witty and attractive talking heads playing a game called politics. In being brought the world we were more able to be detached from it. So we watched the war in Ukraine for months until we became discreetly bored with it and our absence of agency. There really was so little point in planning.

One of the consequences to recognizing a golden age is the retrospective captioning of history. The way of organizing it, not just so that it can be taught or written about, but to give us the illusion of conducting progress as a kind of plan or purpose. So a while ago, I talked about England in the ninth century as a battleground for Saxons, Vikings, and then Normans—with burned cakes for tea. This scheme is natural and well-meaning but in so many ways it is a travesty of how societies progress.

One can outline a book like this as going through the pioneering stage of television, into how the new medium overcame cinema, then by way of the networks into cable, and so on, up to the point of having the domestic screen surpassed by all our smaller screens. This sounds like a plan, and humans and institutions can claim agency at different points along the line. Equally, one can see nothing more or less than the impersonal advance of technology and the secret separation of ourselves from reality when all along that has been the unaddressed policy of television. I think it's possible that Snoop Dogg (as presented for Corona) had a better instinct for what was happening than Newton Minnow.

I felt early in the twenty-first century that long-form television was in its heyday, and something to watch. Over seventy-five years, I felt impressed by the way a medium had gone from *Dragnet* to *Ozark* (from meek endorsement to searching criticism), and I daresay that "improvement" or "realism" encouraged Icarus to take flight. I wanted to write about a number of shows I had seen, and I've done my best just as Lucy and I look back on a lot of fun.

But as I spent a couple of months looking at Snoop, Andy, and their beer, there seemed to be less worth watching on TV, or less feeling for creative danger. There you are: if you allow yourself a golden age, then you can hardly resist a feeling of letdown, tarnishing, and diminution. If you watch a lot of television, it's easy enough to slip into the despondency over how a lot of it is too like the rest of it. That happened with movies, and it has surely happened with TV. Those media told so many stories that we became as jaded as scriptwriters running old routines. Movies began to be versions of old movies; the technology and the commerce made sure of that. The diet of copies can make you forget the sudden unexpected moments in life, not to mention rare afternoons when life pauses in excitement as you contemplate the view.

One flaw in screened stories is that the people do what they are told to do in the script (when you know how the screenwriters have given up the ghost). After a hundred years a good deal of freedom has been abandoned.

It's essential to say something about bad TV.

I think I've seen this before. Isn't she going to fall down the stairs?

You're right. Toni Collette is going to fall down the staircase. We are talking about an incident in the True Crime genre.

In 2001, Michael Peterson was living in an affluent suburb of Durham, North Carolina, with his second wife, Kathleen. He was fifty-eight. He had worked for the Defense Department and served in Vietnam. He then wrote a series of novels about war and crime and failed in a run to be mayor of Durham. He and Kathleen lived with a gang of children: two by his first marriage; two more—the children of friends who died—whom Michael adopted; and one who was Kathleen's daughter by a previous marriage. That's five children who all become characters, and if you can't recall the family tree I don't blame you.

Michael and Kathleen had a large house, and one night in December 2001 Kathleen died there. Michael said she had fallen down a narrow, curved back staircase and apparently bled to death. But the district attorney was suspicious. He believed a blow from a blunt instrument had been involved. There was debate over her wounds and the blood splatter on the staircase wall. Motive was not clear though it turned out that Michael had a gay life which possibly Kathleen had just discovered. So they had had a big row? Michael said she had always accepted his gay affairs. The DA elected to charge Michael with murder. He was convicted in the trial, and sent to prison for life. He said justice had failed. People do fall down staircases: apparently that is how Ivana Trump died in July 2022. And murders can be uninteresting.

There's a great deal more detail in the Peterson case, and while one has natural sympathy for victims of murder, and the relatives of the deceased, and a lingering interest in "courtroom dramas," I believe this case is boring, hard to explain, and harder still if you are hoping to identify with anyone. To care? Never mind, murder trials do not have a duty to entertain us. They have every right to be humdrum and forgettable, as well as cases in which the more you learn the less likely you are to rely on anyone.

There is no mercy. In France, on hearing about the case and its trial, a documentary film was proposed, with a French crew being sent to North Carolina to film as many of the unfolding events as possible. This was mounted by Canal Plus, with Jean-Xavier de Lestrade directing. He had won an Oscar for *Murder on a Sunday Morning,* about a killing in Florida. Eight episodes of this Peterson documentary played in France, and on Netflix in the U.S. in 2004. Later on, there would be another five episodes as the case went to a retrial and then at last to Peterson being released on an Alford verdict. What was that? Well, you might say it was a legal proceeding invented by script-writers that lets a convicted person go free after a formal admission of culpability. Having your cake and eating it in an age that might be seeing a new motive for murder: to get on TV.

This French show was called *The Staircase* in the U.S., and it amounted to thirteen episodes of about fifty minutes each. I've seen it all, and it was tough going.

Then HBO Max determined to redo the story as a dramatization. This venture, again called *The Staircase,* was created by Antonio Campos. He helped write it (another eight episodes of more than an hour each), and he codirected it with Leigh Janiak. It ran on HBO in May and June of 2022. Peterson was played by Colin Firth; Kathleen was Toni Collette; the chief defense lawyer was Michael Stuhlbarg; Parker Posey was notable on the prosecution team. Among the children you could find Sophie Turner, Dane De-

Haan, and Rosemarie DeWitt. It was a class act, even if the factual basis was so uninteresting. The French documentary team was included in the American drama, and that introduced the editor on the French show, a part filled by Juliette Binoche so appealing that it was easy to believe she and Peterson had grown "close."

These were good actors, working hard, though Collette hardly had a character to grasp. Murder victims tend to be written off, or down. Firth was more solid than Michael Peterson had seemed in the documentary, and that was hard luck for the real man (he soon deplored Firth's performance—he said he would have preferred Brad Pitt). But even Firth looked nonplussed at trying to negotiate the long and inconclusive story or in knowing how to play it. The real Peterson (he is alive still, aged seventy-nine) seemed a little flighty or scattered in the documentary. That made him more interesting. Why should living people be plausible or coherent? Whereas Firth seemed determined to stay dogged and real, but rather bad-tempered. As so often in his work, he conveyed a watchful fiber, but still I didn't care a damn. Moreover, in the last shot of the HBO show, where he stares enigmatically into the camera, I had a hunch that Firth had reached the same terminus. (Did he have a ghost of a grin?)

Several times in the drawn-out hours and years I told myself I was sticking with it for you, but now I have little to offer you. *The Staircase* was dreary TV, and while long ago I grew to accept that ocean of doldrums, still it's important to stress that this vacant and excruciating show—or the two shows—served no other purpose than occupying screen time. Being on. I recognize that TV programing is easily drawn to "true crime" as a genre, and I am in favor of that when it turns out to be the coverage of the January 6 Committee, in which there is so much happening, so much character and drama, so much hanging in the balance, that you feel burstingly alive and anxious. But true murderers need to shape up if they reckon to get on TV.

Supper? I was thinking of genuine brown bread and butter, and a cold beer. Plus there's a new season of Peaky Blinders.

It seemed a long time ago that *Peaky Blinders* was something daring under the forbidding light of the English Midlands. It was a BBC show that started in September 2013, created by Steven Knight, a rare talent, versatile but inconsistent. He had been a co-creator of the game show *Who Wants to Be a Millionaire?*; he scripted *Eastern Promises* for David Cronenberg; and he wrote and directed that unique feature film *Locke.* Yet he's unaccountable— he also wrote *Spencer* (2021)—never more so than in his signature work, the six seasons of *Peaky Blinders.*

The Blinders are a gang in the Birmingham area, veterans of the Great War and disillusioned by that ordeal. They are also Romani, inclined to violence (the show's title refers to razors inserted in the peaks of their caps), as loyal as Corleones, and avid for beautiful women. Because of the Romani element, the period setting, and the use of old industrial locations and neglected landscapes north of the Midlands, the show seemed fresh and quirky, even if its format owed a lot to Coppola and Sergio Leone.

The gang leader was Tommy Shelby (Cillian Murphy), aloof yet somehow stricken (it was nearly Jason Statham in the role). In the first season he was sustained by a mighty opponent in an Ulster police inspector played by Sam Neill. He also encountered a woman, a spy for the inspector, and soon Tommy's beloved. There was a lot of sex and violence, as well as striking modern music, some of it by Nick Cave. The 1920s seemed racy and entertaining, and there were hints that the show could get into the troubled politics of Britain in the years between the wars. Winston Churchill appeared briefly as a rascal opportunist.

I took pleasure in the shuffle of originality and throwback; I admired the brave women—Annabelle Wallis, Charlotte Riley, Gaite Jansen, Sophie Rundle—and was amused by tasty supporting performances from Tom Hardy as a Jewish gangster, Adrien Brody as a Mafioso come over from the U.S., and Paddy Considine as a malignant priest. There were also two other potent family members: Paul Anderson as Tommy's gloomy, pathological brother Arthur, and Helen McCrory as their radiantly dangerous aunt Polly. Wasn't she the best female gangster screens have ever had? These two were as explosive as Murphy's Tommy was taciturn. He seemed stilled by his power. That left a hole in the heart of the show, and Knight never found a way of filling it.

So the show deteriorated and became an anxious copy of itself. That process is common in commercial TV, and it can lead to unwitting self-parody or hysteria. There can be a feeling by season 2 or 3 of many shows that they are being pushed on because they are too profitable a band wagon to abandon. But there was a potential in *Peaky Blinders* for digging into the English crises of the 1930s, and it might have focused on the arrival of the fascist leader Oswald Mosley (Sam Claflin) as a character. This offered a doorway into an English *Babylon Berlin,* but Knight was content to make Mosley just a cruel, flashy cad. Those qualities existed in the man, but there was a chance of more. Mosley had a time when he was torn apart by thinking about why Great Britain needed a new order. He was a member of the Labour Party before he was a fascist. He and the Shelbys had similar vague but heady notions of radical change. Maybe the business decision was taken that the *Blinders* audiences should not be challenged with material they did not know about.

There were five seasons with a steady decline, and then a pause before a sixth (in 2022) that was a disaster. It was handicapped by the recent death of Helen McCrory, and the retreat of Arthur as a role—was the actor ill or weary? It was no compensation that the sixth season led Tommy into ponderous soul-searching, when he had never shown enough of a soul before. At the end of series 6, Tommy was still there, numb but in charge, while the show mourned Polly. If only she had had a chance to grapple with Mosley and reveal the cracks and gulfs in English society. The Blinders could have been reds. The function of crime on the screen is to make us wonder whether our scheme of law and order needs to be changed.

You would want that?

You bet your life I would.

What would you say to a defiant seventh season of *Blinders* in which the Shelbys are invited to Downton Abbey?

And they trash the stately place?

They dismantle its hierarchy. They set fire to pretty pictures by Romney and Gainsborough. The grooms and gamekeepers ravish the ascendancy. Wallis Simpson and her sad man are introduced. The Countess of Grantham becomes the new Polly. Her fierceness is something the Blinders understand. The tone should be comic yet frightening.

I can smell the mayhem.

All seventh seasons should gravitate to farce.

Is that Montaigne or Chuck Barris?

There were things we were waiting for in the summer of 2022. There was the war in Ukraine; it had not gone away just because our attention and "concern" were wavering. So the Russians were incendiary-bombing wheat fields waiting to be harvested. The grind of combat had become a weather system. It was not clear that the "sanctions" were turning out to be a plan. The shortages of energy were bearing down on Europe, and in July the summer turned to temperatures that were a new metric. They seemed unnatural, and prompted anger at one wrong word. The quest for air conditioning took on a spiritual aspiration. If the world was ending, why not now? Who cared to miss that view?

In the United States, theories of legislation were collapsing as Lake Mead ran lower still, exposing the historical corpses that had been dumped there in the cause of vengeful monetization. As if that imperative any longer had a chance of saving us. There was a pressure of violence growing. Didn't America have its history of armed gangs running the show?

And other things like that.

Not least the disclosure that the mighty Netflix was in some pain. For the second quarter in a row it had lost subscribers. It still had more than 200 million, but the market was panicky without growth. Netflix had a rescue plan. It would declare that its stream could not function without advertising. And so the gripping atmosphere of its stories might have to be interrupted by delirious shit. Fresh news of assassination and annunciation would be broken in on by promos for some tech refinement of our intel calm. Once upon a time the ads had said, drink this beer, suck the ketchup off this burger, and ogle these seven dreamboats on the beach. But now they spoke of "business assurance" and digital analysis. Such nerve.

There had been a time when the advertising could be assessed as an unfortunate convenience, a vulgarity we would learn to endure. But wasn't it clear now that it had compromised any attempt at honesty in the medium? The commercials never spelled this out, but they had said that lying was natural and OK. That's how we let our membership in fact lapse and turn camp.

We let it in, and can't get it out.

31

Old Men and Older

I got in first; it was like playing white in chess. We were desperate for something to see since so many new shows withered before our eyes. We were in a heatwave, triple-digit temperatures, without air conditioning. We were at a point of still telling ourselves, This heat can't go on forever. But we were uncertain. The weather may rise and fall. It is not obliged to be a narrative. But sometimes we grasp how close it is in its momentum to being free of story.

What shall we watch tonight? I asked Lucy. I didn't mention the World Cup coming up—if we could hold on for that.

There's this Jeff Bridges show, she said. The Old Man. *You know he's golden. I like to feel he wouldn't have done the show unless it was OK.*

Wasn't he ill as they made it? Didn't it stretch out over years? How old is he now?

Bridges was only seventy-two as we spoke. He had had a cancer as well as Covid as *The Old Man* got under way, so that had slowed the mechanics of a new series. That kind of hiatus can intervene if a fruitful January start is interrupted; pick it up again in October and you may have lost the drift or even the characters' names, like an old man getting up in the morning and being uncertain how breakfast functions, or why.

Our friend Phil had warned us. People brood over TV series as if they were last weekend's weather. He had said *The Old Man* started out fine, but then at about an episode and a half it lost its way. He wasn't aggrieved about this. These days a decent episode and a half can be a viable evening. We don't feel a right to ask for much more. It's as if we have no more choice than with the weather. "You could have turned it off," we're told. But that seems to risk losing contact. Aren't we in the habit of starting off a series, feeling hope and energy in its pert setup, yet guessing it will lack the stamina to see us through?

The Old Man is from a novel, by Thomas Perry. I haven't read the book, and to do so now would only lead to pointless turmoil. But as written for television, by Jonathan E. Steinberg and Robert Levine (with the esteemed executive Warren Littlefield hanging around), it offers Bridges as Dan Chase, a retired or withdrawn CIA man who lives alone in the country. In the book this is Norwich, Vermont, where Lucy and I lived once—we were married there, by a justice of the peace. It rained that day, light and sweet, and we walked home down the hill sharing an umbrella.

Dan is a widower; he has a grown daughter at the other end of his phone, and he worries over his cognitive functioning. He might be losing it; he has to pee several times during the night. You can see why that thought concerns his dogs, two exemplary Rottweilers, who act together as deftly as Walter Brennan and Gary Cooper in *Meet John Doe*.

Then his past reaches out to claim him. I must tell you that I could not follow what used to be called "the plot" of *The Old Man*. I wonder whether anyone did. But the daft show is blithe about this, as if to tell us, just be like those dogs, bright-eyed and wagging your tail, and giving Dan uncritical allegiance.

That was fine with me.

Just hold on to something secure with this sketchy synopsis. Dan Chase has a dark past with the CIA. In somewhere like Afghanistan, he wooed the wife of a local chieftain and stole her away. And I believe that in the process he laid hands on a sum of treasure while being caught up in obscure betrayals. This may have been shaming work, but still it *is* Jeff Bridges and you will recall that more or less he has played honorable guys with a straight face, as if that stature could distract him from all the compromise in being a Hollywood movie star for fifty years—it comes to that now. He *is* the Dude.

In other words, we like Jeff enough to stomach Dan's sins, or whatever.

Questions of his cognitive dysfunction, not to mention his physical fragility, are set aside once hostile operators come to get him. He dispatches them so adroitly, while knowing that his life and liberty are curtailed. He is going to have to put his dogs in his car and go under cover, just because fate is resolved to take him off the map. Don't ask why this should be, or how the incompetent CIA behaves so flawlessly. If we're going to sit still for this stuff there are things we must agree not to dispute. Or you could simply give up watching television and take your own dogs for a walk in the hills. One thing I like about our here is that there is wild country twenty minutes away. I like the idea of emptiness being so close.

I feel that on the street.

I haven't told you this yet, but Dan also acquires Zoe, who is played by Amy Brenneman. She is fifty-eight now (*Heat* was a while ago), but still she is a pleasing companion for a man Bridges's age who may not be quite sure which room is his bedroom. Zoe does clear up that doubt.

You are confused? Very well, but you understand that when series television has set up confusion, the best way it knows to erase doubt is to pile on more plot. Thus the Dan dilemma and the efforts to find him for elimination are turned into an assignment for an old colleague at the CIA (this is the excellent and unfazed John Lithgow). His austere professional is aggravated by the presence of Dan's daughter, who is also in the CIA—don't we all deserve to be there, as the centrality of Intelligence strives to suppress every contrary indicator in the world?

I would tell you this daughter's name but she seems to have several, and after four episodes I was not even sure whose daughter she was. Judging by the elusive performance by Alia Shawkat I suspect she is not sure either—like Ingrid Bergman's Ilsa in *Casablanca,* waiting to be told whether she is going off with Bogart or Paul Henreid.

This is looney tunes, yet occasionally compelling. Isn't that our rhythm on the sofa? There is a good scene where Zoe tells Dan the deal she is prepared to make with him (to have half of all he owns and to stay with him;

or to walk away now for significant cash money)—this after she has been prisoner in the trunk of his car (she doesn't even get to ride with the dogs) as he drives across the country, seemingly from Vermont to Montana. Brenneman is impressively fatalistic in that deal-making scene.

I had a suspicion that the frustrated actress might have told everyone on the show, hell, forget what we're calling our ridiculous script, I'm just going to have my say.

It's a prime moment, and the show is clever enough to keep us supplied with amber performances and jittery situations in which Dan handles himself like any superhero, forget the cancer, peeing three times a night, and a straying memory. There is a point in careers and the nonsense of so much material where actors realize that the "story" will be whatever they do and say.

The Old Man got attention in the press, and Hulu decided, well before the first season was over, that it would order up season number 2. I was mildly cheered by this facade of success, but disenchanted at commerce trampling on the nerve ends of story. I am not encouraged in watching a show unfold in which I feel Dan *needs* to be removed finally—like, with prejudice and moral emphasis. That would permit a closing tableau where Zoe and the daughter, John Lithgow and the Rottweilers stand over his shattered body and say something like, Truly, this was some kind of guy, instead of just a figment on television. But how can a second season function if Dan is dead?

You take what you can get these days. I suspect Bridges could play Dan as the Dude of Sheba and that would still fly.

Hold your breath. We still have three episodes to watch in this first season. The night is young.

Or younger than we are.

We watched the rest and it was intolerably vacant, as if any test of narrative demands had been abandoned for the lure of one more season, done in the name of business calculation and uncaptioned shame. We get the television we deserve, as if our civilization is breathing, but asthmatic.

Good night to the Dude.

32

To Call This Fun

If the Dude is gone, is that farewell to Snoop Dogg, too? Does the charm of those lighthearted dropouts burn off in a commercialized sun?

Some of us keep old friends from screens who may not stand the test of time better than the Dude—like Charlie, or Groucho; plus Tom and Jerry; that Mr. Smith who went to Washington and sat at the rear window; with Gary Cooper, so strong but rarely at peace, even after noon; with Ingrid, Marilyn, Mary Tyler Moore . . . all the way to Sybil Fawlty and Lucy Ricardo.

These dreams can get confusing. I have written this book for Lucy Gray, and with her, but the Lucy on the page is less than the woman I live with. I hope in the book she is funny and tender and wise, and those traits are hers in life. Plus mischief. But she may scold me for putting words and bad lines in her mouth. And in life she can cry out in fury as well as delight. A wonder. Isn't that what we feel talking to companions in our silent heads as much as out loud in the living room? Lucy here is no more Lucy Gray than Lucy Ricardo. But there are resemblances, and a kind of incoherent affection, wounded as well as blissful, in which I hold them both. Being in love at last is a matter of keeping company and doing dialogue.

This book began as the admission of how this upstart medium had stolen our consciousness from "cinema" or "movie." So it felt natural to find a format where Lucy and I were on twin couches in our TV room. I was also held by the notion that since 2016 we have been going to hell with a hellmaster unmatched at being on TV. Haven't we been living under his foul occupation? Isn't that the fatigue we feel in listening to the liar?

We are asking now whether an audience could be a community active in its own vital decisions. Or was being an "audience" just a way of betraying that potential?

A trick to keep us sweet.

Is a mass medium a useful construction, or a way of canceling out such plans? Is that medium a model of participation, or a disguise for futility? This question was a shark in the water during the pandemic when we were hiding from having no answers to our worst questions. "What can anyone do about this?" we sighed over the weather. So TV amounted to a spurious insurance scheme. It was cold comfort on burning nights, feebly tempted by Snoop Dogg's warning about plans.

Can a commercial be the most important message on TV?

Isn't that why it plays over and over again?

The Covid lockdown was a window of opportunity for what became known as streaming, or the binge-watching of television. From Amazon to Netflix, platforms enjoyed a sudden increase in subscriptions, and so they entered into an intense period of program generation. You may have noticed that they invested in many series that did not deserve their chance. Nevertheless, the business believed it was daring, and it was apparent that the large audience was holding back from going to see movies in theatres. But that retreat had started years and decades before Covid. Remoteness had been coming.

There was another temptation—to see these changed circumstances as part of a great flourishing in TV quality. There's some truth in that. So I have looked at a number of series or shows in the course of this book that can be gathered under the optimistic umbrella of a golden age.

There are always golden ages in show business—it is like the recurrence of "Magic!" as a mantra. One occurred in the time of *Birth of a Nation* (whether we like this or not—never mind the nation, a business was born). There was another in the last few years of movie silence. There was a heyday in the late '30s; another spurt of daring after the Second World War. And then a brief empire of network TV in the 1950s, perishing as it bloomed. There was a last outburst of brave and somber films in the late '60s and early '70s. The last?

The gold comes and goes. And I suspect that is as true of the range of long-form television series at the start of the twenty-first century as it is of all the other days of splendor.

I am not mocking them; I have enjoyed so many of them: but I wonder whether they have exhausted the medium's inventiveness and our patience. The production of cinema at different moments in our history only taught us that movies tended to be alike. If you watched long enough you realized you were seeing the same old stories and sits. And you became jaded or ironic over the repetition. The movies seemed like so many ads. In habit, we face the depletion of imagination. So the movies and the TV shows became campier versions of themselves. The dynamic and the tedium of fashion hang over these things.

During Covid we went from rejoicing in the advantage of one good show after another to seeing that not enough of them could be that good or piercing. There is no need to moralize over such things; the medium has no conscience or thoughts of a future. But in the time spent writing this book, I feel the material has grown less compelling. It seems predictable, with action and lines that are recited rather than delivered as for the very first time. So in success a blameless entropy sets in as creation seeks to repeat what has worked before. *The Sopranos* changed us all; sheepishly, we entered its gang. But its prequel movie, *The Many Saints of Newark* (2021), left us cold.

So what are we going to do, beloved?

What are you going to do?

You're asking me? You're writing me!

Do you recall: we were talking about *The Forsyte Saga*, in Britain in 1967, and I said that on the show *Late Night Line-Up* the BBC offered an immediate commentary on the Forsytes, talking to people on the street as well as stuffed pundits in the studio.

With a Joan Bakewell as the host.

Exactly. It was not that the late-night debate was brilliant or intense, let alone "right." But it contained a useful idea: that we, the audience and the people, should think about what we were seeing, and argue with it. Television need not be an unapproachable monster. It was a creature we could talk to, even if Bakewell and those putting on a show were not omniscient. But we had a place in the firmament, a need to answer back. This book is founded on that principle.

I realize I have to do my own book. It's terrifying.

We all of us do. We have to reprimand the medium and our parents: they let this thing in the house and never bothered to ask how it worked.

When for centuries we had been given time to understand what words were, how to read and compose, how to try to deal with the substance of discourse.

Yet no one in our education ever paused to ask us what a shot was, a sequence, or how this thing called editing guided us in thinking as much as sentences and paragraphs had done. We let it in the house and left it to its own devices. It's as if those handsome Rottweilers in *The Old Man* had turned into ravenous aliens.

Bursting out of our chests. As if we were consumed already. That was such a piercing image. And I walked out on it in New Hampshire. I should have shouted at the screen for its outrage. People in the movie audience had begun to be like slaves. Long ago, we should have been so much more determined if we meant to save the world.

Time and again, for years, we have stayed silent. Sometimes we are hardly there. Ever since the start of cinema we have known the flow goes on without us.

But as a practical matter, how is this to be done? How does it fit in a schedule— or the budget? You said Late Night Line-Up *went on for as long as it needed? Open-ended. How* did *that work?*

Awkwardly, I'm sure. There were times when the talk became boring, so viewers went to bed. But then there were nights when the conversation was so good, so challenging, that you didn't want it to stop.

What about the show that was coming next?

Nothing came next. Nothing but the night. There was a point where some producer said enough, or Ms. Bakewell thought she had better things to do, and the show stopped. And all of BBC Two stopped.

That's all, folks? The network closed for the night?

It was like reading *Mrs. Dalloway* or *Pale Fire* and coming to a point where you put the book aside, and fell asleep in your chair, dreaming of the story.

No shows came after it? The night took over? That's as frightening as feeling someone has come into the house in the dark. But how can you run television like that? It's not practical.

You make the decision—and it is a large matter for society, education, and politics, but it insists on the audience having identity.

So in 1967 people called in and interrupted the show? That would be chaos.

That may be so, but saying that the audience exists and that this whole medium needs to be challenged is admitting we have a lifetime quest—beyond entertainment.

We have a quest? We don't just stumble along in the dark?

We like to hope so. But just because it's dark we cannot give up the principle of searching. It's hard if the light is just a fancy effect. There is no question as urgent as why are we watching? The answer to that may turn on our having souls in a world that is chaotic. Three hours a night, or maybe four. A month from now will you recall what you saw?

So nothing matters. This is too much Bartleby and Herman Melville. I have to go to bed.

We came back next night with energy for the argument, and ideas that had germinated in the night.

This is what I want to know. The BBC dropped Late Night Line-Up *long ago? Right? The best ideas get discontinued. But are there other shows that have done what you are asking for?*

I can think of a few things where the attempt has been made, where the medium has felt like a forum for argument over its own nature.

Monty Python's Flying Circus—no matter how comic or surreal it was in sketches and episodes—was forever getting us to ask, "Is this really a TV show we are watching, or has something happened? Have devils come in and carried out a coup at the BBC?"

That would be good. And maybe Laugh-In *had a little bit of that, though it always seemed more organized. As if being cute would dull the sharp edge. America is so scared of disorder.*

But you often felt its real subject was TV and the ways of being funny in that medium. I have an urging not just to review particular shows but to question the nature of the medium. To do things that make you say, "But you can't do that on TV!" Like *Fleabag*.

There were other things, and many of them were what we'd call documentary. Like John Berger's *Ways of Seeing*. Adam Curtis launched a line of movie essays that set out to cross-examine the process of understanding and its failure. He is still at it, like a lonely preacher. You should see *The Century of the Self, All Watched Over by Machines of Loving Grace, HyperNormalisation,* and *Can't Get You Out of My Head*. Adam Curtis is as vital as Dziga Vertov and Chris Marker.

I'm building the list. All Watched Over by Machines of Loving Grace— *that's a great title.*

It's from a poem by Richard Brautigan. Add in several hundred editions of *Arena,* led by Anthony Wall.

What's that?

Essays or ruminations on creativity and society. That's the show that made the movie about *Wisconsin Death Trip*. Anthony Wall just retired, yet I believe he was "let go."

Wall and Curtis may have alarmed the business people who run the medium. Those young suits want to believe they are in control, just as we yearn to feel a benign authority behind the screen. But Curtis and Wall aim at shows like nothing you've seen before. They recall the idea that people who disagreed could dispute each other in live talk. That's a good idea for us, but the forces in control were edgy over it in case some rogue energy would escape.

And, of course, Garry Shandling was one of these subversive geniuses.

Maybe the kindest of them all.

I think kindness does very well on TV. Edith Bunker, Bob Newhart, Mr. Rogers, Marge Simpson . . . Vanna White . . .

Or once upon a time, at the end of the day, a BBC announcer would speak to us and tell us good night, because the BBC was closing down. It was a soft voice, gentle and reassuring.

We want to feel the medium loves us.

Whereas a while ago the movies were taken over by unkindness.

Didn't Kenneth Tynan say "Fuck" one night on TV? Was that 1965? Did he mean it as a warning, or encouragement?

He was a naughty boy. It was as innocent as that. But we are always waiting for outrage, like Fukushima or that January 6, when the insurrection went on for hours. But imagine if he, himself, the golden ogre Untruth, had come on air, in a cardigan, by a fireside, and said, please don't be alarmed—we have this all under control.

Good night and sleep well.

January 6 was the medium going out of control. And it was live. But all too soon this openness to dispute and being unsettled turned into people who knew they were right being interviewed by sweet hosts who served up lob questions for them to volley away. That pattern operated on MSNBC as much as on Fox.

Rachel Maddow was always posing long questions—they are statements really—and asking experts to tell her yes, she got it right. So the experts don't have agency. They are hired in like supporting players. They all agree with Rachel. We know this in advance. It curtailed her critical faculty, or her rage. And left us shocked if her good guys lost out there on the streets or at the polls.

So we don't get live, ugly arguments. Or degrees of attack. Or genuine angry fights over issues. No one in America watches a parliamentary procedure. So the violence keeps being put off for another day.

That was cowardly of us.

Yet the medium is pledged to not alarming us, to saying everything will be all right.

When the medium is so scary.

Something similar has worked in pornography. Once upon a time it was unthinkable that the medium could show us having sex. Then that changed and began a new process of female subjugation. As if the animal individuality of sex could be house-trained. How do we tolerate pornography? How do we not know it has dismantled the way we make love? Time and again the medium seeks a formula it can cling to, and so liveliness goes to sleep. Why can't we have people making love on TV and talking about it? As if they have discovered Antarctica.

And yet again . . .

You are funny about it sometimes, yet you feel such dismay at the advertising on TV.

It is worse than any chainsaw massacre, worse than the Bates Motel, or the footage from Abu Ghraib. Because it seems so placid, so accepted. That's why *The Truman Show* (1998) is more disturbing than most conscientious blood-sachet horror movies. It's the stupid calm that is nightmarish and so American.

There you are—is it the being American that makes you sad?

America is gripped by the dread of being un-American—held in place—as if it had never understood that its experiment was to be different, or unlike original casting. The campaign to make America great again is an infantile derangement—because "great" is an assertion of power and superiority, and overlooking the squalor of the built-up country, the ceaseless racism, the fear of science and evidence, the suppression of women, and the addiction to branding that can make "greatness" like a war cry, a "Magic!" All the emotional stress is on "again," as if we feel wronged or stolen from. It was the same with Brexit and the wombward motion it wanted: "Take back control."

Yet you became an American citizen?

A silence follows, a loss of words. Like the howling of an old wind in an empty tunnel.

You know what I think about the advertising? There was a time, the '70s, when the ads seemed smart and witty. We waited to see them. We treasured the mockery. It was all very sexist—babes, beer, and burgers a lot of the time—but that let you feel TV was somehow working class. And the jokiness in the ads was part of that, telling us what chumps we were. But still the ads were as loaded with desire as the burgers reclined in ketchup. There was fun.

A young woman being educated.

And I knew the menu was shit. But now, so many ads are for things I don't understand—not just products but the way desire has been tranquilized. So my old Dad is expected to understand yet more digital refinements in the new phone, how system sophistication will ease arthritis, or why those damned emus are gangsters for life insurance. He is not going to care.

We don't want to be an audience anymore. We know we are a dumb mass being manipulated.

There you are—the ads aren't even selling these days. My Dad and I, we don't give a fuck about what we're being offered. There is no desire. Isn't that what killed the movies?

I thought your Dad died twenty years ago.

That's what the loss of desire will do for you. So movies say they're going to horrify us with cruelty, but I'm left like our little Nick, just wondering how their cleverness peeled the face off the skull. Not afraid. And I can't recall the last time I felt two people in a movie were falling in love—as opposed to getting ready to have sex.

I want to read the book you're going to write.

But you still believe television should be run by some kind of BBC?

Isn't it pathetic to think that? When the BBC is a ghost town now. But I think in its nature television should belong to us, and I like a scheme of administration that is respectful of that. The airwaves are part of the environment. The medium has a relationship with fact, or its pursuit, that must not be abandoned.

So there should be a universal license fee and the revenue from that determines the shows that are put on?

It is the best decent chance we have had. I recognize the dangers of stupidity and prejudice in charge. But we run those risks already and we do believe in the theory of talent—think of that as variations in uniformity. We have to remove the burden in which whatever television says is compromised by the poison of having to advertise a magic medicine that does not work.

This has mundane instances, benign enough, it seems: a commentator on a Giants game in San Francisco, Jon Miller or Dave Flemming, makes a description of a play that can approach eloquence as well as shrewdness. Then almost in the same breath he has to read a promo, for house paint or auto repair. And it is not that those products are worthless or ignominious. But the liveliness of the commentary has had shame slipped into it for twenty seconds. The same voice goes from one to the other, without apology or any deflection to signal indignity.

And all I ever thought was that baseball commentary was sometimes pretty tedious. Don't you think those guys, Jon and Dave, can handle the transition? Like a cool double play.

They are very good. They are our friends on the air. But none of us can make that play reliably. I should also tell you that as the economic tightening in streaming platforms intensifies it is likely that they will require more advertising. This may come gently at first, but that seldom lasts. And if people protest at the intrusion, then the premium price for staying free from advertising will mount. Those most oppressed financially will have to drink the slow poison and the polite contempt for what is being streamed.

You're still thinking about saving TV to save the world. Just remember what you said—we let it in.

If television is the best metaphor we have of ourselves and our chance at a society that can deal with its game of progress, then the discourse must be level and free from any other message than itself.

Blah and blah, dearie. I fear you may be right, and I forgive you for that. But remember Sullivan's Travels *and how its chain gang prisoners found a little comfort in a silly picture show. I think of our friend Doug—he watches Turner Classic Movies so much of the time—and he has one of the best attitudes I know. Like Fred Astaire. Maybe we'll just keep watching TV as the other lights in life go out? But now you are saying the new shows are not going to be as good as they were.*

A decline is always there. In the *Guardian* the other day, writing about the wretched sequel to *American Gigolo,* Joel Golby said it was typical of those shows "half-watched while looking at your phone."

The small screen gnaws away at the larger one. Like a virus. That had to come.

So, like Doug, we'll watch old shows again. Keep dancing the old dance.

There's another chance, a leap forward in the mechanics. I'd say it is a certainty. Not that it will be our decision. As always in the past the technology will lead us on, whether we like it or not. Sometimes we never even notice it.

A new Magic!

Just consider, by 1815, the world had had Shakespeare, Rembrandt, and Mozart. Humans had staked their claim. Independence had been declared; that new America project was alive. Britain had abolished slavery by law, if not practice. Bonaparte had been defeated and sent to Saint Helena to stare at the streaming sea. There were dawnings of a new era of science and industry, full of health and hope. Dickens was three, Wagner was two, Julia Margaret Cameron was about to be born (June 11, in India). And no one could guess what we'd be in 1915, or in another hundred years when Tom Cruise would come skidding across our screen on the slipstream technology of his smile. And other wonders. But then a hundred years after the fresh prospects of 1815, our grimmest century began.

So we should wait patiently for the next ghost of Tom Cruise? You're breaking my heart.

Something will happen. Just as pretty and abrupt. It may start with our phones. The screen will become smaller yet more infernal. It will be a computer to shame us, with its screen in our brain. With imagery playing there all the time, subject to our wishes. We will be our own remote. We will see whatever we think of, awake or asleep. Our successors will keep the files of our memory, the way we still look at photographs in albums.

That feels deathly cold.

To get through it all, we may have to be something less than humanist. That plan was always a long shot.

I think this Lucy may settle for the chain gang. I don't think I would have the heart to watch without you.

You couldn't do it alone?

The idea of loneliness is already so oppressive.

And so, in our habit, we chose our couch, turned off the lights in the room, and summoned the suffuse glow on the screen with its remote signals of enlightenment and affection. Gently, the door rattled against the doorway in the evening draft, enough to conjure up the street outside. But we were not perturbed, not yet. Another night chez nous.

Here it comes, the precious light.

To think this might be fun.

33

Not Quite Fine

A few days later, in the afternoon, our friend Douglas McGrath was in his office in New York. Soon he would have to be on his way to the theatre where he was appearing in his one-man show, *Everything's Fine,* which was getting excellent reviews. Lucy and I had gone to New York for its opening night (October 13) and been thrilled to see him command the stage in the memoir he had written. Doug deserved an audience and treated us with fond respect.

Not that its title covered every aspect of the play, or its awkward situation during Doug's youth in Midland, Texas. But there was something in the claim that matched Doug's optimism.

Not that this could contain the distress on November 3, 2022, when the one-man cast did not make it to the theatre. He was dead of a heart attack in his office. Suddenly, at sixty-four. We'll never know, but maybe doing the show, and making the awkwardness eloquent, had tired him to the depth of his being. Fred Astaire was dead at eighty-eight; the esprit catches up with you.

I cannot take it in, said Lucy. *Time stopped. I need to talk to him.*

Like her I expected a friend to share the news with in some wry e-mail. But for years that friend had been Doug. I think he would have appreciated the irony in being both onlooker and designated victim. Was it Groucho who said, "Hello, I must be going"? I should ask Doug; he would know.

If only because we had mentioned Doug in the last chapter, as a devotee of Fred Astaire, I wanted to close by honoring him. He was a very talented man, and the kindest, most cheerful and happy person I've ever known.

Those are large things. He had an airy nobility that was like Astaire's non-chalance on dance floors. I can't be the only person around who had learned from Doug to look on the bright side, and cling to the wisdom in that shaky advice.

Not that I am the best student in that policy. But I'm going to end here, a few days before the midterm elections of November 8 and then the World Cup. And I will trust you to reconcile those results with what I have been saying in this book. You'll be watching it all, I daresay, on television. It is where we look nowadays, some middle distance between the sky and the street.

It's quiet in the house this time of night, apart from shivers in the structure from the wind. That abiding Gestapo. Here in San Francisco, we can't rule out the chance of a tremor, and alarm if it lasts more than twenty seconds. But I have stayed up late just to get the last word in—you may agree, I deserve that. Still, in case he wakes, it may be tactful to drop the fussy italic, so if he sees words appearing he will believe he has written them himself. Such a dope.

There, I hope that works.

What I want to tell you is that that night when he found me à la *Poltergeist* I wasn't sleepwalking, though sleep can be a dance of seven veils. I felt I was playing a small subterfuge that he would appreciate—the way in *Vertigo* Kim Novak pretends to be unconscious in that (implicit yet unseen) moment where Jimmy Stewart quietly removes her wet clothes. Do you recall—she had jumped into the Bay and needed to be saved?

I did not let on when he led me back to bed, for over the years we had discussed the curious charm of static on the screen. I enjoy those passages where some digital error turns the image into a mosaic of maddened tiles. In many plodding story scenes that frenzy can be a dance.

Thus, I played the game. It can happen in marriages that we collude (without direction, script, or music) in passages of romantic splendor, or being distraught beyond endurance, as if rehearsing our play. And more or less the mood stays playful.

Like an amateur actor, I was caught up in the spell that night. I began believing that the screen was alive and that there was a spirit it had brought into the house. An angel and a demon.

You can call this dreaming, but we know the risky pleasure in making ourselves afraid. In 1960, when Marion Crane arrived at last at the Bates Motel, I felt she was home, at the lip of the place where fear lived.

And home—he did say this at the outset, give him credit—is the preoccupation of television, a mass medium that functions domestically, yet keeps teeing us up for disruption in our sanctuary. This need not be Gestapo; it might be Ricky Gervais at the Golden Globes or the rocket arc of *Babylon Berlin.* But those outbursts are masks for the anxiety we nurse that, one day, turning on the set, nothing will appear. Contact and assurance will have been lost. Every "they" we've supposed will have vanished.

We once thought of our TV room as the place we had chosen for the show, where some of our mortgaged square footage and the worn furniture had been rearranged as a small theatre. That seemed nice and safe, a convenience that let us stay in charge. Yet sometimes that "room" is no longer part of our house. It is like the mouth of a tunnel of access or a gate at an airport in an abandoned city.

But what has happened to that city? Does the television keep us from going mad or feeling alone? Maybe the profusion of its stuff—all there if we can find it—is the iceberg of our futile plenty. Sometimes I scream and throw the error-filled remote on the floor; the batteries spill out like severed pearls. It might be better to try alone. That's my first word in Wordle every day.

Wake up, sleepyhead.

Acknowledgments

If this is an adventurous book, the credit goes to Yale; if it is reckless, that is my fault. If it is both, the burden of decision is yours. When I say "Yale" I mean the university press and its leader, John Donatich, who went with this scheme and its subject and made so many saving suggestions and edits along the way. The underlying thought, that television is a weather system, as out of control as our real weather, owes so much to John's friendship and support. Beyond that, I am grateful for the expert and amused copyediting of an old friend, Dan Heaton, and the generous and tactful control of our showrunner, Susan Laity. And I am not forgetting the contribution of John's assistant, Abbie Storch.

There are several other people with whom I have talked television over the years. That group includes Mark Feeney, Will Balliett, Steve Wasserman, Michael Barker, Laura Morris, Greil and Jenny Marcus, Phil Kaufman, Jean-Pierre Gorin, Anthony Wall, Richard and Mary Corliss, Molly Haskell, Lili Anolik, and Michael Ondaatje and Linda Spalding. And two vital friends who died in the past year: Tom Luddy and Douglas McGrath. The holes they have left in my daily existence only remind me of a much earlier loss, Kieran Hickey, the best friend I've ever had.

Such thoughts overlap with family, the people with whom I have watched and talked back to television the most. That includes my mother, Norah Thomson, my first wife, Anne, the children—Kate, Mathew, Rachel, Nicholas, and Zachary—and other close ties: with Steve Haines, Michelle O'Callaghan,

Sean Arnold, Annie Bishai, and Julie Reilly. There is a society in our sofas, despairing and hopeful, incredulous but suckers. I think that for many of us, watching television is one of our warmest and most useful ways of being together.

Which brings me to Lucy Gray, my essential companion, steadfast, witty, creative, and endearing, and as she has sometimes been heard to say, more than I deserve. But we all deserve someone too good for us.

Index

INDEX